Eileen O'Shaughnessy, in Her Own Words

Angela Smith · Sylvia Topp

Eileen O'Shaughnessy, in Her Own Words

The Complete Letters of George Orwell's Wife

Angela Smith
Media Centre
University of Sunderland
Sunderland, UK

Sylvia Topp
Kingston, ON, Canada

ISBN 978-3-032-03366-6   ISBN 978-3-032-03367-3 (eBook)
https://doi.org/10.1007/978-3-032-03367-3

© The Editor(s) (if applicable) and The Author(s), under exclusive license to Springer Nature Switzerland AG 2025

This work is subject to copyright. All rights are solely and exclusively licensed by the Publisher, whether the whole or part of the material is concerned, specifically the rights of reprinting, reuse of illustrations, recitation, broadcasting, reproduction on microfilms or in any other physical way, and transmission or information storage and retrieval, electronic adaptation, computer software, or by similar or dissimilar methodology now known or hereafter developed.

The use of general descriptive names, registered names, trademarks, service marks, etc. in this publication does not imply, even in the absence of a specific statement, that such names are exempt from the relevant protective laws and regulations and therefore free for general use.

The publisher, the authors and the editors are safe to assume that the advice and information in this book are believed to be true and accurate at the date of publication. Neither the publisher nor the authors or the editors give a warranty, expressed or implied, with respect to the material contained herein or for any errors or omissions that may have been made. The publisher remains neutral with regard to jurisdictional claims in published maps and institutional affiliations.

Cover credit: KRIllustrates/Colin Smith

This Palgrave Macmillan imprint is published by the registered company Springer Nature Switzerland AG
The registered company address is: Gewerbestrasse 11, 6330 Cham, Switzerland

If disposing of this product, please recycle the paper.

Forewords: By Three People Who Knew Eileen

Richard Blair, Warwickshire, UK

This new book, collected and annotated by Professor Angela Smith and Sylvia Topp, brings together many of the well-known letters written by Eileen Orwell (neé O'Shaughnessy), some well documented, but some new ones that have come to light in recent years.

This collection of letters, I think, helps to dispel some of the negative things that have been said about Eileen and George Orwell, especially what Orwell said about Eileen. My father always liked the company of women who had something intelligent to say, or perhaps amusing. In Eileen he found both. Eileen was a young middle-class well brought up woman, well educated to the point of having graduated from Oxford University.

Eileen met my father at a party and he was smitten, telling people that "this was the woman I would like to marry". And in due course he did so, in June 1936, much to his shortcomings, as was warned by both his mother and his younger sister Avril. Nevertheless Eileen went ahead and married George, and there is no doubt in my mind that they were happy together in spite of what many people thought was an unorthodox relationship. Eileen writes to her friend Norah Myles at one point early on in the marriage: "*The next letter you get will be a round robin saying that I have murdered George*". Some people took this to mean that the marriage was a little under strain. This was not the case. Eileen had a wicked sense of humour and no doubt she may well have been a little exasperated by

George's apparent desire to write something every day, but I don't think there was anything seriously wrong in the marriage. My mother was the equal to my father, but she was happy to play second fiddle to someone she recognised as having an extraordinary writing ability, and she believed he would succeed in his profession.

I suppose if there is one criticism one must level at them both, it is their total disregard for their health. Firstly, my father's health broke down after the Spanish Civil War with a bout of TB, and then my mother's health was not good during the Second World War, culminating with her death in a Newcastle private clinic, through what some people might call neglect. But probably she didn't realise how ill she was, something that could be levelled at my father, with his subsequent death in January 1950.

Looking at their marriage for the short time they were together (nine years) and having just adopted a baby son, there is no doubt had they looked after their health they would have continued to be in a loving, if not slightly unorthodox marriage. The glue that would have held them together would have been their adopted little boy, me.

Mary Catherine O'Shaughnessy Moncure, Washington, DC

I was too young to remember Eileen but there was always talk about her while I was growing up.

These stories came to me through many different sources; my mother, Dr Gwen O'Shaughnessy; Lydia Jackson, Eileen's friend; Miss Elizabeth Bradford (Braddy), my mother's dispenser; Mrs Florence Taylor, my nanny and Mrs Mayna Patrick, who worked with my father.

These people all said Eileen was gracious to everyone and treated people all the same no matter who they were, teacher or pauper. She could make a commoner feel like a king or chat to the most intellectual person in the room.

She was intelligent, good looking and had a great sense of humour, so I was told.

She also had the task of taking us children, Rick, my brother Laurence and myself up to Durham to get away from war torn London. Not an easy thing to do in those days especially as she wasn't well.

Mayna told me that Dr Eric was a "very difficult man to work with" so I imagine he was more comfortable with Eileen typing out his papers than using a stranger from the typing pool.

Braddy, who was working in the dispensary when Eileen went into hospital, told me that Mummy had a premonition that things would not go well and asked her to let her know the minute the phone rang. When it did, they closed the surgery and patients were rescheduled.

My mother didn't talk about the past very much but I know she missed Eileen. She was the link to her late husband.

Quentin Kopp, Chesterfield, UK

Why have I been asked to write this short piece for this significant book on Eileen Orwell's first wife, who was very significant in his development as a writer? My Mother was Doreen née Hunton, George Kopp's second wife. Doreen knew Eileen from early in her sister Gwen's marriage to Eileen's brother Eric O'Shaughnessy.

The centre of the family after Gwen and Eric returned to England from the Sudan was 24 Croom's Hill, Greenwich. Gwen had her GP practice there and Doreen and Arthur their brother lived there. It was where my parents met after my Father's release from the NKVD Checkas in Spain in 1938.

Doreen described Eileen as a highly intelligent, open and engaging person who was adored by all. She also said that she felt that Eileen never received the recognition she deserved for the contribution she made to Orwell's development as a writer. Each night Orwell and Eileen reviewed the work he produced, which became *Coming up for Air* when they were in Marrakech. Most importantly, it was her idea to write *Animal Farm* as the allegory, which enabled it to be published and has endeared it to young and old ever since.

My regret is that Doreen did not live to read Sylvia Topp's thoroughly researched biography of Eileen, *Eileen the making of George Orwell*. She would have been delighted to see Eileen recognised at last as the intelligent, vivacious, capable and warm person she was.

Acknowledgements This book would not have been possible without the encouragement and collaboration of a number of individuals and archives. In particular, the help of Bill Hamilton has been invaluable. The archivist at St Hugh's College, Oxford, has given us permission to reproduce unpublished reminiscences by Eileen's fellow undergraduates. Louise North at BBC Written Archive has helped us bring to light for the first time Eileen's letters written when she worked for the Ministry of Food during the Second World War. Molly Beck at Palgrave has championed this project. Richard Blair's encouragement has helped us redress the balance of interpretations of his mother's letters by the gathering together of the complete collection of these for the first time. Along with Quentin Kopp and Catherine Moncure, Richard is one of the few people who still have a direct link with Eileen, and we are very fortunate in that they have kindly contributed Forewords to this collection.

Sylvia

First, I must thank Christopher Hitchens. In 2010, just before he died, I told him I was considering writing a biography of Eileen and he replied, "What an excellent idea". That was all the encouragement I needed. Second, I'm indebted to D. J. Taylor, who invited me to lunch at his home in Norwich and has been very supportive of my work ever since. When I met Quentin Kopp, in 2012, he wanted to be sure that I was aware of what he was told as a child: that Eileen had been a huge influence on the writing of *Animal Farm*. This came as a welcome highlight in my introduction to the significant creative influence Eileen had on Orwell. In 2013, Richard and Eleanor Blair invited me to their home, where we had a fascinating conversation about what life had become for Richard, as the only child of a world-famous author. The creation of the Orwell Society had suddenly propelled him into the spotlight. I also want to thank Catherine O'Shaughnessy Moncure, Gwen's adopted daughter, who was very helpful in getting me started on my years-long research and writing adventure. And, finally, I must mention Peter Davison who, against some resistance, had insisted that Eileen's letters be included in his book of Orwell's letters—well aware of how much his own wife had assisted him.

Angela

Most thanks have to go to the legend who is Alex Fairlamb, who introduced me to Quentin several years ago. In turn this led to meeting Sylvia, whose idea it was to write this book in the first place. Huge thanks also to Laura Brewis of We Make Culture, Sunderland, whose inspirational idea of raising the profile of remarkable women connected to Sunderland led to the Rebel Women of Sunderland project, and Eileen's inclusion. Chris Sharpe has helped unearth information about Nell Heaton which has helped us piece together Eileen's movements in the last few months of her life. Finally, thanks to Anthony and Kerry for putting me up on my visits to London over the years, and always taking an interest in what I am doing when not helping them sample gin.

Competing Interests The authors have no competing interests to declare that are relevant to the content of this manuscript.

Contents

1	**Introduction**	1
	Brief Biography	4
	A Note on Names	5
	Book Structure	6
	Note on the Letters	8
	References	8
2	**School and Juvenilia (1905–1921)**	11
	Scholarships	27
	University and Beyond	29
	Primary Sources	31
	References	31
3	**Oxford and London (1922–1934)**	33
	Introduction	33
	References	48
4	**Meeting Orwell and Marriage (1935–1936)**	49
	A Meeting of Minds	49
	Marriage and Homelife	53
	References	69
5	**Saving Orwell Twice (1936–1938)**	71
	References	104

6	**To Marrakesh (1938-1939)**	107
	References	138
7	**At War (April 1939–April 1941)**	139
	References	153
8	**Eileen at the Ministry of Food (1941–1944)**	155
	Animal Farm	199
	References	202
9	**Last Letters (1945)**	205
	References	236
Bibliography		237
Index		241

List of Figures

Fig. 2.1	Eileen O'Shaughnessy and friend in school uniform. About 1920. UCL Orwell Archive ORWELL/T/3/B/1/1	15
Fig. 5.1	Eileen Blair with Orwell at Aragon Front, Huesca. UCL Orwell Archive ORWELL/T/2/D/6	82
Fig. 8.1	Ministry of food letter from Eileen Blair, signed "Emily". Dated 19 August 1942. BBC written archives centre, R51/285/2	176
Fig. 9.1	Eileen Blair with Richard Blair (July/August 1944). UCL Orwell Archive ORWELL/T/3/B/1/14	208

CHAPTER 1

Introduction

Eileen Maud O'Shaughnessy Blair was a remarkable woman who, in her brief 39 years, helped forge the reputation of one of the greatest writers in English—that of her husband, Eric Blair: George Orwell. However, like many women in history, her story is one that has been largely ignored and forgotten. That is, until recently, when in 2020 Sylvia Topp's biography of Eileen brought to light the story of a precociously intelligent young woman from the North East of England.

Eileen's intellect was more than a match for that of her future husband. We can get tantalising glimpses of it in her few remaining letters that we explore in this book. From these, we get a clear picture of a young woman with a sardonic eye, whose humour sparkles off the page. However, without the full picture of her life and influences, this humour can read like a complaint at her lot in life, particularly when the couple moved to a dilapidated cottage after their marriage. Our discussion of the wider context of each letter helps recreate the context in which they were written and read.

Eileen has been largely excluded from all but the most recent biographies of Orwell, mainly as there had been very little evidence of Eileen's part in his life until the discovery, in 2005, of letters written to her university friend Norah. The edited collection in this book shows for the first time the full range of Eileen's letters currently known. These letters are mostly from Eileen to family and friends, including four long letters to

© The Author(s), under exclusive license to Springer Nature Switzerland AG 2025
A. Smith and S. Topp, *Eileen O'Shaughnessy, in Her Own Words*,
https://doi.org/10.1007/978-3-032-03367-3_1

Orwell himself, written just before her death. But there are also letters of business during the time Eileen acted on her husband's behalf when dealing with publishers. Later, she develops a clear professional identity of her own, which we can find in the letters she wrote whilst working for the Ministry of Food during the Second World War. We also show, through interviews with family and friends, just how far Eileen influenced the writing of *Animal Farm*.

In popular imagination, Orwell is the solitary creative genius, with *Animal Farm* being read by generations of school children who hear little about the creative process of the novel. The 2019 film, *Mr Jones* (Andrea Chalupa), set in 1933–35, is based on the true story of investigative journalist Gareth Jones, who uncovers the devasting famine (or "Holodomor") which resulted in the deaths of millions of Ukrainians because of deliberate mismanagement by the Soviets. In this film, Jones is shown explaining this to his publisher, who in the film is also Orwell's publisher. Jones and Orwell meet, and Orwell is inspired, by Jones's findings, to write *Animal Farm*. Whilst this makes a literary connection between disillusionment with the Soviets, *Animal Farm* was not written until ten years later. In fact, as we shall see, Eileen and Orwell's early months of marriage in 1936 were influenced by socialism to the point that both went out to join forces with the anti-fascists (mostly communists) in Spain in early 1937. In the version above, Eileen's influence on the writing of *Animal Farm* is completely erased, her place being taken by a male journalist.

Only the most iconic novels have merited critical attention that extends beyond academic study. James Joyce's *Ulysses* is one example from the early part of the twentieth century, but Orwell's *Nineteen Eight-four* has moved beyond literature and into everyday language, with phrases such as "Big Brother", "Newspeak", "Thought Police", "Ministry of Truth" and "Room 101" passing into everyday use. The novel has also been used as a central device in other novels, and recently it formed the plot device in a short story by William Boyd, "Bethany on Jura" (commissioned by *The Guardian* in 2017), later developed into a radio series on BBC Radio 4 as *The Jura Affair* (BBC 2025). Dorian Lynskey's 2019 book, *The Ministry of Truth: a Biography of George Orwell's 1984*, is one of many that seek to explore the influences and relevance of Orwell's most famous novel, explaining this to a lay rather than academic audience. Whilst Lynskey offers passing comment about Eileen's input into *Animal Farm*, he tends to treat *Nineteen Eighty-four* as a novel that emerges from a literary tradition rather than being a look at social influences. In so doing, Eileen's work at the Ministry of Information is missing, and along with that goes the visual reference to the building that becomes the Ministry of Truth. As we shall see in the course of this book, Eileen's influence may even have extended to the title *Nineteen Eight-four*, the inspiration for which has been much debated since the novel first appeared in 1949.

The massive undertaking of compiling the complete letters of both Orwell and Eileen by Peter Davison in Davison's *Complete Works* often overlooks the contribution of his own wife, Sheila, who acted as his editor. Other recent research has highlighted the influences of the wives of the "great writers" of the nineteenth and twentieth centuries. Whilst it has been well known for many years that William Wordsworth had the help of his sister, his wife and his daughter, the more widespread silent contribution of women is less recognised. In Wordsworth's case, famously he was inspired to write his best-known poem, "Daffodils", after reading a description in his sister Dorothy's journal. Dorothy became his editor and scribe, a role she later shared with his wife Mary and then daughter Dora.

Looking further afield, Popoff (2010) shows how Sofia Tolstaya acted as Leo Tolstoy's scribe and agent, laboriously copying out *War and Peace* seven times before it was ready to be sent to the publisher. Anna Dostoevskata started out as her husband Fyodor Dostoevsky's stenographer, and he later credited her with inspiring him and being his soul mate (Kaufman, 2021). In the twentieth century, we now recognise that Vera Nabokov's influence is inseparable from her husband's work. He even observed, "Without my wife I would never write a single book" (Boyd 2016 p41). The poet T. S. Eliot was a friend of Orwell's, and Eliot's second wife, Valerie, became editor and annotator of his work (Ackroyd, 1984). So, although the men's names are celebrated, their literary reputations are built on the unpaid, unsung support and influence of the women in their lives. As Topp has shown, Eileen's life fits with this exceptional but largely unheralded pattern. Our book expands on this by exploring her letters, so her personality emerges clearly and produces a startlingly original voice in her own right.

Brief Biography

Eileen Maud O'Shaughnessy was born in South Shields on 25 September 1905. Her parents, Laurence and Mary O'Shaughnessy, had moved to South Shields after a somewhat peripatetic lifestyle owing to Laurence's job as a customs officer. Laurence's family came from County Kerry in Ireland, where he was born. Eileen's mother, Mary Westgate, was born in Nottingham. They married in Gravesend on 7 February 1900, although no one is quite sure how they met. Laurence's job then took them to Sunderland, which was a busy port town as well as being a centre for coal mining and ship building. Their first child, a son called Laurence Frederick, was born there in December 1900. He was known as Eric to the family to avoid confusion with his father, but in turn this would be something that would later cause some confusion for Eileen when she met and married Orwell. The small family moved up to Lerwick, one of the most remote parts of the UK in the Shetland Isles, within a year of Eric's birth, when Laurence was transferred there. Laurence eventually was promoted, and so able to move to a less isolated port: he was made Head Collector and Surveyor of Customs in South Shields. The family moved to South Shields in June 1905, and Eileen was born three months later. Eileen inherited her dark hair and pale "Irish" looks from her father's side of the family, and with her Irish-sounding name, many people would later assume she was Irish.

Laurence O'Shaughnessy's promotion meant that the family were comfortably off. In 1908, they settled into a newly built house that comprised eleven rooms. They named their home Westgate House, after Mary's side of the family. The 1911 census shows that, in addition to the four O'Shaughnessys, the household included a live-in governess and a domestic servant. Mary O'Shaughnessy had worked as a teacher before her marriage, and the senior O'Shaughnessys were ambitious for both their children. Eric was sent to boarding school, but the census shows that the governess had been kept on and so Eileen's education was clearly something valued by her parents from an early age. As we will see in Chapter 2, her parents were keen for Eileen to continue this education and so sent her to Sunderland Church High School at around the age of 10, in 1915. In this period of the First World War, the 15-year-old Eric insisted on leaving school and doing the sort of war work that was available for those too young to fight. In his case, it was working as a look-out on the North Sea coast, allowing him to live back with his family in South

Shields. In 1918, he took up a place at medical school in Newcastle, from where he graduated in 1923. Three years later, in 1926, he passed his surgeons' exams and was made a Fellow of the Royal College of Surgeons, which qualified him to work as a surgeon in the UK. Eileen's education was significantly more academic than was available to most girls at this time and suited her well. She was very close to Eric, but also fiercely competitive intellectually, thus her own education runs in parallel to his in terms of school then university. Their education was paid for by their parents, although in Eileen's case, as we shall see, this was supplemented by the scholarships and exhibition prizes she won.

The O'Shaughnessys continued to live in their house in South Shields until 1925 when Laurence retired. They moved to Hillingdon in North-West London. This retirement was short-lived as Laurence had contracted tuberculosis. He died on 5 November 1929, aged just 63. Eric was practising medicine in the Sudan at this time, so Mary's care was assumed by Eileen, who moved into the Hillingdon house. Mary became part of Eileen's life to an even greater extent than before, and because of this, we have some of Eileen's letters to her mother, which help us understand her life in this period.

Eric returned to the UK and finally settled in Greenwich, London in the early 1930s. He was building a career as a highly respected cardiothoracic surgeon, perhaps spurred on by his father's illness. He had married a fellow doctor, Gwen Hunton, when they met whilst working in the Sudan. She eventually became a well-respected general practitioner. Like Eric's, her family came from the North East of England.

A Note on Names

Throughout this book, we refer to Eileen's husband, Eric Blair, as "George Orwell", or more frequently just "Orwell". When they married, Eileen took her husband's surname of Blair, and this is the name she carried with her throughout her life from then on. She referred to herself as "Mrs Blair" in formal contexts, never "Mrs Orwell" (contrary to the subtitle of Funder's book, *Wifedom: Mrs Orwell's Invisible Life*). Although he had already started to make a name for himself under the pseudonym "George Orwell", Eileen initially referred to him in her letters as Eric. It is only when he became better known by his pen name that she switches to referring to him as George. Everyone around them referred to him by that name, and it also served to distinguish him from Eileen's brother Eric.

We will see in several letters Eileen playfully teasing the recipient about this confusion. Eileen herself adopted the name Emily when working for the Ministry of Food in 1942–1944. She was known by everyone who worked there by that name. For consistency's sake, we continue to refer to her as Eileen throughout.

Book Structure

The chapters in this book are organised chronologically, offering us a chance to better understand Eileen's life. We will be able to show that Eileen's love of word play and drama did not emerge after her marriage, but instead follow a pattern that starts in her school days. In so doing, we are able to better understand her humour and so not fall into the trap of others, such as Anna Funder in *Wifedom*, who have taken her letters from the turbulent early months of their marriage and treated these as stand-alone examples of Eileen's frustration at her "dominating" husband.

Although Eileen was a prolific letter writer, very few of her letters remain. This is partly due to the ephemeral and prolific nature of her letters: why would someone want to keep a letter when they knew another would arrive soon? We know she and Orwell wrote long letters to one another frequently when apart, but only one of those he wrote to her remains, mostly as it was sent when they were in Spain. It is thought that this one exists since it was mixed up with other papers in the chaotic escape from Barcelona. The couple seem to have been a singularly unsentimental pair in this respect. Of all of Eileen's letters to Orwell, only four remain: these are the last ones she wrote to him, and three were received after she died. Their existence shows a rare example of sentiment on Orwell's part but offer us a fascinating insight into their relationship.

In addition to these personal letters, there are letters of business. Eileen acted as Orwell's agent on occasion and so we have her letters to his publishers, as well as letters relating to the occupancy of the cottage at Wallington. Of great interest are the recently discovered letters held in the BBC Written Archive, which come from Eileen when she was working for the Ministry of Food during the war. There may be other letters still lurking in other archives, but these have thus far evaded the extensive investigations of researchers.

This book starts not with a chapter of letters from Eileen, but with an exploration of her juvenile writings as found in the school magazine. Understanding Eileen's early education is vitally important to how we understand her later letters, and so the inclusion of juvenilia is relevant to this book.

Chapter 3 explores Eileen's life between school and marriage. Her years as a student at Oxford see her forming friendships that continue for the rest of her life and later provide us with rare examples of letters. We can also start to understand how she worked and lived after university as a highly educated single woman in the interwar years.

Chapter 4 is the start of our real exploration of Eileen's letters after she meets and marries Orwell, recounting in amusing and mischievous detail her life with him in letters to her Oxford and London friends. She is also found to be working (unpaid) for Orwell, acting as his literary editor and communicating with his editors.

Chapter 5 sees the most dramatic first year of marriage played out in letters. After Orwell's decision to go and fight with the anti-fascists in Spain, Eileen is left in charge of the production of *Road to Wigan Pier*, and the letters to the publisher show her to be a highly efficient executor. After following Orwell to Spain, she writes letters to her mother and brother from Barcelona. The drama of Orwell's injury after being shot in the throat is played out in her letters to her brother, and the escape from Spain shows Eileen at her most innovative. Once back in Britain, she is then forced to act very quicky to save Orwell's life for a second time when he suffers a massive tubercular haemorrhage.

Chapter 6 sees Eileen and Orwell travel to Marrakesh for the winter, in an attempt to alleviate his tubercular problems. Without a telephone, Eileen kept in touch with family and friends by letter, and we are fortunate to have several of these. They show us the chaos and inconveniences of life in Marrakesh, all told through Eileen's whimsical and quirky writing, a narrative that only hints at her own health problems.

Chapter 7 sees Eileen and Orwell back in England, in time for the start of the Second World War. As they move from their cottage in Wallington to London, we have letters of business from Eileen as she sorts out the tenancy for the cottage, whilst also keeping her friends updated on their movements. The horror of war is never far away, and there is a gap in the chronological run of letters at this time as Eileen grieves for her beloved brother who died during the evacuation from Dunkirk.

Chapter 8 is by far the longest chapter in the book. This is simply because it contains the most letters. These letters cover Eileen's main contribution to the war effort, working for the Ministry of Food as liaison with the BBC. The BBC Written Archive contains a large number of letters from Eileen (writing as Emily Blair, for reasons we speculate about in this chapter). Whilst these are primarily letters of business, they continue to show glimpses of Eileen's mischievous and playful character that we have seen since her juvenilia. These letters also show how hard she was working, trying to keep the public informed about changes in food rationing whilst also calming the frequently troubled waters between the Ministry and the BBC in their tussle for control over the broadcasts. Also in this chapter, we show how, whilst working for the Ministry of Food, Eileen was also helping Orwell with drafts of *Animal Farm*. Through the recollections of family members, we can learn about her input into this much-loved novel.

Chapter 9 is our final chapter of letters. This chapter covers the last year of Eileen's life, as the couple finalised the adoption of their son, and Eileen adjusted to being a mother whilst her husband was away in Europe reporting on the war. As mentioned earlier, we have four of Eileen's letters to Orwell, written in early 1945 as she waited to go into hospital for an operation that she trusted would "cure" her. The heartbreakingly poignant final letter is one she wrote whilst in hospital, waiting for the anaesthetic to take hold, and as such is not finished.

In structuring this book around the chronology of Eileen's life, we hope to show how she had a style of writing that developed as she grew older. Even in her final letters, she shows much of the humorous word play that we first encountered in the juvenilia.

Note on the Letters

The majority of Eileen's personal letters have previously been published in Peter Davison's works, where they have been interspersed with Orwell's letters. As such, we have retained the punctuation and spelling that Davison used. Where the letters and other written texts by Eileen have been sourced from elsewhere, we have used the spelling and punctuation as it appears in the original. This is particularly the case in the letters in Chapter 8, which come from the BBC Written Archive and have not been published in full previously.

References

Ackroyd, Peter (1984), *T. S. Eliot: a life*, Penguin, London.

Boyd, Brian (2016), *Vladimir Nabokov: the American Years,* Princeton University Press, Princeton.
Funder, Anna (2024), *Wifedom: Mrs Orwell's Invisible Life,* Penguin, Harmondsworth.
Kaufman, Andrew (2021), *The Gambler Wife: A True Story of Love, Risk, and the Woman Who Saved Dostoyevsky,* Riverhead Books, New York.
Popoff, Alexandra (2010), *Sophia Tolstoy: a biography,* Free Press, New York.
Topp, Sylvia (2020), *Eileen: the making of George Orwell,* Unbound, London.

CHAPTER 2

School and Juvenilia (1905–1921)

In order to explore how Eileen's distinctively playful writing style developed, it is useful to start with her early schooling. We will also see how the specific school she attended affected her future life.

Eileen's birth in South Shields on 25 September 1905 saw a period of stability for the family. Her father's work as Collector of Customs had previously led to a very peripatetic life, but Eileen's birth coincided with changes in the way the role of Collector of Customs was organised, and her father remained in South Shields until he retired in 1925. The family comprised Eileen's mother, Mary; her father, Laurence; and her older brother, Laurence Frederick (born in Sunderland in 1900). Her brother always went by the name Eric, the abbreviation of his middle name, and probably not "Laurence" to avoid confusion with their father. The family moved around South Shields for several years before settling in a newly built house in Wellington Terrace. It was a large house, over three floors, and had a separate entrance for servants. The 1911 census return shows that the family employed a governess, Florence Watt, who lived in the house and presumably taught Eileen and Eric before they entered formal schooling. In Eileen's case, this would be the fee-paying South Shields High School junior section. Her birthday of 25 September meant that she was one of the oldest children in her school year. Little is known of her time at South Shields High School, but in September 1915 she transferred to Sunderland Church High School. This would have been

© The Author(s), under exclusive license to Springer Nature Switzerland AG 2025
A. Smith and S. Topp, *Eileen O'Shaughnessy, in Her Own Words*,
https://doi.org/10.1007/978-3-032-03367-3_2

a considerably longer journey for her, taking about an hour each way every day (walking to the railway station, then the train to Sunderland and either walking or riding on the school's horse-drawn waggon up to the school itself).

Why did Eileen's parents choose to move her to a more distant school? Her name appears in the *South Shields Gazette* in 1915 under the "Senior Honours" awarded to pupils at South Shields High School for the Cambridge Local Examinations, where she is listed as achieving "distinguished in English" and a "pass in spoken French". Eileen and Eric had a sibling rivalry when it came to academic achievement. Eric was already doing well at his fee-paying school, and it is likely Eileen was keen to pursue an academic course of study that was close to the traditional education Eric was taking.

Sunderland Church High School was one of four independent (i.e., not state-funded) schools run by the Church of England in the area, under the management of the Church Schools Company. Closer to South Shields, and easier to reach, were the schools in Newcastle and Gateshead, with a third further afield in Durham. All of the schools were managed by a board of trustees attached to the Church Schools Company, and had all opened around 1884. As was usual in such schools, girls and boys were educated separately, to different curriculums. The rise of a new middle class during the nineteenth century had led to a need for more schools, particularly for those families willing and able to pay for their children's education. However, this reinforced gender division, with the middle-class girls being educated in "accomplishments" such as needlework, music, painting and dancing, with additional focus on skills that would allow them to manage a household and children. Boys, on the other hand, had an education that mirrored the Classics taught in the traditional public school system, with additional subjects in the sciences and engineering that reflected the middle-class occupations that were opening up for them. It is estimated that only one in fifty middle-class women entered paid employment on leaving school (Holden 2007).

By the beginning of the twentieth century, attitudes were starting to change, partly mirroring the rise in arguments for women's rights that were to dominate gender issues in the first decade of the century, as the disparate groups arguing for different specific rights merged to present a more unified voice calling for the right to vote, and thus to influence the laws of the land (Vicinus 1985). Sunderland Church High School was not immune from this growing move to change gender stereotypes, and it seems this largely came to the school under its most influential head teacher, Miss Ethel Ironside. We will see how her reputation as a moderniser, through a more progressive approach to teaching and learning, may well have been a factor in Mr and Mrs O'Shaughnessy's decision to send Eileen to that school rather than to any of the others that were perhaps in easier reach.

Miss Ironside was educated at Cheltenham Ladies' College, where the legendary Miss Beale had already educated young women in a range of subjects that would be comparable with the studies of young men. Such young women were the first to go to university, where many of the "new" universities were willing to offer degrees to women. The most-esteemed universities, Oxford and Cambridge, were still some years away from allowing female students to graduate (Oxford was the first to break cover and offer degrees to women in 1920, whilst Cambridge held on until 1948). Ironside took a teaching qualification at London University and began a career that would eventually lead her to Sunderland.

Miss Ironside could be seen as being a progressive head teacher. She regularly took part in sports activities with the girls (including swimming and hockey), as well as teaching sciences and mathematics. She was also familiar with "modern" teaching methods, advocating the Fröebel Kindergarten methods at the school. In 1911, she was forced to defend this system of education to parents who were demanding rapid results. At that time, she commented, "Those who trust their children to the care of the Kindergarten must be content to await patiently the results which must ultimately show themselves in quickness of observations and intelligent grasp of subjects" (in Sayers 1984: 27). In other words, Ironside was setting up the school to have a steady progression of girls from Kindergarten up to Senior, and encouraging parents to "stick with the system" for the duration.

At her first prize-giving event in 1908, Miss Ironside set out what would become her philosophy on educating the young women in her charge:

> Our highest hope is to send out into the world a race of women of sane balanced mind, able to take a keen and intelligent interest in all that is going forward, proud of their nation because not ignorant of its great history, wide minded and not insular because they know something of languages and peoples other than their own, imperially minded because they have been taught of the responsibilities and duties of a citizen of such

an Empire as that of Great Britain, eager to read and form judgements for themselves, able to appreciate beauty with both eye and ear, able to reason, able to listen; in short, women with training, and not ignorant, gossiping idle beings, whose chief fault, nay, misfortune, is in being the possessors of ill-stocked minds. What are going to be the problems with this this generation of girls will have to grapple in their turn is not the point; the thing is that they shall be taught to use wisdom along whatever path they may be sent—and wisdom the beginning of which is fear of the Lord. (quoted in Sayers 1984: 28)

If we look at the details of what Ironside is promoting here, we will see she is setting up "her" school as one which will confound the damaging stereotypes associated with women. In patriarchal society, men are associated with rational thought and temperance; women are the ones lacking such attributes. However, in Ironside's view, the girls at Sunderland Church High School will be "of sane balanced mind"; in other words, they are going against the unwelcome female stereotype.

The girls will also be engaged with the outside world, taking a considered and informed view. Again, this refutes the stereotype of female domesticity, where the concerns of women are associated with the private world whilst those of men are associated with the public sphere.

Elsewhere, we see a clear dismissal of the female stereotypical behaviour glossed here as "ignorant, gossiping idle beings", linking the avoidance of this stereotype with the education the school would provide, an education that would, like that afforded to boys, equip girls with knowledge of the world that was useful beyond the home. That Ironside frames this as a "misfortune", with the deliberate correction from "chief fault", is relevant to her over-arching argument that it is through education that we can do good in this world, not just in the home.

In 1907, one of the first things Miss Ironside did was to introduce a school uniform that comprised box-pleated gym tunics, white blouses and ties. This helped create a sense of unity amongst the girls, identifying themselves as belonging to the same school. It also helped ameliorate the snobbery that Ironside had observed amongst some of the girls who regarded their clothing as a marker of social class. The only known photograph of Eileen when at school is one that shows her wearing a slightly later version of this uniform, which has a shorter skirt than that introduced in 1907 (see Fig. 2.1). Another marker of Miss Ironside's desire to level out social differences was the inclusion of elocution lessons for the

2 SCHOOL AND JUVENILIA (1905–1921)   15

Fig. 2.1 Eileen O'Shaughnessy and friend in school uniform. About 1920. UCL Orwell Archive ORWELL/T/3/B/1/1

girls. This continued through to the latter part of the twentieth century, and if we are seeking some idea of what Eileen's accent might have sounded like, we could listen to the BBC's former Chief News Reporter, Kate Adie, who also attended Sunderland Church High School, half a century after Eileen. For the ambitious young woman, such an accent could help her move in elevated circles where judgements are made on the way someone talks.

Another social levelling action was the link Miss Ironside made between the school and the local hospital, the Royal Infirmary. The girls were engaged in charitable work such as sewing garments to distribute in the children's ward and raising funds through "Entertainments", which included staging plays, concerts and tea parties. This was so successful that it was quickly adopted by the other Church High Schools in the region.

The school also formed teams in netball, tennis, swimming and hockey, playing in regional tournaments against teams from other high schools. That said, traditional subjects were still on the curriculum. Needlework, singing and painting, for example, were all still taught, although there was less emphasis on these subjects. The girls were organised in teams and entered local competitions in singing and music. We can see, for example, that the North of England Music tournament in 1922 awarded the school's Senior Girls' Choir second place, a choir that included Eileen O'Shaughnessy (although her first name appears as "Elsie" in the school magazine, *The Chronicle,* in June 1922).

In 1909, Miss Ironside introduced the debating society. The first debate topic was "That women should have the vote and be equal with men". This was carried. It was followed soon by a parade through Sunderland in support of female enfranchisement, and a group of girls from Sunderland Church High took part wearing placards reading: "Votes for Women". This was fully supported by the head teacher of the school. If we look at the topic of the debate, it is more than just Votes for Women: it includes the point that gender equality beyond enfranchisement is also at issue.

A sense of continuity and investment in each girl was further emphasised by the creation of the Old Girls' Guild in 1908, which involved inviting former pupils to engage with the school at various points and in various capacities. The Guild grew, with alumni continuing to be members for many years after leaving school, some of them from their new homes in distant lands. They would also come into Eileen's life as we shall see shortly.

Of greatest relevance to our understanding of Eileen is the school magazine that Miss Ironside set up. This was published bi-annually and took its name from the ecclesiastical context of the school: *The Chronicle*. It was edited by one of the mistresses, but a sub-editor would be drawn from the Lower Sixth and Upper Sixth every year or so. The sub-editor would serve in that role for one calendar year, rather than one academic year. This oddity seems calculated to ensure that the final six months of a girl's schooling could focus entirely on her exams rather than the distraction of a demanding role in editing. The sub-editor's role was to gather stories and reports, and the magazine was professionally printed by a local stationer. Eileen became sub-editor in 1923, when in the Lower Sixth, managing the demanding task of editing whilst also preparing for her university entrance exams. We will return to the editions of the magazine that Eileen edited shortly. The magazine was distributed around the school, to local church luminaries, to other Church High Schools in the area, and to members of the Old Girls' Guild.

Eileen started at Sunderland Church High School in 1915, with the First World War already a year old. The school had raised money for wounded soldiers and their families through garden parties and theatrical performances. Several senior girls and staff worked as Voluntary Aid Detachment staff in the local hospitals. However, school work was not disrupted by the war, and, at the time Eileen O'Shaughnessy entered the school, it was about to adopt the Durham School Certificate (in 1917), which was the local examination board qualification, equivalent to GCSE today.

The year 1917 also saw the introduction of the House system. This was done, according to the former teachers interviewed by Sayers (1984, 37–38), to help foster a greater sense of co-operation and enthusiasm throughout the school, from the Kindergarten up to the Seniors. The decision was taken to follow the system of having four "houses" that was already well-established in boys' fee-paying schools. The girls at Sunderland Church High were divided up according to where they lived, using quadrants on a map. The houses were given names taken from the initials of the school motto *Timor Domini Principium Sapientiae* (TDPS): Tiger (red), Drake (green), Panther (purple) and Swift (blue). Miss Ironside was also careful to note at this time that these shared a name with Royal Naval destroyers. By dent of her home address falling into the northern quadrant of the roughly divided local map that Ironside used, Eileen found herself in Swift House. In this way, the school continued to modernise at a pace, and Eileen was able to take advantage of this (the school report for 1923 notes she is "full of loyal interest in the life of the school", but she was also criticised for untidy work). This is a model of cultural education adopted by the other Church High Schools in the region around this time, but their houses were less imaginatively named: usually these were colours, rather than the well-thought-through animals linked to the school motto that Miss Ironside instigated.

We can thus see that Miss Ironside set about modernising the school, both in its organisation (such as the introduction of the House system), and in its curriculum, with the emphasis on "political and social subjects" beyond the domestic domain. In encouraging debate and engaging with the wider community, the school was outward looking and progressive. This continued into the period of the First World War, with the curriculum's expansion to include a route into university entrance through the Durham University Certification examination. Miss Ironside's influence resulted in a large increase in numbers enrolling at a time when State-run schools were encroaching on the independent school territories. For example, the boys' Church High School in Sunderland closed around 1910 as parents chose to send their sons to the Higher Grade School, later Bede School, in Sunderland, and similar schools in the Tyneside area.

The fact that Ironside was introducing a broader curriculum for the girls at the time of the First World War shows that she was aware of the future necessity for them to earn a living for themselves, without being reliant on a husband to support them. The prescience of Ironside's changes can be seen in retrospect to have been very timely. The interwar years saw young women such as Eileen O'Shaughnessy complete their school education and go to university, and then to earn their own way in life as single women. Single women in the interwar years, women who had never married, reached record numbers in the years following the First World War (Israal, 2002) .

If we look in more detail at Eileen's time at Sunderland Church High School, we can start to see her development of a writing style that would feature so strongly in her letters. By the time the First World War ended, in 1918, we can see that Eileen must have already started to make an impression at the school. She was absent from school for a prolonged period at that time. It may have been a result of the "Spanish Flu" that started in late 1918, a deadly viral infection that spread through the returning troops (and is seen as an early form of the Covid-19 virus a century later). The more serious outbreak of Spanish Flu seems to have occurred in the area in the following year, as the annual reports of the school's sporting exploits for 1919/1920 include mention of Tiger House lamenting their teams depleted by all the boarders being in quarantine for a sizeable part of the year, whilst Swift House celebrated having fewer people in quarantine. The school ledger for the autumn of 1918 notes Eileen's absence: "We much hope for an uninterrupted term [...] We much regret her absence which has made progress impossible". If not Spanish Flu, Eileen may have had any one of a number of different illnesses that would require her to isolate; medical treatment for even common illnesses was very limited at this time, even for the relatively wealthy such as the O'Shaughnessys. There is frequent mention of mumps or scarlet fever being the cause of quarantine and other prolonged absences, so these diseases are also a possible cause. After Christmas 1918, Eileen returned to school and her teachers commented that her progress was "VG", noting, "She has worked splendidly to make up for last term's absence as is clearly shown by her exam results". A year later, in Christmas 1920, the school ledger notes her progress is "Very good; she is growing in depth and strength". The following summer (1921), she is noted under Prizes and Certificates as having won "Senior Divinity. No refusals. Certificate in Inspector's Exam on Church Catechism". What is interesting is that the compulsory study of religion had been removed from the school's curriculum, and so Eileen's achievement here would have been something she chose to do, rather than being part of her routine studies. This could be linked to her marriage in church, 15 years later, as we will see in the next chapter.

From 1921 onwards, Eileen's name appears more frequently in *The Chronicle*. She started to take on leadership roles in the school, such as becoming sub-librarian when she was 16, and she was singled out in school reports as one student to be nurtured for leadership and academic progress. By the summer of 1922, Eileen was described in such a report as being "Full of commonsense and initiative; she has developed in a very satisfactory way". She had formed part of a four-person Senior Reading Team, winning second prize at a North of England Schools competition. She had also had her first poem published in *The Chronicle*.

> SONG
> Oh a rose sky and a gay sky,
> Is the sky of the dawning day;
> And a gold sky and a bright sky

Is the sky when the sun holds sway;
But the sky of skies is pearly grey,
With a rift to show its colours by,
And if it be August or if it be May,
Soft winds will whisper a lullaby,
And the things of the earth will rest.
(*The Chronicle*, June 1922).

In this poem, we see Eileen's sense of optimism. Her stated favourite sky is not the clear blue of a sunny day or the colourful hues of dawn, but the soft grey of a clouded sky that is linked with a sensuously soft wind. Her ability to find beauty in what others might see as dreary or boring is a quality in her that others would note.

In spring 1923, Eileen took on the role of sub-editor of *The Chronicle*. This role was to work under the editorship of one of the mistresses, Miss Dyer. Miss Dyer was also Swift House mistress, and was the tutor assigned to Eileen to help her prepare for her Oxford entrance exams, so Eileen would have worked closely with her in more than one context. The chief job of the sub-editor would be to write a few paragraphs of "notes" after the Introduction letter, which was always written by Miss Ironside. The "notes" section was generally a round-up of school events such as minor in-school competitions and sporting achievements, the names of recipients of awards and scholarships, and visits of any note. The first edition she co-edited, in November 1922, included a second poem:

Satis!
It was a day, a sunlit day
That silvered a late winter's snow,
And those who once had been so gay
Sat vainly wondering what to say,
With heads bowed low.

And one pen squeaked and one went dry,
And one sighed loud and one sighed soft;
Both panic-stricken wondered why
The cuckoo in the clock its cry
Must voice so oft.

> And History with its complex scheme,
> And English with its too deep thought,
> And Essays with unwieldy theme,
> And French and Latin, made them deem
> They were distraught.
>
> But not e'en swift impending doom,
> Nor minds as blank as minds may be
> Bring uniformly settled gloom;
> One joy remained—entered the room
> Two cups of tea.

This poem, with its sense of camaraderie and containment, again offers an optimism that is typical of Eileen's approach to life. She finds humour in the camaraderie of two school girls stuck indoors to write tedious essays, finding no inspiration for their studies. Instead, there is a focus on the distraction of the sound of pens on paper, before the sound of a cuckoo clock rouses them into realising they are wasting time. However, they are saved from despair by the arrival of tea. This is underscored by the title—*Satis!*—which translates from Latin as "Enough!". In other words, the poem is about the frustration of the tedium of school work when there are more interesting things to do, and the realisation that release can come in the form of a cup of tea.

By 1923, Eileen had taken over as Swift House captain (as well as being Hockey Captain). She would therefore be responsible for writing the Swift House Notes. Whilst other House Notes are perfunctory, listing achievements, those produced by Eileen show a lively personality and hint of melodrama: "This last year has not been very successful for the Swifts, for we have only one cup left, for Examination Honours, and our shelf looks deserted and bare".

Eileen's sense of whimsy and playful melodrama seem to have developed around this time in her published writings in *The Chronicle*. This may have been something of a "house style", as it is found in many of Miss Ironside's Introductions to *The Chronicle*. If, for example, we look at the November 1921 edition, Miss Ironside engaged in whimsy to report the departure of a family that had long been connected with the school, referring to them as the "House of Carrick". However, it is the use of melodrama that appears so frequently that bears more attention.

For example, in June 1922, the effect of infectious disease in the school is rendered more dramatic with touches of humour:

> Last term was a miserably disturbed one; to begin with, we came back a fortnight late owing to influenza; we then embarked on mumps in the School House, the last victim being Miss Lunn herself on the very last day of her holidays, after being in such intimate contact with it all through the term that the Doctor said she might almost be considered immune. To her rescue came miracles of help: Miss Hutchinson most generously undertook the VIth and Durham Mathematics [...]

The hyper dramatic use of "miserably" perfectly expresses the sense of despair of both teachers and students, whilst the use of "embarked" to refer to an outbreak of mumps adds a more vividly dynamic sense of an illness. The temporary staff appointments are referred to as "miracles of help" who rescue the school, adding a sense of whimsy to the tedium of consecutive illnesses.

The November 1923 edition of *The Chronicle* opens with Miss Ironside's Introduction:

> A great and devastating cataclysm has come upon the School, and after thirteen years we are to lose Miss Lunn, who has been appointed as Head Mistress of S. Aidan's, Stroud Green.

She continues:

> There was a happening little short of any earthquake when Audrey Sykes' most thoughtless Father allowed himself to be translated to a more magnificent niche, and so bereft not only the Head Mistress of the School that educated his wife as well as his daughter, of her most treasured Secretary, but the School itself of one of its least spareable possessions. The Swifts miss her horribly, so does the English Circle, and the Dramatic will feel itself shorn of more than a Secretary.

Several other contributors attempted to emulate this, but none as successfully as Eileen. The whimsy that is found in her later writings can be glimpsed in her Notes, such as this short paragraph from an otherwise quite dry list of visitors:

> Our only other visitor was Canon Hughes, who came not to speak but to sing to us. Of his singing we can only say that we hope he will give us a speedy opportunity of hearing it again, even if we are to pay the penalty of another general knowledge test.

Eileen's playfulness can be seen here in the rhetorical flourish of "came not to speak but to sing", carrying the Shakespearean echoes Mark Antony's speech on the Citadel in *Julius Caesar* in its use of contrasts. She finishes the paragraph with the implicature that the girls had been subjected to an ad hoc general knowledge test by Canon Hughes, which they had not enjoyed.

In the last edition of *The Chronicle* co-edited by Eileen, her Notes section includes a rare piece of punning: she refers to the absence of Miss Lunn in what could be seen as being a piece of clumsy rhetoric, but is actually cleverly constructed:

> We cannot begin to say how much we miss Miss Lunn.

There are several other alternatives to this repetition of "miss", and Miss Dyer's pen is seen editing various other areas of the text in most issues, but not here. It must be the case that Miss Dyer saw the wit of Eileen's writing and chose to leave in the polysemic pun.

We can also see direct links with Miss Ironside's use of melodrama in other areas of Eileen's writing in *The Chronicle*. For example, in June 1924's Swift House report, Eileen begins with:

> To our sorrow we have started this term without Miss Gregersen, but we are especially glad to welcome again Miss Chalmers, who deserted us some time ago, and we have been lucky enough to lose only one other member of the house.

This combination of melodrama and hyperbole (Miss Chalmers "deserted" the sports team, rather than "dropped out") mirrors what we have seen in Miss Ironside's contributions to the magazine. However, Eileen goes on:

> Membership would mean for each individual a continual and vigorous effort. Laziness and tepidity are the sins into which we fall most easily, and we are glad that we can only lay them to the charge of the very few, while congratulating the many on a really active co-operation.

Here, we can see a sharper side of hyperbole where a lack of enthusiasm is rephrased as "laziness and tepidity", which are collocated in a religious frame as "sins". These accusations are ameliorated by the inclusive pronoun "we", which allows the less enthusiastic Swifts a way back into the in-group of the more active members via the sympathetic understanding that these sins are easy to fall into. Added to this, we can also see that Eileen, in her last term at school and with the pressures of exams, is exasperated by the lack of co-operation. It is not too far from the frustration of *Satis!*, as we saw earlier.

The notion of the House being a community is one that Eileen had used in the November 1923 report for *The Chronicle*, which marked her first year as House Captain. In her report, she welcomes new Swifts to the active House membership:

> We hope that they are as glad to join us as we are to welcome them, and that the old Swifts will see that the newcomers feel that they belong to a House which not only realizes but practices the ideal of fellowship and co-operation.
> The shelf beneath our shield is better furnished than it has been lately, but there is still room for several more cups without overcrowding. In the Sports we lost considerably on Team Races though we did quite well in individual events, but we hope in future that we shall not fail through lack of co-operation, but realize that in a House as in a kingdom "Unity is strength".

Eileen presents the Swifts as being a community, one which embraces solidarity as an ideal. It is interesting that she notes the apparent lack of team achievements she has inherited, with more success by individual sporting achievements. She finishes her report with a noteworthy merging of religious rhetoric—"in a House as in a kingdom"—and socialist slogan, "Unity is strength". It is tempting to see this as Eileen demonstrating both her religious education and her burgeoning political awareness.

It should also be noted that Eileen's House reports are very different in tone to those of other House captains. If we look, for example, at the rather bland note of welcoming new members by Panthers House Captain, Christal Robson:

> We take this opportunity of wishing all the Panthers who have left us the best of luck, and hope that those who are still here will do their best to make all the new members happy with us.

There is no mention of lofty ideals, and the lively prose of Eileen's report stands out as an example of her own lively personality. Eileen's successor as House Captain records in the November 1924 House Notes that "We were very sorry to have to say good-bye to three Swifts last term, and especially to Eileen O'Shaughnessy who captained us so splendidly during the year".

Elsewhere, if we look at the content of Eileen's Notes sections, there is little that distinguishes her writing from that of the other sub-editors who did a similar job of rounding up records of speakers, sporting and academic achievements, and Old Girls' news. However, if we look at some of the more detailed descriptions of the content of speakers' talks, we can see as hints of her future interests in politics, as well as an understanding of personal deprivation. For example, in *The Chronicle* of November 1923, Eileen writes an account of a talk by a Mr Whelan who was promoting the League of Nations:

> [Mr Whelan] put into words the great ideal of the League—friendship between the nations of the world, and, by the destruction of hatred, abolition of war, and told us besides of the practical results which had been achieved in countries suffering from national and individual poverty, famine, and disease—Poland, Austria, and Russia. To this, and to an address which Mr Whelan gave later to the Sunderland Branch of the League of Nations, we owe our own branch, whose activities are reported elsewhere.

The years immediately after the First World War saw many people questioning the logic of warfare. The war also was often referred to as "The War to End All Wars", so great was the shock of that conflict on the population. The League of Nations became the forerunner of the United Nations a quarter of a century later. Sunderland Church High School was inspired by Mr Whelan's speech to set up its own branch of the League of Nations: Eileen was the first chair of this.

Many of the other speakers were missionaries, who would have been sponsored by the Church and so connected to the schools. Such schools were rich recruiting grounds for missionary work at this time, and so it is not surprising that the majority of speakers at Sunderland Church High School came from this calling. The religious zeal of such missionaries is clearly seen in one description by Eileen, from November 1923:

> Miss Graham, whom most of us remember very well, came again this term to speak on Missions. She said that Missionary work solved the problem of how to live side by side with the rest of the people in the world, and that the Western peoples must make good their civilization and conquer the prejudices of the East, which arose merely from social misunderstanding. This applied specially to India—the dim and mysterious—which was composed of many races united by a common hatred of the white peoples, and which was the special responsibility of Great Britain.

Superficially, this is a typical account of the sort of missionary talks that the girls were subjected to, where Christianity is seen as a civilising force for good. However, there may be some hint that Eileen was not entirely convinced by this. She uses indirect speech ("she said that…") which distances the writer from the speaker and so leaves room to question the veracity of the sentiment. This contrasts with the style of reporting used by other sub-editors who used more involved indirect speech, such as "she explained that…" and "she spoke of…" In these cases, there is less room to challenge the point of view of the speaker. Miss Graham seems to have specifically highlighted the problem of India, where "many races" are united by a common hatred, particularly of the British rulers. Eileen adds her own sentiment to this passage through the parenthetical "dim and mysterious" adjectival description of India, reflecting perhaps her own passing interest in the subcontinent (note that it is not "dark and dangerous"). Given her future husband's links with India, this is an interesting early example of how Eileen is already forming opinions about this nation.

We can thus see that there is the beginning of a witty, whimsical and politically engaged young woman in Eileen's writing when at school. She had a role model for this in Miss Ironside, who would have shown that such a style of writing was acceptable for publishing. Miss Ironside's curriculum innovations and her changes to the culture of the school all positively affected Eileen. Beyond this, there is another area to Miss Ironside's changes to the school that Eileen was able to take advantage of: university scholarships.

Scholarships

As Holden (2007) has commented in relation to the tracking of census statistics at this time, more than half of the women who were single in 1921 had not married by the time of the 1931 census. Although the percentage of women who were unmarried (including never married and widowed) in 1921 was remarkably high, this was mostly caused by the huge rise in the number of women widowed by the war. By 1931, however, the number of widows had returned to a level comparable with 1911, as most of them had remarried (Smith 2013). This greater likelihood of having no male head of household who could support them was something many young middle-class women became alert to as the attritional realities of the war unfolded. Rosamund Essex's (1977) oral history of this time records testimony from women from middle-class backgrounds that reveals they were warned by schools and universities about the shortage of men and that they should make career choices with this in mind. This chimes with the changes Miss Ironside made to the curriculum and culture of Sunderland Church High School around the time of Eileen O'Shaughnessy. In fact, Ironside's report in the November 1917 *Chronicle* directly addresses this. She warns against the lure of short-term war work in banks and offices, and cites government concerns of a looming teacher shortage. She writes there is an:

> urgent necessity of women training for Education, [encouraging in particular] girls who were in doubt as to whether they aught to spend money on Oxford or Cambridge when they could quite well be earning a weekly salary with no training at all [...] If she has a special love for small children, she should certainly take the Fröebel Course, and if for older children she must begin working as soon as may be for an entrance to one of the Universities, or if possible for a scholarship. (*The Chronicle*, November 1917)

Whilst teaching is seen here as the most desirable profession for young women, the need to gain a university education is marked out for special attention because of the financial implications. To better enable girls to go to university, Miss Ironside instigated a system of scholarships. These were specifically aimed at girls who would go to Oxford or Cambridge universities. At that time, even though neither university allowed women to graduate, the value perceived of an education offered at these two universities was temptation enough to apply. Such was the esteem, the school allocated a mistress to coach potential entrants: Eileen's coach was Miss Dyer, the mistress who also edited *The Chronicle* as well as teaching English and Latin.

The first scholarship was set up in 1918, and was funded by the Old Girls' Guild. This was open to any girl who applied to go to any university in the UK and would pay £30 per year. The scholarship was not awarded every year, but the school record book shows that Eileen was awarded it in both 1925 and 1926. A note in Miss Ironside's report in the November 1925 edition of *The Chronicle* shows that Eileen was still very much in the minds of her former colleagues as the previous recipient of the Old Girls' Scholarship graduated and so was no longer eligible for the award. Miss Ironside notes:

> Eileen O'Shaughnessy, who is reading English at S. Hugh's College, Oxford, has been elected as their new scholar.

Thus the scholarship was awarded to Eileen, who was already a year into her studies. It was not awarded to any other Old Girl who was already at university, nor to any of the girls who would be in a position to start university the following academic year. The Old Girls' Scholarship shows the changes Ironside had made in the school in bringing a greater sense of collaboration and responsibility, even after leaving school. The criterion for the awarding of the scholarship was not financial need (which would have been rather odd, given the fact that this is a fee-paying school and attracted affluent middle-class families), but rather exceptional promise, which undoubtedly was seen to be found in Eileen.

A second scholarship was instituted in 1919: the Everett Scholarship. This had been funded by the Everett family who donated a £1,000 War Loan to the school for the scholarship as a thanks-giving offering for the safe return of their son (a former Old Boy at the since-closed Boys' School) from the war. Their daughter, Dorothy, had been an Old Girl and she continued to manage the scholarship for many years, ensuring it was safely invested and able to keep up with rising costs. To begin with, Oxbridge entrants were eligible for a grant of £20 per year for three years. Like the Old Girls' Scholarship, this was based solely on academic merit.

In setting up financial incentives to apply to university, the school was encouraging its young women to prepare themselves such that their education could be of value beyond the home. In perusing the carved wooden prize boards at the school, it is noticeable that Eileen O'Shaughnessy is the only person whose name appears on plaques for both the Old Girls' Scholarship and the Everett Scholarship. Granted, the 1930s saw a change in rule so that any one individual could hold only one scholarship at a time. Nonetheless, it does show us something of the exceptional student who was Eileen O'Shaughnessy. In keeping with this, her list of achievements whilst at the school is remarkable:

> Head girl
> Head prefect
> Swift House captain
> Sub-editor of *The Chronicle*
> Sub-librarian
> President of the League of Nations Branch
> Whitaker Thompson Memorial Prize winner

This latter prize is named after Mr Whitaker Thompson, who had been Chairman of the Church Schools Company for many years and had left a small legacy in the form of this prize in his will. The prize was open to entrants from all the Church High Schools in the region, so Eileen's success in winning this particular prize hints at her talents being recognised more widely than in just Sunderland Church High School.

As Swift House Captain, too, Eileen can be glimpsed as a motivational and enthusiastic leader. Overall, it seems Eileen's leadership and organizational qualities were recognised throughout the school, not just in Swift House. Her editing of the school magazine hints at Eileen's future life as editor of Orwell's work. Furthermore, we can also see her interest in politics and international affairs in her involvement in the League of Nations branch, something that she might well have drawn on as a common interest with Orwell when they first met.

University and Beyond

Eileen went to St Hugh's College, Oxford in the autumn of 1924 to study English Language and Literature. This is recorded in Miss Ironside's column in *The Chronicle* in June 1924:

> Eileen O'Shaughnessy has brought great honour to the School with her English Bursary of £20 per annum for three years at S. Hugh's College, Oxford; and Margaret Ellis also with her entrance to S. Hugh's on her

History Scholarship paper. We congratulate them most heartily, and their coaches, Miss Dyer and Miss Curran.

The Chronicle from November 1924 continues in the same tone, describing Eileen and two other university-bound former girls as "real props of the school". The bright, enthusiastic outstanding schoolgirl embraced university life, supported in part by the scholarships she had won from Sunderland Church High School as well as the Oxford bursary, which in her case was for £20 per annum for three years. As we will see in the next chapter, Eileen's dream of out-performing her brother Eric in academic achievement by obtaining a First at Oxford was thwarted. Eileen's initial dream of spending her days as an academic immersed in Literature were never realised. Instead, she tried her hand at teaching. There is a later mention of Eileen in *The Chronicle*, where the November 1927 edition does not record her degree, as is found in the case of other Old Girls, but her career: "Eileen O'Shaughnessy is teaching English at Taplow". It seems Eileen did keep in touch as an Old Girl, which is unsurprising given her various scholarships from the school. However, the same report that notes her career also urges Old Girls to keep in touch: "There is very little news of Guild members this time. We would like more letters telling of your doings and any interesting happenings. This Magazine travels to most parts of the world, so there should be lots of interest". Thus, we can see that Eileen was keen to continue as an active Old Girl at this point, although there is no further mention of her in the magazine until her contribution to the 50th anniversary edition in 1934. From then on, she appears in the list of events, such as her marriage in 1936, a change of address (to the Wallington cottage in 1937) and, finally, her death in 1945. It would appear that she retained a subscription to the magazine all her life and heard of the call for contributions for the Golden Anniversary edition of the magazine that way rather than through any individual invitation.

What we can tell from the updates on previous students is that most of the Old Girls who had recently graduated seem to have gone in for teaching. Teaching was by far the most popular profession for single women at that time; indeed it had been her mother's pre-marriage occupation. By 1931, it was estimated that more than half of the single professional women aged 35–45 in the UK were teachers: that is one in eleven women who were in paid employment. Until 1944, married women would be obliged to resign their posts. Another option for the highly educated young women was in the civil service, which again had a marriage bar in place until 1946 (or until 1973 for the Foreign Service) (Civilservantorg.uk). Exacerbating the injustice still further, women at this time earned on average 60–80% less than men for doing the same or a comparable job. This gender disparity continued well into the latter part of the century, and it took the efforts of Second Wave feminists in the 1960s to bring about political action for equal pay. Education could only help so far, in a context in which society was still orientated towards a patriarchal stance.

Primary Sources

The Chronicle (School magazine for Sunderland Church High School).

November 1917
November 1918
June 1922
November 1923
June 1924
November 1924
November 1927
June 1934
June 1936
November 1937
June 1945

Additional primary sources from Sunderland Church High School's archive held at Sunderland Antiquarian Society are reproduced with the consent of that organisation.

References

Bell, Rudolph and Virginia Yans (2008) (eds), *Women on their Own: interdisciplinary perspectives on being single,* New Brunswick, Rutgers University Press.
Civilservantorg.uk Women in the Civil Service: a history, https://www.civilservant.org.uk/women-history.html [Accessed 27 July 2022].
Essex, Rosamund (1977), *Woman in a Man's World,* London, Sheldon Press.
Holden, Katherine (2007), *The Shadow of Marriage: singleness in England 1914-60,* Manchester, Manchester University Press.

Israal, Betsy (2002), *Bachelor Girl: the secret history of single women in the twentieth century*, New York, William Morrow.

Sayers, Audrey B. (1984), *Sunderland Church High School for Girls: a centenary history*, Privately printed.

Smith, Angela (2013), *Discourses Surrounding British Widows of the First World War*, London, Bloomsbury.

Topp, Sylvia (2020), *Eileen: The Making of George Orwell*, London, Unbound.

Vicinus, Martha (1985), *Independent Women: work and community for single women 1850-1920*, London, Virago.

CHAPTER 3

Oxford and London (1922–1934)

INTRODUCTION

In 1924, when Eileen O'Shaughnessy arrived in Oxford, only four colleges accepted female students, and it was just four years since the university had deigned to award degrees to women. The first cohort of women allowed to graduate from Oxford occurred in 1920, but amongst these were some of the women who would become well-known writers: Vera Brittain, Winifred Holtby and Dorothy L. Sayers. Of these, Brittain's autobiographical account shows post-war Oxford to be an uncomfortable place for those more mature students: these women had all started their studies before the First World War, but had suspended them in order to take in war work, particularly voluntary nursing. When they returned to Oxford to finish their degrees, they found themselves having to live and study amongst younger women who had not experienced the adventure and drama of war. In *Testament of Youth* (1933), Brittain writes of the feeling of isolation and alienation from the gaiety of the younger women. Sayers, on the other hand, uses Oxford as the backdrop to her 1935 novel, *Gaudy Night*, where her protagonist, Lord Peter Wimsey, plays second fiddle to Harriet Vane. Harriet is represented as a former graduate of a fictional Oxford college who returns for a Gaudy Night celebration and recalls her happy times as a student in her youth, referring to "the grey walled paradise of Oxford" (1988, p. 22), with an approximate graduation date that would coincide with Eileen's. Harriet is given a biography of having obtained a First in English, and is making a living as a mystery writer who has achieved notoriety for being tried for the murder of a lover in an earlier book (*Strong Poison*, 1930), before being acquitted through the detective work of Lord Peter. In many ways, we can see through Sayers' fictional account that an Oxford education for a young woman at this time could be liberating and exciting.

St Hugh's College was some distance to the North of the main campus, but Eileen was put in accommodation close by. At the time, St Hugh's was the largest of the women's colleges at Oxford. We have no record of Eileen's arrival beyond her entry in the official registry on 10 October 1924. Eileen shared her digs with two other St Hugh's students: Esther Power and Norah Myles neé Symes. Esther was American and has left us a vivid record of her own arrival, offered as part of a collection of remembrances to celebrate 100 years of St Hugh's, in 1986 (see St Hugh's Archive). She writes of the cold and dampness of Oxford, but things brightened up when she "met two of the liveliest English girls, Eileen O'Shaughnessy and Norah Symes, who shared with [her] the same digs". The three young women quickly became very close friends and remained in touch long after graduating. Eileen's letters to Norah in later years continued to use the nickname she had acquired at Oxford: Pig. It is not clear how this nickname came about. Topp (2020) suggests that, given evidence from cast lists showing she played minor parts in student plays, it might have been a nickname she acquired having played the part of a pig. However, given her teachers' and tutors' comments about her general untidiness, it may be that there was a joke about the mess in her lodgings—a "pigsty"—that led to this nickname being fondly adopted by the housemates.

Life at Oxford for the female students was rigidly set out. They were expected to be dressed in academic caps and gowns at all times, even when riding bicycles. Page after page of rules dictated things such as curfew time, chaperone arrangements, and rules on conduct at dances. The fifty female students who enrolled at St Hugh's with Eileen would all have been privately educated and came from relatively wealthy families. In addition to her scholarships, Eileen's life at Oxford would have been supported by her father.

An active Literary Society invited well-known speakers to visit, speakers such as Vita Sackville-West and G. K. Chesterton. One of the main attractions of Oxbridge universities was—and still is—the links and networks students can make. Esther's recollections include attending Lady Astor's

Ball in London, where the Prince of Wales was in attendance. It would not be unlikely that Eileen accompanied Esther on such trips, and, in later years, Orwell was impressed that Eileen seemed to know so many important and influential people who could be called on when needed.

Eileen studied English Language and Literature, although the "Language" side would have meant translation into and out of Latin or Old English rather than the more recent development of English Linguistics. The syllabus was a traditional survey from Anglo-Saxon to the Nineteenth Century. Amongst this, Eileen would appear to have found a particular love of the Romantic poets, as books of such poetry travelled with her to Spain ten years later. Students were taught by a mixture of new academics and more experienced ones. Amongst the new academics were J. R. R. Tolkien, who started at Oxford in 1925 and taught Anglo-Saxon literature to Eileen and the other students. He was one of Eileen's four viva examiners when she was sitting for her final exams in 1927. Another lecturer was C. S. Lewis, whom Esther remembers as being dismissive of female students. It would seem that, for some academics at least, women were still not welcome at Oxford.

Whilst we have no recollections of Eileen for this period of her life, we do have some of the reports written about her by her tutors. One of them, Miss Francis, reported:

> Miss O'Shaughnessy has a sense of style and when she translates correctly her work is quite good. But the weakness, which her prose composition discloses, is a hinderance to her in a general way. She is a hard worker, and I hope will get up to standard on her set books.

Another tutor, Miss Ritchie, commented encouragingly on Eileen's translation of Latin into English:

> Latin Prose & Unseen: Miss O'Shaughnessy's work is clear-headed & intelligent, & she seems to be well grounded. Her prose is on the whole better than her unseen; but she should pass in both without difficulty.
> Pliny & Virgil: Both papers were satisfactory & pleasant to read. Miss O'Shaughnessy's style is good. Her knowledge of the subject matter might have been better.

Later in the year, Miss Francis was still critical of Eileen's work:

> Set Books: A good collection paper. Miss O'Shaughnessy has distinct ability.
> Prose: Unfortunately this is very weak. Miss O'Shaughnessy has a sense of style and often selects her vocabulary well; but her work is constantly marred by careless errors of a very serious kind. I am much afraid this may plough her.

Another tutor at the end of her first year, Miss Stopford, is more encouraging:

> Miss O'Shaughnessy's work has been most satisfactory. Her essays show wide reading & appreciation. She has a certain sense of style and her work, on the whole, is promising.

It would seem that Eileen's tutors were recognising her ability to write in terms of style, and that she was a hard worker. Perhaps the weaker area of her academic knowledge, at this stage at least, was the translation work. Yet her tutors were encouraging and could see her as a hard worker.

After a summer break with her family in South Shields, Eileen returned to Oxford in the autumn of 1925, where she took on the role of second year representative for *The Imp* magazine; Norah is listed as Treasurer. This magazine had been started in 1918 as a student literary publication, but by 1920 it had expanded to cover a broader range of topics. The Orwell Archive holds a fragment of a comic play that Eileen wrote when at Oxford, so it may be that she was writing contributions to the magazine as well as producing performances. As none of the contributions to the magazine are attributed to specific authors, we cannot be sure of any other creative work she wrote at this time.

However, Eileen's name vanishes from copies of *The Imp* within the year. Topp suggests that she moved to work on a strongly suffragist magazine, *The Fritillary*, which was jointly run by the four women's colleges at Oxford. There is a photo of students parading through Oxford with placards urging people to buy the magazine, and one of these students is thought to be Eileen. Again, the contributions to the magazine were anonymous.

In the remaining tutor reports for Eileen's second year of studies, we can again see a distinction between her English Language and Literature studies. In Language, Miss Buckhurst writes:

> Miss O'Shaughnessy is capable of very good work but does not always produce it. A more sustained effort is needed, both in phonology and translation.

This contrasts with her Literature papers, where Miss Seaton reports:

> Miss O'Shaughnessy did some good work in her Collections papers & had worked with capability, & some enthusiasm & humour. She needs to read even more widely to bring her matter up to the level of her excellent arrangement & style.

Eileen's struggles with Language continued into the summer term of 1926, with Miss Buckhurst lamenting:

> I still feel Miss O'Shaughnessy does not always give her best in her language work; she generally seems content with a moderate achievement, but at times shows that she is capable of almost first-class work. Her fluent style in translation sometimes covers a slight uncertainty as to the exact meaning.

Thus, Eileen entered her final year at Oxford with work still to do to meet the highest standards, particularly in English Language. Miss Buckhurst seems to have recognised the improvement in her work:

> Miss O'Shaughnessy has produced extremely good work in language, both in translation and written papers. Her work is clear and accurate and is generally well arranged.

Such a report must have been a huge relief to Eileen! However, a new tutor—Frank Wilson—had arrived at Oxford and was less enthusiastic about her Literature work:

> Her work has no great depth or penetration, but is pleasant and attractively fresh. She writes with point and edge and with good taste and discrimination.

The strategy of damning with faint praise is seen here, where Eileen is implicitly accused of being shallow in her understanding. At the same time, she is implicitly praised for frivolity. There is a gendered element to this, and perhaps gave notice of the attitude of her examiners in her forthcoming viva (Wilson was one of the four appointed). However, it was not all faint praise. An un-named tutor's report comments on her work in Romantic Literature:

> A well written thoughtful paper, showing independence of judgment & sound taste. The answer on Coleridge as a critic was excellently presented, that of Keats & Shelley unusually sane & discriminating. She writes from a full knowledge & has a real critical gift.

Eileen's love of the Romantic poets is recognised in this report on her work, whilst she is also praised for writing a "sane" essay, which could hint at a superficial appearance of frivolity in her personal manner.

At the end of her final year came exams week. Esther writes of the experience of this high-pressure environment, describing the exam hall. This description mentions her friend: "I saw Eileen O'Shaughnessy sitting at the end of the next row. She was opening a little box and eating aspirins, apparently trying to assuage her neuralgia pains". There was very little written by or to Eileen about her own discomfort or health, but this early description of "neuralgia" appears in Esther's account as being something that was not unusual for Eileen. Neuralgia can take many forms, and perhaps here it could be linked to migraine (and it would not be unusual for any student sitting high-pressure exams to suffer from such), or it could be linked, for example, to chronic period pain. In any case, this medical problem is one that Eileen is battling with during the most important exams of her life. Students had to endure the written exams as well as an oral examination by four academics. In Eileen's case, these were Mr A. O. Balfour; J. R. R. Tolkien, Mr Frank Wilson and Professor Ernest de Selincourt. At the end of the examination period, the results were posted on the St Hugh's noticeboard: no one had obtained a First. Eileen must have been devastated, with Jackson recording that she was "bitterly disappointed" (1976, p. 343). She had set her sights on becoming an academic, but access to that career was dependent on obtaining a First Class degree. Instead, Eileen was one of ten students who obtained a Second Class degree, with Norah and Esther only obtaining Thirds. Out of the 50 women who had started at St Hugh's with Eileen, only 33 completed their degrees. Another student from Sunderland Church High School, Margaret Ellis, had dropped out of her degree after finding it too challenging. Others had left to get married. However, Eileen had stuck with her studies, paying off the faith in her that the scholarships from

Sunderland Church High School had anticipated. And it was the friendships and other links she made at Oxford that would prove to be of more use to her in the future. Her competitive relationship with her brother had also been another factor in her desire to get a First: Eric O'Shaughnessy had managed only a Second Class degree in Medicine, but had already started on what would become a brilliant career in medicine, moving to work in Sudan in 1924.

The world Eileen entered on graduating was very different from that of previous generations, but one that Miss Ironside's educational vision had started to prepare her for. Eileen was entering a world of work, where women could earn enough money to be self-sufficient. For young women with degrees, the most common employment was teaching. By the time of the 1931 census in the UK, more than half of single educated women in the UK were employed as teachers: that is 6:11 women. At this time, a marriage bar still existed, with married female teachers being forced to resign (similar marriage bars existed in other professional employment opportunities such as the Civil Service and nursing). Eileen's mother had been a teaching assistant before her marriage, and so it is not unexpected that the first job Eileen obtained after graduation were as a teaching assistant. This was at a fee-paying girls' school, Silchester House, in Taplow, Buckinghamshire. Her parents were living in Hillingdon in North-West London by this time, where they had moved following her father's retirement in 1925. This meant it was within commuting distance for Eileen, who could save money by living with her parents whilst working at the school. Eileen wrote to Sunderland Church High School to update them on her progress, and this is one of the last mentions of Eileen that appears in *The Chronicle*, in November 1927. However, Eileen loathed teaching. She lasted only one term at Silchester House, telling a friend she was "engaged mainly in making a humorous study of the species of female who own and staff such schools" (Jackson 1960, p. 115). It would seem that even in the midst of a miserable teaching job, Eileen was able to find humour, even if this is tinged with a sharp criticism of fellow female employees.

The years following Eileen's graduation were transformational for women in Britain. The general election in May 1929 was the first time women had parity with men when it came to voting rights. It was also the second time a Labour government was elected, under Ramsay MacDonald, an MP whose constituency of Seaham was next to Sunderland. Sunderland returned its first female MP, Dr Marion

Phillips. Disparagingly, this election was called "the Flapper Election", highlighting the lowered age of female enfranchisement at a time when young women were carefree, frivolous and generally lacking in respect for authority. However, not all young women were able to lead such carefree lives, and Eileen was amongst that latter group.

Eileen's father, Laurence, died of tuberculosis on 5 November 1929. His will revealed very little by way of savings, despite the well-paid job he had enjoyed. Eileen and her mother continued to live in the family home in Hillingdon, and it would seem that around this time Eileen took a shorthand and typing course. In Eileen's tutors' reports from her time at Oxford, it seems that phonetics and phonology were part of her English Language studies, being used in the translation of Old English into modern English. Miss Buckhurst's report from Eileen's second year comments on a need to improve in this area. However, it does seem to have helped Eileen in her search for work after graduation: in her shorthand and typing class, her knowledge of English phonetics would be invaluable in picking up Pitman shorthand.

From Topp's research, we can piece together that Eileen was engaged as a shorthand typist at the agency W. B. Gurney & Sons of 47 Victoria Street, London. As an alumni of St Hugh's, Eileen kept the college updated with her various employment positions, but she was somewhat vague about just what these involved. For example, in early 1930, she wrote to inform the college that she was working on the "Archbishop's Advisory Board for Prevention and Rescue Work", which was a committee of do-gooders who were intent on "rescuing" sex workers. As Eileen's name does not appear in any of the membership or associates lists for this committee, it is most likely that she was working as a shorthand typist (Topp's detective work has traced an advertisement for such a post at this time). However, Eileen's time at Gurney's was short-lived. She wrote to a friend that the office was "run by a neurotically sadistic woman" who "took pleasure in humiliating her employees, criticising their work in a most severe, destructive way and keeping them under a permanent threat of dismissal" (Jackson 1976, p. 343). Whilst it might be tempting to see the context as that of a lively, intelligent Eileen being perceived as a threat by someone less well educated, and thus that person taking a dislike to her and wielding power over Eileen with such threats of dismissal, Jackson (1960, p115) records a testimony from another former employee that reports much the same behaviour, commenting that the female boss "revelled in reducing all her female staff to tears". Eileen had been trained in leadership whilst at school, and had experience of what good leadership and management looked like. Although we lack any detail of what she actually did at Gurney's, she wrote that before she resigned she "led a successful 'revolt of the oppressed' against [the boss] before [she] walked out in triumph" (ibid.). The mischievous nature of Eileen's character is shown here to be aligned with a sense of social justice that also harks back to her leading role in the formation of the League of Nations whilst at school.

Eileen's next job was rather different. In 1931, she went to Birmingham to act as "reader to Mrs George Cadbury"; the Mrs Cadbury was actually Dame Elizabeth Cadbury. The job of companion to an elderly women was the role many educated young women had taken up throughout the nineteenth century and into the twentieth, and it was generally perceived to be a one of low status and tedium. Thus it is a curious choice for Eileen, were we not to understand more about Dame Elizabeth Cadbury. The Cadbury family were wealthy through their innovations as chocolate makers and were philanthropists who chose to focus on social inequalities. Dame Elizabeth was well known for her work in fighting social inequalities and had a long-standing interest in promoting women's welfare. In an echo of Miss Ironside's teachings, Dame Elizabeth believed that well-educated woman should have a life of service. However, for whatever reason, Eileen's time in Birmingham was short-lived. By December 1931, she was living and working in London.

Eileen and her mother had rented out the house in Hillingdon and instead were sharing a flat at 22 Albany Mansions, Albert Bridge Road, in South West London. In December 1931, Eileen wrote to Oxford University that she was "Proprietor of an office in Victoria Street for translation, typing and secretarial services". This was Murrell's Typewriting Bureau, a business Eileen had bought from its founder, Grace Murrell. It was next door to Gurney's. Eileen employed an assistant, Edna (later Edna Bussey), who was just 15 years old. In a letter to the Orwell Archive in 1968, Edna recalled her time working at the bureau with Eileen. She paints a picture of Eileen as someone who was genuinely trying to help her clients, with little interest in making money. She writes:

> They were very happy days as [Eileen] was a very happy person and had a very vivid personality. I don't think she ever made very much money as she was too generous and I fear most unbusinesslike. She was untiring in her efforts to help people [...] There was a Mr Tereshenko, he was a white

Russian, who was writing a thesis for his professorship, being taken under [Eileen's] wing. She literally re-wrote his thesis for him and I have always felt that it was she who earned the professorship [...] Writing was her love I think. (Bussey, 1968)

It would seem that Eileen's experience of editing *The Chronicle* when at school was now proving itself to be invaluable. She was able to use her skills as a writer to make a non-native speaker's thesis perfectly comprehensible, building on the "translation" that had been part of her undergraduate degree.

Eileen's brother Eric returned to the UK in 1932. He had been working in the Sudan Medical Service since 1924, meeting and marrying Gwen Hunton there. Gwen was also a doctor, and her family also had close links with the North East of England. Eric and Gwen returned to England to live, settling in 59 Trafalgar Road, Greenwich. In 1933, Eileen and her mother moved to 59a Trafalgar Road, probably a flat in the same building. Eric specialised in thoracic medicine, possibly motivated by their father's suffering from TB. Gwen worked as a general practitioner but with a specialist interest in ophthalmology. Eric was building a reputation as a leading doctor in his field, publishing papers on his research. These papers were mostly written with Eileen's help, as it was well known that Eric's written English was infamously lacking in clarity. The Orwell Archive holds many pages of Eileen's shorthand notes, dictation taken from Eric. He published in the most prestigious journals, such as *The Lancet*, and worked on scholarly tomes with the renowned German surgeon, Ferdinand Sauerbruch. All of this was done with the help of Eileen. In what would become a pattern with Eileen's editing work, it was never acknowledged by the benefactor, and it would seem that she had no expectation that it would be.

In 1934, Sunderland Church High School celebrated its 50th anniversary. As an Old Girl, Eileen would have been aware of this through the regular delivery of *The Chronicle*, and she would also have seen the call for Old Girls to provide a written contribution to a special edition of the magazine to mark this milestone. This was a period in which the rise of fascism in Europe was just beginning to be seen as a looming threat to world peace. Winifred Holtby's posthumously published novel, *South Riding* (1936), finishes with the looming menace of conflict on the horizon; Holtby died in September 1935. Like Eileen, Holtby had been a member of the League of Nations when at school and had been an active member of the Labour Party. It should not be a surprise to learn, therefore, that Eileen's contribution to a special issue of *The Chronicle* in 1934 contains traces of this concern with politics.

Whilst many of the Old Girls contributed short stories about their time at school, only two of them contributed poems: Eileen is one of these. Her poem, "End of the Century, 1984", looks both back at the previous 50 years and forward 50 years.

> END OF THE CENTURY, 1984
> Death
> Synthetic winds have blown away
> Material dust, but this one room
> Rebukes the constant violet ray
> And dustless sheds a dusty doom.
> Wrecked on the outmoded past
> Lie North and Hillard, Virgil, Horace,
> Shakespeare's bones are quiet at last.
> Dead as Yeats or William Morris.
> Have not the inmates earned their rest?
> A hundred circles traversed they
> Complaining of the classic quest
> And, each inevitable day,
> Illogically trying to place
> A ball within an empty space.
>
> Birth
> Every loss is now a gain
> For every chance must follow reason.
> A crystal palace meets the rain
> That falls at its appointed season.
> No book disturbs the lucid line
> For sun-bronzed scholars tune their thought
> To Telepathic Station 9
> From which they know just what they ought;
> The useful sciences; the arts
> Of telesalesmanship and Spanish
> As registered in Western parts;
> Mental cremation that shall banish
> Relics, philosophies and colds—
> Mañana-minded ten-year-olds.

> The Phoenix
> Worlds have died that they may live,
> May plume again their fairest feathers
> And in their clearest songs may give
> Welcome to all spontaneous weathers.
> Bacon's colleague is called Einstein,
> Huxley shares Platonic food,
> Violet rays are only sunshine
> Christened in the modern mood.
> In this house if in no other
> Past and future may agree,
> Each herself, but each the other
> In a curious harmony.
> Finding both a proper place
> In the silken gown's embrace.

The world of 1934 was indeed alarming. In this poem, Eileen envisages the stifling and destruction of a world of culture and the arts, with Hitler already using art and culture to both elevate Nazism and denigrate those whom he deemed un-Germanic. Eileen would have received first-hand accounts of life in Germany through her brother, who continued to travel there as part of his on-going research collaborations.

Eileen's poem starts with "Death", and perhaps can be read as her own sadness at not having time to read her beloved poetry books any more, where her work as typist and editor leaves her literary knowledge "outmoded", and how this is reflected in a lack of attention given to the literary arts in society in general as it rushes to modernity. In "Birth", she dips into a futuristic present (in much the same way as Stella Gibbons' 1932 novel, *Cold Comfort Farm*, does), disapproving of the emphasis on science and technology. In referring to "sun-bronzed scholars", there is also a link back to her earlier poem in *The Chronicle*, "Satis!", which depicts the bored and hard-working scholars at work indoors, gazing out of the window at the forbidden freedom. However, this freedom to languish outside in the sun is not beneficial, as these scholars do not need books, but are fed information via Telepathic Station 9, and that information is limited to what they need to know. This leads to a lack of mental curiosity, here described as "mental cremation". This foreshadows Orwell's dystopian vision in *Nineteen Eighty-four*, where there is only one accepted truth. Orwell's novel is not a prediction about the future, but a warning. Eileen, on the other hand, envisions a "curious harmony" where science and literature, ancient and modern, can work hand in hand. This optimistic view comes in "The Phoenix" section, which is looking forward 50 years to 1984, and sees that the world has rectified itself.

Eileen's love of poetry never left her. Even in the tedious world of her typing bureau work, she would escape into literature whenever she could. Writing in 1945 to Orwell, she recalled how poetry and Oxford were her solace, not too distant from the "grey-walled paradise" that Harriet Vane recalls in *Gaudy Night*.

> When I lived in London before I was married I used to go away certainly once a month with a suitcase full of poetry and that consoled me until the next time—or I used to go up to Oxford and read in the Bodleian and take a punt up the Cher if it was summer or a walk in Port Meadow or to Godstow if it was winter.

However, Eileen had realised that she could not make a living for herself through writing, no matter how hard she tried. Reading her beloved Romantic poets was a life-long pleasure, but her own creativity was not quite good enough to allow her to make a living. Instead, she seems to have looked away from the arts and into new-fangled science.

The world of academic study was developing new disciplines in the 1920s and 1930s. One of these new disciplines was educational psychology. One of the first courses in this area in the country was at University College London. Perhaps inspired by her short stint as a teaching assistant, and then by the quality of her own education, Eileen felt sufficiently intrigued by this discipline to enrol in a two-year Master's course in autumn 1934. This would also be of interest to her through her witty and pithy observations about human behaviour in the various contexts she had found herself over the years. The course at UCL was run by Professor Cyril Burt. In 1934, he was 51 and already a prominent educational psychologist. He had pioneered IQ testing, and had established that girls were equal to boys in general intelligence, something that was quite ground-breaking in the early part of the twentieth century, when women were still excluded from education on the grounds of their gender. He was particularly known for his belief that everyone should be given the chance of a good education.

The course involved traditional lectures and seminars, but also practical psychological experiments. Such experiments included word association and memory tests, and the students would be drilled in rigorous recordings of their experiments. For someone steeped in the arts, this was all new and exciting.

Such courses attracted a wide range of students and were part of an opening up of higher education to more people at this time. Eileen herself became part of this movement when, in her first year of studies, she ran two short courses on psychology for Young Workers' organisations. At UCL, Eileen met Russian-born Lydia Jackson, a fellow student who was ten years older than her, and recently divorced. Lydia and Eileen became good friends. Another student was Rosalind Obermeyer, who was South African. The eclectic range of students in the course made for a lively social world.

Eileen's Master's thesis topic was decided at the end of her first year, and involved giving intelligence tests to a large sample of children. Lydia recalls "she was a brilliant student and was greatly encouraged to go on with this work by the Head of Department [Cyril Burt]" (Jackson 1960, p. 118). In Lydia's description of Eileen, we get a glimpse of the hyper dramatic story-telling that was found in her early writing for *The Chronicle*, describing how her "eyes could dance [...] like a kitten's watching a dangling object" even as "you knew that she habitually embroidered her stories, that things did not happen quite as amusingly or unexpectedly as she described", adding that her "exaggerations were rarely malicious" (Jackson 1976, p. 344). The comment that she was "rarely" malicious leaves room for us to see that Eileen could be scornful of certain types of people, such as she had been in her House Captain report in her final term at Sunderland Church High School.

It is through Lydia that we also get a vivid physical description of Eileen at this time. Like most others, she describes Eileen as attractive, and says she is "tall". Eileen was actually 5'5", which would be slightly below average height a century later, but in 1935 this would be above the average adult female height of 5'1". Lydia also comments on Eileen's "Irish" colouring of dark hair, blue eyes and pale skin, observing that "her shoulders [were] rather broad and high, giving an impression of a slight stoop", making her look "rather gawky in the way she moved" (Jackson 1976 p343). Like most people, Lydia also mentions Eileen's slender body.

Lydia was often a guest at the O'Shaughnessy house. They had moved to a larger home in Montpelier Row, Blackheath, close to Greenwich Park, around this time. Eric was doing very well in his medical practice and the family employed several staff to help run the house. Lydia recalls additional guests being welcomed by the O'Shaughnessys, who assumed their staff would be able to cope with extra mouths to feed. Amongst these guests was a friend of Eric's, Karl Schnetzler. He was an engineer who had left Germany in 1935 owing to a dislike of living under Nazism (he settled in England, but was interned between 1939 and 1943). Lydia notes that Eileen and Karl got along every well, and Eileen kept in touch with him for many years. Eileen had many male friends with whom she corresponded, and, as Orwell would later note, she was exceptionally well connected, perhaps partly as a result of the maintenance of such friendships. Ever keen to speculate, Lydia suspected Schnetzler of being in love with Eileen, although he always denied any sort of romantic relationship. For her part, Eileen left no clue as to her relationship with him, despite his reappearance in her life in 1943 after his release from internment (which we will discuss in Chapter 8).

By 1935, Eileen had graduated from Oxford and started a Master's degree in Psychology at UCL. In between these education events, she had drifted from job to job, never really finding a focus beyond a willingness to help others write their academic papers. There is some evidence she engaged in ad hocjournalism during this time, but records that could prove this decisively have long since been lost. Her brother, Eric, was doing very well in his medical practice, and was managing to support not only his wife but his mother and sister in quite luxurious style. Yet Eileen continued to be interested in politics and issues of social inequalities. Her Master's degree shows us that this could be a future career move for her, leaving behind her typing bureau business.

Like many educated, single women in these interwar years, Eileen had an active social life and a wide circle of friends with whom she could socialise without the need for a chaperone. If we place this in the context of mid-1930s, this is now established as a world where Edwardian social mores have been swept away. The idea of chaperoning was largely obsolete, despite the best efforts to retain it by the Oxford colleges. Attitudes towards unmarried sex for women were also changing, and perhaps we can see just how far that was true if we return to Dorothy L. Sayers' novels. Harriet Vane has at least one lover before marriage (she refers to living "with a man who was not married to her" (1988, p. 8), yet her eventual marriage is to a member of the aristocracy. Harriet appears as an increasingly prominent character in the extremely popular Lord

Peter Wimsey books from 1930 onwards, which reinforces the idea of the acceptability of educated young women having more liberty than their mothers would have had. This is found in both the storyline created for a popular female character by Sayers, and in the fact that her publisher, Victor Gollancz, did not request this aspect of the narrative be changed to make it more acceptable. There was also much more information available about contraception with the publication in 1918 of Marie Stopes' book, *Married Love*. Stopes gave advice on contraception that was both practical and reliable, such as the use of "dutch cap", which was available from pharmacies, or even the use of olive oil as a highly effective spermicide. This book was widely passed around, although rarely talked about.

In many ways, Eileen had been in the right place at the right time to take advantage of the many new opportunities available for women in the first decades of the twentieth century. However, she had also run up against the existing prejudices in society when it came to women in the public sphere, and the eight years following her graduation were largely aimless. All this, however, was to change as we shall see in the next chapter.

REFERENCES

Brittain, Vera (1997, first published 1933), *Testament of Youth: an autobiographical study of the years 1900-1925*, Virago, London.

Bussey, Edna, Letter to Ian Angus, 19 September 1968, Ian Angus Archive, UCL.

Jackson, Lydia (writing as Elisaveta Fen), "George Orwell's First Wife", in *The Twentieth Century Magazine,* vol 168, August 1960.

Jackson, Lydia (writing as Elisaveta Fen) (1976), *A Russian's England*, Paul Gordon Books, Warwick.

Sayers, Dorothy L. (1988, first published 1935), *Gaudy Night*, Hodder and Stoughton, London.

St Hugh's Archive, Collection of submissions for Penny Griffin (ed), *St Hugh's: One Hundred Years of Women's Education in Oxford*, Palgrave Macmillan, 1986. Reproduced here by kind permission of the Principal and Fellows of St Hugh's College, Oxford.

CHAPTER 4

Meeting Orwell and Marriage (1935–1936)

This chapter explores the two surviving letters that cover the period from when Eileen first met Eric Blair to the point when they both head off (separately) to Barcelona in the winter of 1936/37. During this time, the couple settled into married life, and these letters from Eileen to her university friend, Norah Myles, help us see more clearly the lively, intelligent, playful voice of the woman who so captivated Orwell on first meeting.

A Meeting of Minds

By the spring of 1935, Eileen had settled into her Master's degree and made friends with other women on the course. Amongst these was Rosalind Obermeyer, who lived in a large flat at 77 Parliament Hill in Hampstead, and rented out a smaller bedsit attached to hers to a relatively unknown writer called Eric Blair. Blair, who wrote under the pen name George Orwell, had decided by the spring of 1935 that he was sufficiently well enough published to celebrate with a party, and he asked Rosalind to jointly host this in her larger flat. Rosalind invited Eileen and Eileen's good friend Lydia, both single, who were enticed to the party by the promise of meeting two published authors there (the other being Richard Rees). Eileen was almost 30 years of age whilst Lydia, a few years older, was recently divorced. As both were ad hoc writers, they were sufficiently curious to turn up.

When they arrived, the party was already in full swing, and they immediately noticed two very tall men in deep conversation by the fireplace. According to Lydia, "Their clothes were drab and their faces lined and unhealthy", and in particular they were "rather moth-eaten" (Jackson 1976 p345). One of the men stopped talking to the other and walked straight across the room to introduce himself to Eileen as Eric Blair. Eileen and Orwell spent the rest of the evening in deep conversation. As Eileen told a friend later, she had been "rather drunk, behaving my worst, very rowdy" at this party (Topp 2020 p99). At the end of the evening, after walking Eileen and other guests down to the bus stop at the end of the road, Orwell returned to Rosalind's flat and declared, "Now *that* is the kind of girl I would like to marry!" (Obermeyer 1974).

The next time Rosalind met Eileen in class, Eileen had started reading *Burmese Days*, quite likely on Orwell's recommendation. Eileen's educational achievements would have equipped her with an understanding of what made "good writing", and she may well have seen this in Orwell's early work. It is also likely that she was quite pleased to have found a man who was not intimidated by her education and intelligence, whilst Orwell himself was happy to have found a woman who could match him intellectually (if not exceed him in this). Like Orwell, Eileen had a love of language play, something we find again and again in her letters. Whilst Eileen was undoubtedly highly intelligent, she was also strikingly attractive. Orwell described her as having "a cat's face" and Lydia recalled her face "was rather short, soft in outline, the nose slightly uptilted, the eyes large and round with a look of disarming innocence" (Jackson 1960 pp. 115–16). Her Celtic colouring of dark hair and pale skin added to this striking appearance.

As the summer progressed, Eileen and Orwell spent more and more time together, often taking a train into the country on a Sunday afternoon for a long walk in the surrounding countryside. Orwell recreates their country adventures together in *Keep the Aspidistra Flying*, which he was in the middle of writing when he met Eileen.

After a surprisingly brief courtship, Orwell proposed to Eileen and she accepted. This was not a popular decision amongst Eileen's friends and family. Lydia, for example, found it difficult to understand what Eileen saw in Orwell. By way of explanation, Eileen joked io Lydia: "I told myself that when I was thirty I would accept the first man who asked me to marry him" (Jackson 1960 p 116). Eileen's mother knew that Orwell lacked the means to support a wife, and she believed that he was a horrible choice as a husband for her daughter.

Meanwhile, Eileen's brother Eric O'Shaughnessy's medical career had progressed in leaps and bounds and he was making a name for himself in the field of pulmonary medicine. He had bought a large house in Greenwich to accommodate his own growing family, with plenty of room for Eileen and her mother to stay as guests. Over dinner with Orwell, the two Erics exchanged political opinions, particularly about the rise in Fascism across Europe at this time. Orwell is on record telling Richard Usborne, in 1947, "As to politics, I was only intermittently interested in the subject until about 1935", [Davison 2011, p xi], so Eileen was obviously going to affect his thinking when it came to politics in particular.

Eileen and Lydia were amused that Eileen's brother and lover shared the same name. "Being psychology students, we commented on and agreed about the significance of her marrying a man whose first name was the same as her brother's", Lydia wrote later (Jackson 1976 p349). Eileen routinely continued to call Orwell "Eric", even after his adopted penname of George became the one by which most other people referred to him and which he now used in his correspondence. In her early letters, Eileen often distinguishes between brother and husband through parentheses and cross-outs, although she later abandoned this and began to call Orwell "George" in most of her letters.

Around this time, Eileen and Orwell began discussing where they would live after they were married. They both agreed that, in order to live cheaply, they would have to find somewhere outside of London, and the challenge of country living appealed to them both greatly. In January 1936, *Keep the Aspidistra Flying* was despatched to his publisher, with a print release date of April. Orwell had set himself the ambitious target of writing one book a year, and his publisher encouraged this by suggesting a departure from fictional writing into writing a report on unemployment and general living conditions in the industrial north of England. The idea appealed to Orwell, not least as it came with a modest advance payment, allowing him to give up his job in the bookshop and start to make more concrete plans for the wedding. However, before any marriage could take place, Orwell was keen to do the necessary research for this report, and he set aside two months to visit various sites around the industrial north (although not the "north" of Eileen's childhood, which was actually more than 150 miles further up the county than where Orwell focused his tour).

Starting on 31 January 1936, Orwell visited poverty-stricken towns and villages, walking between locations and briefly experiencing some of the working conditions of the people in the coal mines. Never in robust health, he frequently found himself having to take to his bed for days on end to recover, although, as with his health in general, he downplayed the seriousness of his incapacity. No letters remain between Orwell and Eileen during his time away, although in a letter to his former schoolfriend, Cyril Connolly, Orwell wrote that he would have liked to stay in the north doing his research for much longer, but "it means being away from my girl" (in Davison 2000 vol. 10 p426).

In the meantime, Orwell's Aunt Nellie offered them the use of a cottage in the village of Wallington, about 35 miles north of London, where she was living at the time. Whilst he was away, Eileen inspected this cottage, and told Orwell that, although it was in an extremely primitive condition, and the nearest train station was four miles away, she was willing to share the difficulties with him after their wedding. Whilst not discouraging to guests who would frequently visit the cottage, it would turn out to be at the very least inconvenient to the couple in moments of crisis.

Rather surprisingly to almost everyone, Eileen embraced the idea of life in a house without electricity, hot water or the basic comforts even bedsit life could offer. Eileen had been born into middle-class comfort, with her private education and a brother whose status as a leading doctor meant his household included servants. But ever since her Oxford days, Eileen had loved spending time far from the big cities. Perhaps this was the point at which Eileen saw how she could be of use to Orwell in other ways: aside from helping a brilliant husband in his literary ambitions, she was practical and attracted to rural life.

Orwell returned from his fact-finding tour of the north in early April and moved straight into the cottage. Added to the obvious lack of amenities, the main doorway was only about four feet high, an obvious inconvenience for Orwell, who is variously described as being either 6'3" or 6'4". However, he was enchanted by the cottage, even by the recent addition of a corrugated tin roof which rattled alarmingly in the wind and rain. One positive feature of the cottage, which was of great appeal to the self-sufficient aims of the couple, was the possibility of sustaining a large garden and adding some chickens for eggs and a goat for milk. Also, the cottage had served as a small village shop, and this was something Eileen and Orwell hoped to reinstate to cover the very small rent charged. With the shop up and running, Orwell worked very hard preparing the garden in the two months before the wedding, while also making a start on *The Road to Wigan Pier*.

Marriage and Homelife

Eileen and Orwell married on 9 June 1936. Both families had great reservations about the match, not least as Orwell was still not earning much money. Although neither Eileen nor Orwell were regular church-goers, they married in the parish church of St Mary's in Wallington. Eileen's education in a church-sponsored school might have had a bearing on this, and indeed she had asked her local vicar from South Shields, John Woods, to perform the ceremony (he had also baptised her as a baby). That, however, is largely where the traditional marriage conventions end: Eileen and Orwell walked down the lane from their cottage to the church together, and Eileen chose to remove the promise to "obey" her husband from the traditional vows. Another notable aspect of the marriage is that Orwell listed his occupation as "author" on the marriage certificate, whereas Eileen simply put a line through this box, to indicate no profession for herself. It was as if she was leaving her independent life and potential career in child psychology to devote herself to acting as literary editor and housekeeper for her new husband. Eileen clearly embraced her new life, seeing it as an adventure. In the nine years of their marriage, there is nothing to suggest that Eileen ever regretted her decision.

There was no formal honeymoon, partly through lack of money but mostly as Orwell was committed to his writing. He had a deadline for an article just three days after their wedding, and continued to write numerous book reviews and the first draft of *The Road to Wigan Pier* throughout this early period of married life. The couple frequently hosted guests in their spare room, and various friends who visited reported the couple squabbling and sometimes arguing passionately. But this should not come as a surprise. Two previously completely independent people needed time to learn how to live as a couple, sharing a tiny, inconvenient cottage, especially since each of them had lived quite separate lives until then. She and Orwell together had chosen this difficult life. And for the first six months, at least, they were proud of their successful struggles to such an extent that Eileen felt comfortable enough about them to make these arguments form part the humour in her letters, as we shall see. Other guests who stayed at the cottage commented on the obvious feelings of love that the couple expressed toward each other. Mabel Fierz, for example, believed Orwell "was very happy. That was the only time in his life when he was really happy. He was devoted to [Eileen]" (Wadhams 1984 p 40). Geoffrey Gorer also saw this positive change in Orwell: "I think the only year that I ever knew [Orwell] really happy was that first year with Eileen" (Stansky and Abrahams 1979 p154). And the people Eileen worked with in Barcelona all mentioned how much Eileen was in love with Orwell and how pleased she was with her marriage.

The couple's life at the cottage in those early months of the marriage, when not entertaining guests, focused on Orwell's writing. Eileen's experience working for her brother as editing assistant and typist, as well as running her own editing and typing business before she met Orwell, equipped her with the practical skills she needed to assist her husband. They worked out a system whereby Eileen would type up Orwell's manuscripts mostly during the times when he was out of the house working in the garden or tending to the goats. Eileen showed she could be a perceptive critic and offer intelligent suggestions for improvement in the course of typing up his work, something their friends were aware of (Shelden 1991 p 209), and Orwell himself of course appreciated immensely.

Eileen had assured her family and friends that she would complete her Master's in Educational Psychology after the wedding, with just the dissertation left to complete. With Lydia's help, she was planning to work with the schoolchildren in Wallington to provide data for this dissertation, "The use of imagination in school essays" (Meyers 2001 p122). However, the school at Wallington had only five or six children, and so was too small a sample size for her project. A glimmer of hope arrived in the opportunity to intervene in the education of a "backward" child at the school, called Peter. He was 10 years old at this time and was given little hope of progressing to grammar school. Eileen conducted an IQ test on Peter and this showed him to be above average intelligence. Lydia recalls that Eileen "then volunteered to coach him in reading and arithmetic for several months, which resulted in his winning the coveted scholarship" (Jackson 1976 p 378).

Eileen and Lydia continued to work on the dissertation over the summer, with the hope that this would offer a lucrative job in education after graduation. However, the self-sufficiency drive of Eileen and Orwell proved more successful than they had initially thought, with their rent for the cottage covered by takings from the shop. As a result, there was a less pressing need for Eileen to gain external employment. Her editing and typing workload was increasing, with both her brother and her husband relying on her, and in the end she gave up working on her Master's dissertation and shifted her attention from helping needy children to helping her husband and her brother.

Although life at the cottage was largely governed by Orwell's writing, the couple did have ways to amuse themselves. Eileen had moved her collection of beloved English Literature books into the cottage shortly after their marriage. And they each had their own typewriter, which they used for any arrangement of visits with friends. Without electricity, there was no radio or record player, of course. The Orwell family were not musical, although it is not known whether Eileen continued her interest in music from her school days (Smith 2023). Orwell once joked, as he was recovering his voice after being shot in Spain, that perhaps he would soon be able to sing again, adding, as an aside, that his singing voice might not be universally enjoyed.

If the couple ever went out for the evening, it would be to the local pub, The Plough, where Orwell would stubbornly insist on everyone drinking dark ale, irrespective of their personal preference (Cooper and Crick 1984 p164). Eileen was widely reported to have been tolerant of her husband's stubbornness in this respect, treating it as a quirk of his character to be lightly mocked. This is apparent again in the "marmalade" story. When Orwell objected to Eileen putting a full jar of marmalade on the table, rather than using a jam dish, even though they didn't have one, her friend Lettice reported that Eileen was greatly amused at finding that there were still small gentilities that Orwell set great store by. Their friend Patricia Donahue observed that "Eileen had a good sense of humour and was given to telling funny stories. And funny stories about George, which he didn't seem to mind. In fact I think he rather liked being made fun of by Eileen. I don't think George was an easy man to live with, but they did get on quite well. I had the impression it as a very happy marriage" (in Wadhams 1984 p 118).

In November, after they'd been married five months, Eileen and Orwell made their first visit to Orwell's family home in Southwold, where they stayed for about a week. Eileen and Orwell were both prolific letter writers, and certainly had kept in touch by mail while he was doing research up north, as well as at other points before their wedding. But, unfortunately, they apparently didn't save each other's letters, so we have no record of how this visit was arranged.

Luckily, during the nine years since graduation, in 1927, Eileen had also been exchanging letters with Norah Myles, her best friend from their Oxford days. For some reason, Norah began saving Eileen's letters just after she was married, and the one below is the first letter written by Eileen that has been recovered so far. Her lively, witty writing style in this letter, as well as her use of humorous exaggeration and irony, are apparent in all her letters that have survived. As Lydia noted, "One could never be certain whether she was being serious or facetious [...] Her Irishness was revealed most clearly in the ease with which [rather outlandish] remarks rolled off her tongue [...] with a slant and a degree of whimsicality all her own" (in Topp 2020 p98). As Orwell's friend Richard Rees wrote, "This seems to have paired nicely with Orwell's "genuine streak of old-fashioned conventionality sometimes [bordering] on whimsy" whereby it was not always possible to be "quite certain if he was serious or not" (Rees 1962 p39). Also, the two main characters in *Keep the Aspidistra Flying* occasionally "quarrelled vigorously, according to their custom" (1363 p 23) and delighted at one another's absurdities. This suggests that Orwell and Eileen might actually have enjoyed arguing about some of their disagreements. Given the fact that Orwell was writing this book at the same time as he was developing his relationship with Eileen, perhaps it is not too great a leap to suggest that this might reflect his expectations for a companionship of intellectual equals. Therefore, it is an avoidable mistake to take Eileen's exaggerated complaints in her letter to Norah literally. If the first months had been that bad, there's no doubt she would have dissolved the marriage. She and Orwell together had chosen this difficult life. And for the first six months, at least, they were proud of their successful struggles.

Eileen's six surviving letters to Norah almost all begin with vague dates and no salutation. They are also all signed "Pig", a nickname that it's only possible to speculate on, but also very curious, considering the main characters in *Animal Farm*, which was written many years later. However, as discussed in the previous chapter, Eileen's notorious untidiness might be the most obvious inspiration for this. The letters to Norah were not discovered until 2005, and we are very lucky to have them, since they contribute many facts about Eileen and Orwell's marriage that are extremely important in order reflect on their 10 years together.

Eileen's first letter to Norah is handwritten, and is dated simply Tuesday. However, we can surmise that it was written on November 3 because she mentions meeting Norah in London on either November 18 or 25, and she would need time to hear back from Norah as well as to return to Wallington before she could manage a trip to London. Eileen immediately displays her casual attitude toward that kind of detail, which, as we shall see, will cause problems later on.

This could actually be the first letter Eileen had written since her marriage in June. She was surprised and a bit disappointed at first, it seems, as she and Orwell struggled with agreeing on a daily routine. Also, there were very real problems setting up life at the cottage that perhaps neither of them had actually anticipated. It took a while, but eventually Orwell realised that the woman he loved and who loved him also had great editing and typing skills, which would improve his writing as well as allow him to finish his books and essays more quickly. Eileen also had a profound knowledge of socialist politics and psychology, two areas Orwell hadn't taken too seriously before meeting her. All the early conflicts in the marriage are touched on in this first letter.

36 High Street

Southwold, Suffolk

Tuesday

I wrote the address quite a long time ago & have since played with three cats, made a cigarette (I make them now but not with the naked hand); poked the fire & driven Eric (i.e George) nearly mad—all because I didn't really know what to say. I lost my habit of punctual correspondence during the first few weeks of marriage because we quarrelled so continuously & really bitterly that I thought I'd save time & just write one letter to everyone when the murder or separation had been accomplished.[1] Then Eric's aunt[2] came to stay & was so dreadful (she stayed <u>two months)</u> that we stopped quarrelling & just repined. Then she went away & now all our

---

[1] Eileen assumes that she would survive the arguments herself, joking that she might even resort to murder.

[2] This would be Orwell's aunt, Nellie Limouzin, who was one of his favourite relatives and gave him vital support in his writing career in various ways.

troubles are over.³ They arose partly because Mother drove me so hard in the first week of June that I cried all the time from pure exhaustion⁴ & partly because Eric had decided that he mustn't let his work be interrupted & complained bitterly when we'd been married a week that he'd only done two good days' work out of seven.⁵ Also I couldn't make the oven cook anything & boiled eggs (on which Eric had lived almost exclusively) made me sick. Now I can make the oven cook a reasonable number of things & he is working very rapidly· I forgot to mention that he had his 'bronchitis'⁶ for three weeks in July & that it rained every day for six weeks during the whole of which the kitchen was flooded & all food went mouldy in a few hours. It seems a long time ago now but then seemed very permanent.

I thought I could come & see you & have twice decided when I could, but Eric always gets something if I'm going away if he has notice of the fact, & if he has no notice (when Eric my brother arrives & removes me as he has done twice⁷) he gets something when I've gone so that I have to come home again.⁸ For the last few weeks we have been completely broke and shall be now until Christmas because the money we expected in October for Keep the Aspidistra Flying won't be paid until April and the next book won't earn its advance until December anyway and possibly January.⁹ But I must be in London for some days this month. Is there a

---

³ No doubt a bit of an exaggeration.

⁴ Eileen's mother tried to convince her not to marry Orwell.

⁵ Orwell turned out to be more difficult to live with than Eileen had at first imagined.

⁶ Eileen puts this in quotes, as if she hardly believes his complaint at first.

⁷ Eileen's brother occasionally brought her back to London to work with him, editing his books.

⁸ Clearly, Eileen didn't realize before the marriage how serious Orwell's bronchitis was, which might explain why she puts the word in quotation marks. At this point, she appears to believe that he is using these episodes in order to prevent her from going off on her own. But she still resents his attempts to curtail her freedom. There is also probably a bit of exaggeration here, as Eileen mentions visits with other friends and the couple are staying with the Blairs when she writes this letter. Therefore the impression that she is stuck in the cottage is not quite as dramatic as it sounds.

⁹ The poverty Eileen complains about is far from the abject poverty of the people Orwell had visited in *The Road to Wigan Pier*. Both Eileen and Orwell had affluent families whom they often visited and could fall back on when in need. In Eileen's case, it was her beloved brother, Eric, whose house in Greenwich offered hot running water for baths and servants to prepare delicious meals. Orwell's family were less affluent but

chance of one of these Wednesdays? If so & if you tell me which I'll make my visit to fit it. I must see Eric (brother) a bit about his book, the proofs of which I'm now correcting, & also have some intelligence testing to do with Lydia.[10] Could you come either on the 18th or on the 25th? I think they're Wednesdays—anyway I mean Wednesdays. I want passionately to see you. Lydia must have a bit of notice & indeed at any minute is going to descend on me in wrath (against Eric on social grounds not against me, for I am perfection in her eyes) & force me to go to London exactly when I don't want to. So if you were to send a postcard-----

This is our address for the rest of this week. We are staying with the Blairs & I like it. Nothing has surprised me more, particularly since I saw the house which is very small & furnished almost entirely with paintings of ancestors. The Blairs are by origin Lowland Scottish & dull but one of them made a lot of money in slaves & his son Thomas who was inconceivably like a sheep married the daughter of the Duke of Westmorland[11] (of whose existence I never heard) & went so grand that he spent all the money & couldn't make more because slaves had gone out. So his son went into the army & came out of that into the church & married a girl of 15 who loathed him & had ten children of whom Eric's father, now 80, is the only survivor[12] & they are all quite penniless but still on the shivering verge of gentility as Eric calls it in his new book which I cannot think will be popular with the family.[13] In spite of all this the family on the whole is fun & I imagine unusual in their attitude to me because they all adore Eric & consider him quite impossible to live with—indeed on the

nevertheless are thought to have paid for his clothing (most of Orwell's clothing was made by the family's tailor in Southwold). They also paid for his medical care as his bronchitis worsened over the years.

[10] In order for Eileen to complete her Master's degree.

[11] It was actually the Earl of Westmorland, not the Duke.

[12] The talkative Eileen has collected part of the family history from Orwell's father, adding a few important details to what Orwell scholars had already discovered. She clearly is interested in the family history of making money in the slave trade and then eventually going broke when "slaves had gone out". Orwell had apparently hidden this notorious family history from her, possibly because he was ashamed of it. Eileen's light-hearted discussion of this is distasteful to modern sensibilities but at the time would have been seen less unfavourably.

[13] This information does not appear in any Orwell book, so he apparently decided to delete a section that perhaps Eileen had suggested would upset his family. This also suggests that Eileen was already working with Orwell on his manuscripts.

wedding day Mrs Blair shook her head & said that I'd be a brave girl if I knew what I was in for, and Avril the sister said that obviously I didn't know what I was in for or I shouldn't be there. They haven't I think grasped that I am very much like Eric in temperament which is an asset once one has accepted the fact.

If I'd written this from Wallington it would have been about the real things of life—goats, hens, broccoli (eaten by a rabbit). But it would be better perhaps to tell you because this has got out of hand. Poor girl, [not legible] it all out except the bit about the Wednesdays & say you can come on the 18th or the 25th to meet Pig.

The previous summer, as Eileen and Orwell carried on enjoying their "merry war", elsewhere in Europe there were rumours of another war building. The rise of Fascism was clearly seen in Italy, Germany and Spain. When Franco marched towards Madrid in the late summer of 1936, the Spanish workers' resistance to this was widely praised by left-leaning people around the world. Eileen and her brother Eric, and most likely their parents, were socialists. As we have seen earlier in this chapter, Orwell's interest in politics coincides with his meeting Eileen. With civil war starting in Spain, the couple attended a nearby Marxist conference. They even invited one of the speakers, E. C. Large, back to the cottage for tea. Orwell later seemed pleased when he told a friend about Eileen "almost falling in love with [him]" in a letter to Jack Common (Davison 2000 vol. 10 p507). Visitors to the cottage during the autumn of 1936 reported Orwell and Eileen discussing the war in Spain with great passion, and it came as no surprise to anyone when Orwell announced his intention to travel to Spain, aiming to produce a "report" similar to his work in *The Road to Wigan Pier.*

However, he was also going to fight for the Socialist cause in Spain, not merely report on it. In 1947, Orwell wrote that this was with Eileen's full agreement: "My wife and I both wanted to go to Spain and fight for the Spanish government" (in Davison 2000 vol. 19 p86). Perhaps part of the purpose of their visit to Orwell's family in November was to inform them of their plans. Orwell seems to have been preparing for this commitment for several weeks since, when he packed his bag, he included a letter of introduction from John McNair, the Independent Labour Party's (ILP) representative in Spain (Topp 2020 p164).

So, the first Christmas Eileen and Orwell spent as a married couple they actually spent apart, as Orwell left for Spain on 23 December, Eileen remaining at the cottage where he had entrusted her to manage the final production of *The Road to Wigan Pier*, which was due to be published in March 1937. Eileen had been busy typing the full manuscript of that book to be sent to the publisher before Christmas; the one decent source of income the couple could expect to receive. Orwell told his agent, "During my absence abroad will you please communicate with my wife on all subjects relating to my literary affairs and accept her decision as my own... My wife has my authority to make them on my behalf" (Davison 2000, Vol. 10 p527).

The unsentimental nature of both Eileen and Orwell that saw them spend this time apart is perhaps not so surprising when we realise that they kept very, very few of the letters written to each other in the course of their relationship. It is this rarity that makes the remaining letters so valuable.

Eileen spent her first Christmas of married life in a different country to her husband, seemingly with her full agreement. She had been entrusted with corresponding with Orwell's publisher in the final production stages of *The Road to Wigan Pier*, an essential part of the process, which shows the confidence that Orwell had in her abilities.

Before she could leave for Spain, Eileen had three important letters to write, ensuring that *The Road to Wigan Pier* was proceeding through the publishing process. The first letter was to Orwell's agent's secretary. Gollancz had objected to Orwell's use of the word "copulating", and they were trying to come up with an alternative. Orwell strongly objected to the use of "courting", and they eventually compromised on "treading". As Orwell had realised, Eileen was very capable of handling his editing requests, and her letters to the publisher attest to both her efficiency and her sense of humour.

17 January 1937

[Typewritten]

The Stores, Wallington,

Near Baldock, Herts.

Dear Miss Perriam,

Thank you very much for your letter. My husband said that Gollancz had warned him that the book would have to be rushed through and that it might be impossible to let the proofs out of the office at all, but the final arrangement was that I was to have the proofs even if they could only be spared for twenty-four hours.[14] Perhaps even that wasn't possible—anyway I suppose this means that no alterations have been necessary in the text to conform with any laws and conventions, which is satisfactory, and we must just hope that the proof-correctors have not made too many "emendations."[15]

The word my husband particularly wants changed is in Chapter I, the last paragraph but one. In the manuscript the sentence is: "For the first time in my life, in a bare patch beside the line, I saw rooks copulating." According to my husband, Gollancz and he altered copulating to courting, but he wishes the phrase to read " ... I saw rooks treading", because he has seen rooks courting hundreds of times. Of course if by any chance Gollancz changed his mind and left copulating, that would be better still, but I expect there is no hope of that.[16] If you can get this alteration made, I shall be most grateful again; I'm so sorry the misunderstanding arose, because I'm afraid it is an irritating nuisance for you.

I have had a postcard from Eric from Sientamo,[17] a village where they halted for food, a few miles from the front. He says the peasants are carrying on as though nothing had happened although the buildings have been almost smashed to pieces by bombs and shell-fire.[18]

Yours sincerely,

Eileen Blair.

---

[14] Orwell had such confidence in Eileen's wisdom that he felt comfortable leaving for Spain with so many important details yet to be taken care of.

[15] The use of scare quotes here suggest Eileen is perhaps overly polite about the changes she's requesting.

[16] However, she can't help adding a bit of irony whenever possible.

[17] Siétamo.

[18] It is a bit surprising that Orwell's letter from so near the front has managed to reach Eileen, but the postal service seems to have been operating fairly reliably at this point.

The second letter was written two weeks later, this time directly to Orwell's agent.

31 January 1937

[Handwritten]

The Stores, Wallington,

Near Baldock, Herts.

Dear Mr Moore,

I enclose the signed agreement. I am afraid there was a little delay before your letter was forwarded to me—I got it yesterday—but when I read the agreement I was delighted, as I know my husband will be when he hears the details. I had not fully realised before how satisfactory it was; in your office the other day I was being rather single-minded.[19]

There is quite good news in Spain, though it comes very erratically.[20] Eric has been created a 'cabo', which is I think a kind of corporal & which distresses him because he has to get up early to turn out the guard,[21] but he also has a dug-out in which he can make tea. There is apparently no proper fighting as neither side has efficient artillery or even rifles. He says he thinks the government forces ought to attack but are not going to.[22] I hope no crisis will arise needing his decision as letters take from 7 to 10 days to get here.[23]

---

[19] One can only speculate about what Eileen is referring to here, but apparently she can be pretty adamant when she is arguing for something she knows is important to Orwell.

[20] It is hard to imagine just what good news Eileen was referring to, but it may be her news that Orwell has been promoted.

[21] Orwell is never shy to complain about something.

[22] It's a bit curious that Orwell is so anxious for the fighting to begin, although many soldiers do report their anticipation of the start of fighting being more appealing than a state of inaction.

[23] However, if a crisis did arise, Eileen would surely have handled it on her own.

With many thanks,

Yours sincerely,

Eileen Blair.

The third letter was written from Eileen's brother's home in Greenwich, just as Eileen was preparing to leave for Spain herself.

11 February 1937

[Typewritten]

24 Croom's Hill

Greenwich, S.E.10.

Dear Mr Moore,

Thank you very much for your letter. I do, of course, agree with you that Mr. Gollancz should make the separate edition of Part I of <u>Wigan Pier</u> and I very much hope he will do so.[24]

The news that the book is definitely chosen for the Left Book Club is splendid, and I am glad to have it now because there is a possibility that I may, go to Spain next week—in any case I am hoping to go the week after next, and I am now in town making the necessary arrangements.[25] I will call at your office before I go, in case there is something I should have done and have not done, but there are several matters I can deal with now.[26]

---

[24] Throughout the history of the novel, it was quite common to publish in shorter volumes, and this practice was still in place but falling out of use by the middle of the twentieth century.

[25] Eileen is brave to head off to Barcelona—a battle zone—on her own, but, as we will see, she was not completely alone on her journey.

[26] Once again, Eileen shows just how efficient she is in handling problems for Orwell.

I have arranged with my husband's bank that they will credit him with cheques made out to him and sent direct to them. Would you therefore send any cheques you may have for him to The Manager, Barclay's Bank, Baldock, Herts.? I thought it wise to do this, although I fear it may be more trouble to you, because the mails to Spain are so unreliable. The bank has arranged for me a credit in Barcelona so that I can draw money there as we may need it.[27]

My address in Barcelona will be Hotel Continental, Boulevard de las Ramblas, Barcelona, and from there I ought to be in fairly good touch with my husband.

The only other question to be dealt with, so far as I know, concerns complimentary copies of the book. My husband suggests that I should ask you to send them for him, and I therefore attach a list of the people he wishes to have copies.[28] I do not know whether we shall be given any of the Left Book Club edition, but if so they could be sent to my brother, Laurence O'Shaughnessy,[29] at this address, with his own complimentary copy. I intended of course to do all this myself before going away, but my husband thinks he may get some leave at the end of this month and wants me to be in Barcelona as soon as possible.[30]

With many thanks,

Yours sincerely,

Eileen Blair.

THE ROAD TO WIGAN PIER

---

[27] This sounds like an ingenious idea, and just like Eileen to come up with it.

[28] Yet another very important chore that Orwell has entrusted to Eileen.

[29] It is interesting to note that Eileen does not give her brother the title "Dr". By this time, he had become an established surgeon and in the English system of honorific medical titles, he would be known as "Mr" to distinguish him from the physicians. This is reflected in the list of addresses at the bottom of this letter, where she notes his qualification as "FRCS"—Fellow of the Royal College of Surgeons.

[30] At least Eileen is able to avoid some of the tedious work left to do.

Please send one copy (10/6 edition) to each of the following:

Sir Richard Rees[31], 9 Chesham Place, W. (Please forward)

Henry Miller, esq., 18, Villa Seurat, Paris XIV.

Mrs. Sinclair Fierz[32], 1B, Oakwood Road, Golders Green, N.W.

Mrs. Dennis Collings,[33] c/o Mrs. P. Jaques, Four Ways, Reydon, Near Southwold (Please forward)

Geoffrey Gorer[34], esq., The Elms, Fitzroy Park, N.W.6.

Mrs. Adam,[35] The Stores, Wallington, Near Baldock, Herts.

Mr. & Mrs. R. W. Blair, Montagu House, Southwold, Suffolk.

Laurence O'Shaughnessy, esq., F.R.C.S., 24 Croom's Hill, Greenwich, S.E.10.

And two copies (10/6 edition) to Mrs. Eric Blair, Hotel Contintal (sp), Boulevard de las Ramblas, Barcelona, Spain.

Free copies of the Left Book Club edition, if any, to be sent to Mr. Laurence O'Shaughnessy.

With *The Road to Wigan Pier* finally in print, Eileen was at loose ends at The Stores. She found out, via McNair's office, that he needed an English-French shorthand typist, a job for which she was considerably

---

[31] A long-time friend of Orwell's.

[32] Mabel Fierz was a long-time acquaintance and sometime lover of Orwell, who had acted as his agent in finding a publisher for *Down and Out,* and remained a great champion of his work.

[33] A friend of Orwell's.

[34] A close friend of both Orwell and Eileen.

[35] This would be Orwell's Aunt Nellie.

over-qualified, but very willing to undertake if it meant she could be closer to her husband.

But, before she could leave for Spain, Eileen also had the logistical nightmare of leaving their shop, their garden and the animals to others if she were to join him. Somehow, Aunt Nellie was persuaded to return to the cottage and look after it and the animals for the uncertain duration of Eileen and Orwell's absence. Over and over again, Eileen displays her ability to convince others to do favours for herself and, even more so, for Orwell.

In her informative letter of February 1937 to Norah, Eileen describes her decision to follow Orwell to Barcelona. Written in Eileen's unique and charming style, this letter is also undated, but was likely written around 16 February 1937, while she was staying at her brother's home in Greenwich.

24, Croom's Hill Greenwich

A note to say that I am leaving for Spain at 9 a.m. tomorrow (or I think so, but with inconceivable grandeur people ring up from Paris about it, and I may not go until Thursday). I leave in a hurry, not because anything is the matter but because when I said that I was going on the 23rd, which has long been my intention, I suddenly became a kind of secretary perhaps to the I.L.P. in Barcelona. They hardly seem to be amused at all. If Franco had engaged me as a manicurist I would have agreed to that too in exchange for a salvo conducto[36] so everyone is satisfied. The I.L.P. in Barcelona consists of one John McNair[37] who has certainly been kind at long distances but has an unfortunate telephone voice and a quite calamitous prose style in which he writes articles that I perhaps shall type. But theoretically George gets leave at the end of this month and then I shall have a holiday, willy John nilly John. By the way, I suppose I told you George was in the Spanish Militia? I can't remember. Anyway he is, with my full approval until he was well in. He's on the Aragon front, where I cannot help knowing that the Government ought to be attacking or hoping

---

[36] Salvo conductor: a safe conduct document that Eileen needed to travel to Spain.

[37] John McNair was the Head of the I.L.P. office in Barcelona. He came from Newcastle, which is on the opposite side of the River Tyne to where Eileen was born, so she was most likely teasing him for his Geordie accent, the same accent she would have been familiar with as she was growing up in South Shields.

that that is a sufficient safeguard against their doing so.[38] Supposing that the Fascist air force goes on missing its objectives and the railway line to Barcelona is still working, you'll probably hear from there some day. But letters take 10-15 days as a rule, and if the railway breaks down I can't think how long they'll take. Meanwhile it would be a nice gesture if you were to write a nice letter yourself, addressing it c/o John McNair, Hotel Continental, Boulevard de las Ramblas, Barcelona. I am staying at the Continental too to begin with, but as we have now spent practically all the money we shall have until November, when the Left Book Club wealth will be available,[39] I think I may be doing what the Esperantists call sleeping on straw—and as they are Esperantists they mean sleeping on straw. The I.LP. of course is not contributing to my support, but the Spanish Government feeds George on bread without butter and 'rather rough food' and has arranged that he doesn't sleep at all, so he has no anxieties.[40]

This is longer than I meant it to be—(that should be a long dash, but you have to move the carriage.) Write the letter, because I think it likely that I may loathe Barcelona, though I'd like to see some of the excitements that won't happen. I don't know of course how long we'll be there. Unless George gets hurt I suppose he'll stay until the war qua war is over—and I will too unless I get evacuated by force or unless I have to come and look for some money. But to-day's news suggests that the war may not last very long—I doubt whether Mussolini or even Hitler would feel enthusiastic about trying to push Franco across Catalonia, and certainly they'd need a lot more men to do it.

---

[38] Eileen seems to be joking here, suggesting that Orwell's presence at the front well help deter Franco from attacking there.

[39] *The Road to Wigan Pier* had been chosen by the Left Book Club, which meant that thousands more copies would be sold.

[40] Eileen has been receiving letters from Orwell, and she is joking here that the difficult conditions he has been facing have probably reduced his common anxiety.

The dinner gong is going.[41] Is it not touching to think that this may be the last dinner unrationed available for Pig.

Give everyone my love—even yourself. Eric[42] is lecturing at Bristol, but I think not till May. Hey Groves[43] came to the heart lecture at the College of Surgeons and then invited him to talk to you, but the date isn't settled yet. He has some pretty pictures. I could have come with him—perhaps after all I shall come with him. If you meet Hey Groves tell him to make the date after the war is over.

Could you tell Mary (not urgently) that I simply hadn't time to write separate letters to the two old Oxford Friends—which is simply true.

Less than two months after his departure for Spain, Eileen made her own way there, travelling on her own through France. It was one of her first trips away from Britain, and she was heading into a war zone.

References

Cooper, Audrey and Bernard Crick (eds) (1984) *Orwell Remembered*. BBC Books, London.
Davison, Peter (ed). (2000) *The Complete Works of George Orwell*. Secker & Warburg, London. *Volume 10: A kind of compulsion*, 1903-1936.
Davison, Peter (ed). (2006) *The Lost Orwell*. Timewell Press, London.
Davison, Peter (ed) (2011) *George Orwell: a life in letters*. Harvill Secker, London.
Jackson, Lydia Elisaveta Fen 1960 'George Orwell's First Wife' in *The Twentieth Century Magazine* vol 168. August 1960.
Jackson, Lydia Elisaveta Fen (1976) *A Russian's England*. Paul Gordon Books, Warwick.

---

[41] The gong could be found in most grand and upper middle-class homes, where the servants would use this to signal to the diners that dinner was about to be served. In many such homes, this was an essential part of the dining tradition, as the sound of the gong could be heard around the house, avoiding the need for undignified shouting. To have such a system in place implies a well-run, upper-middle-class household that employs serving staff and also a very large house. This is a dramatic example of the two different worlds that Eileen and Orwell inhabited during their cottage years together.

[42] This is Eileen's brother Eric.

[43] Ernest William Hey Groves was a distinguished surgeon who developed the use of bone grafts in surgery.

Meyers, Jeffrey (2001) *Orwell: A Wintry Conscience of a Generation*. W.W. Norton, New York.

Rees, Richard (1962) *George Orwell: Fugitive from the Camp of Victory*. Southern Illinois University Press, Carbondale.

Shelden, Michael (1991) *Orwell: The Authorized Biography*. Harper Collins, New York.

Smith, Angela. '"A great prop to the school": the important place of Sunderland Church High School in understating Eileen O'Shaughnessy'. *George Orwell Studies* vol. 7/1, 2023 pp. 6-22.

Stansky, Peter and William Abrahams (1979) *Orwell: The Transformation*. Constable, London.

Topp, Sylvia. (2020). *Eileen: the making of George Orwell*. Unbound, London.

Wadhams, Stephen (ed) (1984) *Remembering Orwell*. Penguin, Ontario.

Obermeyer, Rosalind. Letter of 12 November 1974. Crick Archive.

Orwell, George (1936) *Keep the Aspidistra Flying*. Victor Gollancz London.

CHAPTER 5

Saving Orwell Twice (1936–1938)

This chapter contains letters sent by Eileen whilst in Spain, most of which are to her brother and mother.

George Orwell's decision to fight in the Spanish Civil War, as we saw in the last chapter, stemmed from his involvement in socialist politics, both in his writing and in his actions. The participation of artists and writers in military action is one that had been established twenty years before when a combination of idealism and conscription led to a highly literate representation of the First World War in art, literature and music. As Paul Fussell (1975) famously observed, the First World War was the most literate of wars. The rise of fascism in Europe in the 1930s attracted those who had been promised a better world after the First World War, but were instead seeing a threat to peace through Fascist ideology and felt the need to take action. Many academics and writers now see the Spanish Civil War as being an influence on the minds of an entire generation, including Orwell's. The conflict had escalated in 1936 and lasted until 1939. It was a war between the Second Spanish Republic and the fascist forces of Francisco Franco, who was an army general leading an insurrection to restore the monarchy and establish a military dictatorship (something he finally succeeded in doing in 1939).

The war was perceived, among many intellectuals worldwide, as an act of violence by the army against the will of the people. The Nationalist forces led by Franco found their recruits in Spanish colonies such as Morocco and the south of the country while the Republic held the northern and central parts of Spain. An ideological divide between the right-wing Nationalists and left-wing Republic left the world divided as well, for the conflict escalated, with many countries offering their support to each side.

An important symbol for the Republic's cause were the international volunteers, and among them were many writers, poets, journalists, painters and even film directors. Some fought in the trenches, whilst others waged a war against the Nationalist propaganda in a more literary and artistic way, gathering support and understanding worldwide. Many died on the barricades of Madrid and in battles across Spain. The ones who survived often saw that experience as pivotal for their work.

In the roll call of artists and writers who fought in the Spanish Civil War, most were fighting on the side of the Republic. Some, such as the prominent poet and playwright Federica Garcia Lorca, died in the process.

The journalist Arthur Koestler's time in Spain is more nuanced. He was a writer of Hungarian-Jewish origins who acted as an English journalist during the Spanish Civil War. He ended up in Spain in 1936, as a Comintern agent (Communist International), using his journalist credentials as cover. Koestler used this cover to infiltrate Franco's headquarters and conduct an interview with him. Franco was duped into thinking that Koestler was a huge sympathiser of his cause, and thus he gained Franco's trust. Importantly, during the interview, Koestler acquired evidence that Nazi Germany and Fascist Italy directly supported Franco and his army with volunteers, guns and other equipment. However, his cover slipped and he only just managed to escape the headquarters with his life.

Next year, Koestler was again in Spain, as a war correspondent. He was captured in Malaga by the Nationalist Forces and sentenced to death. Instead of being shot he was used as a high-value prisoner and got swapped for the wife of a Nationalist fighter pilot ace, who had been captured by the Republic's forces. After Spain, Koestler became disillusioned with Stalin, who had offered to help the Spanish Republic and instead became a significant factor in its demise. Koestler wrote his novel condemning Stalinism, *Darkness at Noon,* in 1941.

Other prominent literary recruits included the French novelist, André Malraux, who became one of the prominent leaders in the war and was very respected and loved by the Spaniards. In 1938, he toured the United States to raise funds for the cause. That same year he published a novel, *A Man's Hope,* concerning his war experience.

One of Europe's most prominent surrealist poets and the founder of Dadaism, Tristan Tzara, a Romanian by origin, fought for the Republic's cause on several occasions during the civil war. He was living in France when the war broke out and in 1937 participated in the defence of the city of Madrid during the siege conducted by Franco's forces. After surviving the siege, he wrote a collection of poems titled "Conquered Southern Regions". Some of his poems were included in a publication called *The Poets of the World Defend the Spanish People*. As the war became plagued with foreign political interventions and accusations of treason, Tzara took a more ambivalent stand towards the Communist Party of Spain.

It was not just Europeans who were attracted to fight for the Republic's cause. American writer Ernest Hemingway had become famous for portraying his experiences in the First World War in his book *Farewell to Arms*. In 1937, he was sent by the North American Newspaper Agency to report on the war in Spain. Together with Joris Yvens and John Dos Passos, he produced a film, *The Spanish Earth*. He was joined by American Martha Gellhorn, with whom he started an affair. Martha Gellhorn also worked as a war journalist and she continued to pursue her career on battlefields all over the world, after the war in Spain.

Hemingway spent the siege of Madrid in late 1937 writing his play *The Fifth Column* while the city was under bombardment. He left Spain after the battle but returned twice more in 1938. He was present at the Battle of the Ebro, which was one of the Republic's last stands, and he was among the last English and American journalists to leave Spain, right before the inevitable defeat.

The influential American modernist writer, John Dos Passos, joined the Republican side in 1937 as an observer and a correspondent, spending his time in the rural areas. He worked as a screenwriter with Hemingway and Yvens for the film *The Spanish Earth*. Dos Passos changed his views on the Soviet involvement in the conflict after his friend Jose Robles was accused of treason and shot. Robles was a Republican intellectual and a translator of Dos Passos's work into Spanish. This led to a disagreement between Dos Passos and Hemingway, the latter believing that war was an act of chivalry, and the two ceased their collaboration. In later years, Dos Passos wrote of his disappointment:

> I have come to think, especially since my trip to Spain, that civil liberties must be protected at every stage. In Spain I am sure that the introduction of GRU (Soviet military secret service) methods by the Communists

did as much harm as their tank men, pilots and experienced military men did good. The trouble with an all-powerful secret police in the hands of fanatics, or of anybody, is that once it gets started there's no stopping it until it has corrupted the whole body politic. I am afraid that's what's happening in Russia. (in Diggins, 1975: 233)

This disillusionment as expressed by Dos Passos is something that we will see is very relevant to the story of Eileen's time in Spain.

When Orwell set off for Spain at the end of 1936, he was joining a large number of international recruits to the Republic's cause. He travelled for 36 hours from France to Barcelona on a train crowded with these recruits, earning itself the nickname the Red Train. This sense of unification for a cause against fascism only became more nuanced when they arrived in Barcelona. Once there, Orwell headed to the only address he knew in the city, that of John McNair and the Independent Labour Party (ILP). It was McNair who recommended that Orwell join the Workers' Party of Marxist Unification, known by the acronym POUM, rather than the International Brigade. The POUM was more closely aligned with the anti-establishment anarchists, and its members were sometimes disparagingly referred to as Trotskyists, whereas the International Brigade was aligned with the Communist Party and Stalinist Russia. As a former officer in the Indian police service, Orwell had some experience of a militaristic life, experience that was in contrast to many of the volunteers who had arrived in Barcelona. Another factor that marked him out was his height: at 6'3" he was considerably taller than most of his fellow recruits, and in photographs of his time in POUM he is easily identifiable in a crowd.

As for Eileen, after ensuring the *Road to Wigan Pier* manuscript was safely ready for printing, she bravely set off for Barcelona by train through France in February 1937, travelling alone. With McNair's help, she crossed the border into Spain. When she arrived in McNair's Barcelona offices, she caused quite a stir. Through the reminiscences of others, we get a glimpse of the young woman who had so entranced Orwell. Eileen is described by Charles Orr as "a round-faced Irish girl, prim and pretty with black hair and big dark eyes" (Orr 1984, p5). He described her as "friendly, gregarious and unpretentious", which he said was the complete opposite of her husband, whom Orr described as being "tongue-tied" and inarticulate, commenting that he "seemed to be afraid of people" (ibid). Orr also recognised Eileen's intelligence, describing her as "an excellent secretary […] intelligent and self-confident. Everyone liked her, women as well as men" (ibid). Eileen's wit and acumen, attributes that had first attracted Orwell, appear to have been recognised more widely, and are certainly aspects of Eileen's personality that we find repeatedly in her letters. Eileen quickly settled into the Hotel Continental, where she organised social evenings for those associated with the ILP, helping to boost morale.

After a few weeks in Barcelona, Eileen had still not seen Orwell, since he had yet to be granted leave. In frustration, she went to see his commanding officer, the charismatic and enigmatic Belgian Georges Kopp, and talked him into taking her to the front to see Orwell. The trip lasted three days, and Eileen was able to stay with Orwell both in the trenches during the day and in the make-shift barracks at night. In a letter to her mother, Eileen describes her visit to the front.

22 March 1937

Seccion Inglesa

10 Rambla de los Estudios

Barcelona

Dearest Mummy,

I enclose 'a letter' I began to write to you in the trenches! It ends abruptly—I think I've lost a sheet—& is practically illegible but you may as well have a letter written from a real fighting line, & you'll read enough to get the essential news.[1] I thoroughly enjoyed being at the front.[2] If the doctor had been a good doctor I should have moved heaven & earth to stay (indeed before seeing the doctor I had already pushed heaven & earth a little) as a nurse—the line is still so quiet that he could well have trained me in preparation for the activity that must come.[3] But the doctor is quite ignorant & incredibly dirty. They have a tiny hospital at Monflorite in which he dresses the villagers' cut fingers etc. & does emergency work on any war wounds that do occur. Used dressings are thrown out of the

---

[1] Unfortunately, this letter hasn't survived.

[2] A photo has survived of Eileen sitting at the front with Orwell and the other soldiers.

[3] Eileen was even willing to act as a nurse to be near Orwell. In this, as in many other ways, she shows how much she loves and admires him.

window unless the window happens to be shut when they rebound onto the floor—& the doctor's hands have never been known to be washed.[4] So I decided he must have a previously trained assistant (I have one in view—a man). Eric did go to him but he says there is nothing the matter except 'cold, over fatigue, etc.'[5] This of course is quite true. However, the weather is better now & of course the leave is overdue, but another section on the Huesca front made an attack the other day which had rather serious results & leave is stopped there for the moment. Bob Edwards who commands the I.L.P. contingent has to be away for a couple of weeks & Eric is commanding in his absence, which will be quite fun in a way.[6] My visit to the front ended in a suitable way because Kopp decided I must have 'a few more hours' & arranged a car to leave Monflorite at 3:15 a.m. We went to bed at 10 or so & at 3 Kopp came & shouted & I got up & George (I can't remember which half of the family I write to)[7] went to sleep again I hope. In this way he got 2 nights proper rest & seems much better.[8] The whole visit's unreality was accentuated by the fact that there were no lights, not a candle or a torch; one got up & went to bed in black dark, & on the last night I emerged in black dark & waded knee deep in mud[9] in & out of strange buildings until I saw the faint glow from the Comité Militar where Kopp was waiting with his car.

On Tuesday we had the only bombardment of Barcelona since I came. It was quite interesting. Spanish people are normally incredibly noisy & pushing but in an emergency they appear to go quiet. Not that there was any real emergency but the bombs fell closer to the middle of the town

---

[4] As usual, Eileen is probably exaggerating a little, but it definitely was a good decision on her part not to become his nurse.

[5] It's not clear why Orwell did go to this doctor, but apparently it wasn't for anything too serious.

[6] Perhaps she is teasing Orwell here, as she often did.

[7] This probably relates to the emerging habit of referring to her husband as George in letters even to those close to them, and, in Eileen's case, to help distinguish between her husband and her brother in letters to close family.

[8] Kopp made sure they had two nights together, even though he was in love with Eileen himself.

[9] More of Eileen's cheerful exaggerations.

than usual & did make enough noise to excite people fairly reasonably.[10] There were very few casualties.

I'm enjoying Barcelona again—I wanted a change. You might send this letter on to Eric & Gwen, whom I thank for tea. Three lbs of it has just come & will be much appreciated. The contingent is just running out, Bob Edwards tells me. The other message for Eric is that as usual I am writing this in the last moments before someone leaves for France & also as usual my cheque book is not here,[11] but he will have the cheque for £10 within 2 weeks anyway & meanwhile I should be very grateful if he gave Fenner Brockway[12] the pesetas. (In case anything funny happened to the last letter, I asked him to buy £10 worth of pesetas & give them to Fenner Brockway to be brought out by hand. Living is very cheap here, but I spend a lot on the I.L.P. contingent as none of them have had any pay & they all need things. Also I've lent John [McNair] 500 ps. because he ran out.[13] I guard my five English pounds, which I could exchange at a fairly decent rate, because I must have something to use when we—whoever we may be—cross the frontier again.)[14]

I hope everyone is well—& I hope for a letter soon to say so. Gwen wrote a long letter which was exciting—even I fall into the universal habit of yearning over England. Perhaps the same thing happens in the colonies. When a waiter lit my cigarette the other day I said he had a nice lighter & he said 'Si, si, es bien, es Ingles!' Then he handed it to me, obviously thinking I should like to caress it a little. It was a Dunhill[15]—bought in Barcelona I expect as a matter of fact because there are plenty of Dunhill &

---

[10] Of course there was danger if bombs were falling. Again, Eileen's humour is at play, but rather than over-dramatising events, she is downplaying them here. Given she is writing to her mother, the downplaying of the drama is probably to help ease her mind a little.

[11] Eileen often makes light of her "inefficiency", as if she is denying her ability to handle everything very well.

[12] Archibald Fenner Brockway, Baron Brockway (1 November 1888–28 April 1988) was a British socialist politician, humanist campaigner and anti-war activist. His work as a journalist made his name during the General Strike of 1926. It was Brockway who facilitated Orwell's journey to Spain and gave him the necessary papers to join the ILP in Barcelona.

[13] Eileen, as well as Orwell, are always very generous with money.

[14] This comment is upsetting, given that we know what tragic days are ahead for them both.

[15] Dunhill was a well-known maker of quality cigarette lighters.

other lighters but a shortage of spirit for them. Kopp, Eric's commander, longed for Lea & Perrins Worcester Sauce. I discovered this by accident & found some in Barcelona[16]—they have Crosse & Blackwell's pickles too but the good English marmalade is finished although the prices of these things are fantastic.

After seeing George I am pretty confident that we shall be home before the winter—& possibly much sooner of course.[17] You might write another letter to the aunt some time. I have never heard from her & neither has Eric, which worries me rather. I think she may be very sad about living in Wallington.[18] By the way, George is positively urgent about the gas-stove—he wanted me to write & order it at once, but I still think it would be better to wait until just before our return, particularly as I have not yet heard from Moore about the advance on the book. Which reminds me that the reviews are better than I anticipated, as the interesting ones haven't come through yet.[19]

I had a bath last night—a great excitement. And I've had 3 superb dinners in succession. I don't know whether I shall miss this café life. I have coffee about three times a day & drinks oftener, & although theoretically I eat in a rather grim pension at least six times a week I get headed off into one of about four places where the food is really quite good by any standards though limited of course. Every night I mean to go home early & write letters or something & every night I get home the next morning.[20] The cafés are open till 1.30 & one starts one's after-dinner coffee about 10. But the sherry is undrinkable—& I meant to bring home some little casks of it!

Give Maud[21] my love & tell her I'll write some time. And give anyone else my love but I shan't be writing to them. (This letter is to the 3

---

[16] Eileen also did favours for Kopp, a man she was perhaps a bit in love with.

[17] It's not clear why she has come to this conclusion, but perhaps Orwell had discussed the war with her and predicted it would be a short one.

[18] Eileen has no problem asking her brother for favours, and he always complies without complaint.

[19] The mail is working well enough for Eileen to get letters from London.

[20] Another mention of Eileen's capacity for alcohol, which we first heard of the night she met Orwell.

[21] Peter Davison suggested that Maud might have been Eileen's aunt, but this is the only time Maud is mentioned by Eileen.

O'Shaughnessys who are thus 'you' not 'they'.)[22] It is a dull letter again I think. I shall do this life better justice in conversation—or I hope so.[23]

Much love

Eileen

Eileen returned to Barcelona with Kopp, and it was two whole months before she was to see Orwell again. However, she did receive a letter from him a few weeks after her visit, possibly dated 5 April, and written from the hospital while he was recovering from a poisoned hand. This is the only surviving letter from Orwell to Eileen, and it's a mystery just why it did survive, but we're lucky to have it (Fig 5.1).

Dearest,

You really are a wonderful wife.[24] When I saw the cigars my heart melted away. They will solve all tobacco problems for a long time to come. McNair tells me you are all right for money, as you can borrow & then repay when B[ob] E[dwards] brings some pesetas, but don't go beggaring yourself, & above all don't go short of food, tobacco etc. I hate to hear of your having a cold & feeling run down. Don't let them overwork you either,[25] & don't worry about me, as I am much better & expect to go back to the lines tomorrow or the day after. Mercifully the poisoning in my hand didn't spread, & it is now almost well, tho' of course the wound is still open. I can use it fairly well & intend to have a shave today, for the first time in about 5 days.[26] The weather is much better, real spring most of the time, & the look of the earth makes me think of our garden at home & wonder whether the wallflowers are coming out & whether old Hatchett is sowing the potatoes.[27] Yes, Pollitt's review was pretty bad, tho' of course

---

[22] Her mother, plus Eric and Gwen.

[23] Eileen's letters are never dull and neither was her conversation.

[24] It is clear Orwell did value Eileen, so it's rather sad that, in one of the very few times he praises her, he is happy that she has provided him with material goods in the form of cigars and margarine.

[25] Orwell does appear here to really be concerned about Eileen's health, shortage of food, and the fact that she's overworking herself.

[26] Orwell does a good job here being optimistic about his own well-being.

[27] One of Orwell's great loves was the cottage.

good as publicity.[28] I suppose he must have heard I was serving in the POUM militia. I don't pay much attention to the Sunday Times reviews as G[ollancz] advertises so much there that they daren't down his books, but the Observer was an improvement on last time. I told McNair that when I came on leave I would do the New Leader[29] an article, as they wanted one, but it will be such a come-down after B.E.'s that I don't expect they'll print it. I'm afraid it is not much use expecting leave before about the 20th April.[30] This is rather annoying in my own case as it comes about through my having exchanged from one unit to another—a lot of the men I came to the front with are now going on leave. If they suggested that I should go on leave earlier I don't think I would say no, but they are not likely to & I am not going to press them. There are also some indications—I don't know how much one can rely on these—that they expect an action hereabouts, & I am not going on leave just before that comes off if I can help it.[31] Everyone has been very good to me while I have been in hospital, visiting me every day etc. I think now that the weather is getting better I can stick out another month without getting ill, & then what a rest we will have, & go fishing too if it is in any way possible.[32]

As I write this Michael, Parker[33] & Buttonshaw[34] have just come in, & you should have seen their faces when they saw the margarine. As to the photos, of course there are lots of people who want copies, & I have written the numbers wanted on the backs, & perhaps you can get reproductions. I suppose it doesn't cost too much—I shouldn't like to disappoint the Spanish machine-gunners etc. Of course some of the photos were a mess. The one which has Buttonshaw looking very blurred in the

---

[28] Orwell always said that even a bad review was worth having for the publicity.

[29] The *New Leader* was the journal of the ILP, and was where Orwell later published his famous article, "Why I Join the ILP".

[30] And, of course, if Orwell had been on leave earlier, he might have avoided being shot.

[31] This is another example of a soldier wishing for action rather than inaction.

[32] Going fishing was one of Orwell's main enjoyments. Eileen never mentioned her feelings about that.

[33] This could be Thomas "Buck" Parker, another POUM volunteer.

[34] This is Harvey Buttonshaw. He fought alongside Orwell and in later life delighted on recounting the anecdote that he was the one who told Orwell to keep his head down moments before he was actually shot.

foreground is a photo of a shell-burst, which you can see rather faintly on the left, just beyond the house.[35]

I shall have to stop in a moment, as I am not certain when McNair is going back & I want to have this letter ready for him. Thanks ever so much for sending the things, dear, & do keep well & happy. I told McNair I would have a talk with him about the situation when I came on leave, & you might at some opportune moment say something to him about my wanting to go to Madrid etc.[36] Goodbye, love. I'll write again soon.

With all my love

Eric

Meanwhile, Eileen was able to enjoy the heady excitement of this early part of the war. Barcelona was full of interesting and exciting people. There was also no shortage of food and drink, and Eileen was able to write to her mother mentioning this. Eileen had become good friends with Orr's wife, Lois, and the two of them were treated to generous meals by a journalist from the *Daily Express* on more than one occasion, although Eileen was keen to state that she had never divulged any information that could be of use to a writer for a "reactionary and sensational" paper (as she referred to it in a letter to her mother).

Eileen also proved to be attractive to other men who were in Barcelona. She struck up a friendship with the Italian, Georgio Tioli, and was also pursued by David Crook. Both men seemed to find her gregarious nature appealing, and Eileen's letters contain mention of trips out to the countryside with them. However, there is a darker side to this, as both Tioli and Crook turned out to be spies for the Communist Party, perhaps hoping that the gregarious Eileen would also turn out to be loose-lipped. She was, after all, working at quite a high level in the ILP, typing letters and other documents that contained highly confidential material. There is no evidence to suggest that Eileen was indiscreet, and, if anything, both men came to admire her in her own right.

---

[35] It appears that many photographs were taken at the front, so it's a shame that only one survived.

[36] Orwell has decided that he wants to join the Stalinist forces in Madrid, where there is real fighting taking place. However, he very dramatically changes his mind later, turning actively against Stalin.

Fig. 5.1 Eileen Blair with Orwell at Aragon Front, Huesca. UCL Orwell Archive ORWELL/T/2/D/6

Meanwhile Eileen was still conducting business with Orwell's agent about the distribution of *The Road to Wigan Pier*, as described in a letter to Gollancz in mid-April.

12 April 1937

[Typewritten]

Seccion Inglesa,

10, Rambla de los Estudios,

Barcelona.

Dear Mr. Moore,

I hope you received my message of thanks for sending out the two copies of Wigan Pier when it was first published. Now I wish to thank you for the four further copies, two of the 10/6 edition and two of the L.B.C. edition, which came on Saturday. The press cuttings are coming through very well too, and on the whole are very satisfactory. Everyone I hear from is most impressed by the book—I wonder what you thought of it.[37]

I saw my husband a month ago at the front, where, as this is a revolutionary war, I was allowed to stay in the front line dug-outs all day.[38] The Fascists threw in a small bombardment and quite a lot of machine-gun fire, which was then comparatively rare on the Huesca front, so it was quite an interesting visit—indeed I never enjoyed anything more.[39] Eric was then fairly well, though very tired; since then he has had a rest two miles behind the line as he got a poisoned arm, but I think he is now back in the line and the front has been active for the last week. He is keeping quite a good diary and I have great hopes for the book.[40] Unfortunately the activity on his part of the front has interfered with his leave, which is now long overdue, but I hope he will be down here in a week or two.[41]

I should be very grateful if you could let us know whether Gollancz paid the second advance on publication, as he said he was prepared to do. We are still solvent, but when Eric comes on leave we must discuss our future arrangements which will partly depend on the advance.[42] As a matter of fact, there may be a letter now on the way from the bank. The mails are so slow and so irregular that it is very difficult to manage any sort of business.

With many thanks,

Yours sincerely,

Eileen Blair.

---

[37] *Wigan Pier* was getting favourable reviews, but Eileen is again downplaying this as "very satisfactory".

[38] A great example of Eileen's ironic humour.

[39] We have to assume Eileen is overstating her enjoyment.

[40] Orwell must be sending diary notes to Eileen for later use in his book.

[41] Unfortunately, Orwell's leave was delayed, but he did eventually have a short, active few days of leave.

[42] Eileen has hopes that the couple can move from Wallington to a place in southern England with a better climate, as she's concerned, as always, with Orwell's health. He is very resistant to making any move, however.

Another man who also became very close to Eileen at this time was Georges Kopp. They were often in each other's company, and Georges undoubtedly fell in love with Eileen. There has been much speculation as to whether this was ever reciprocated. Crook himself reported back that he was "95% certain that Kopp and Eileen were on intimate terms" (Wildemeersch, 2013, p61). Eileen herself leaves us some hints at her closeness to Kopp in her letters, as we will see later in this chapter.

The busy social life in Barcelona was mixed with the more serious business of working for the ILP, and also in typing up the notes that Orwell was sending her from the Front. The paucity of suitable writing materials at the Front meant much of this was improvised, such as on the backs of envelopes, scraps of paper, and even, on occasion, on toilet paper. Finally, at the end of April, after 115 days at the Front, Orwell got leave to spend time with Eileen in Barcelona. As we can see from Eileen's letter to her brother, Orwell arrived in a shabby state. There is also a great deal of time spent in this letter negotiating money, against a backdrop of increasing danger for Eileen in the previous safety of Barcelona.

1 May 1937

Rambla de los Estudios

Barcelona

Dear Eric,

You have a hard life.[43] I mean to write to Mother with the news, but there are some business matters. Now I think of these, they're inextricably connected with the news so Mother must share this letter.

George is here on leave. He arrived completely ragged, almost barefoot, a little lousy, dark brown, & looking really very well.[44] For the previous 12 hours he had been in trains consuming anis, muscatel out of anis bottles, sardines & chocolate. In Barcelona food is plentiful at the moment but

---

[43] This is an example of Eileen's playful sense of humour. She appears overly sympathetic to her brother's life at home whilst she herself was facing real danger in Spain.

[44] Eileen is so happy to have Orwell back on leave that she is able to joke about his appearance.

there is nothing plain. So it is not surprising that he ceased to be well. Now after two days in bed he is really cured but still persuadable so having a 'quiet day'.⁴⁵ This is the day to have on May 1st. They were asked to report at the barracks, but he isn't well enough & has already applied for his discharge papers so he hasn't gone. The rest of the contingent never thought of going. When the discharge is through he will probably join the International Brigade.⁴⁶ Of course we—perhaps particularly I— are politically suspect but we told all the truth to the I.B. man here & he was so shattered that he was practically offering me executive jobs by the end of half an hour, & I gather that they will take George. Of course I must leave Barcelona but I should do that in any case as to stay would be pointless. Madrid is probably closed to me, so it means Valencia for the moment with Madrid & Albacete in view but at long distance. To join the I.B. with George's history is strange but it is what he thought he was doing in the first place & it's the only way of getting to Madrid. So there it is.⁴⁷ Out of this arises a further money crisis because when I leave Barcelona I shall leave all my affiliations—& my address and even my credit at the bank; & it will take a little time to get connected again perhaps. Meanwhile we spend immense sums of money for Spain on new equipment etc. I did write to you about getting money through banks—i.e. your bank buys pesetas with your pounds & instructs a bank in Barcelona to pay me the number of pesetas you bought. If this can be done will you do it (about another 2000 pesetas I should think), & will you ask the bank to cable. Probably I shall be here for a couple of weeks but I'm not <u>sure</u> where I shall go next & I want if possible to have some money in hand before leaving. If the bank business can't be done I frankly don't know what can—i.e. I must use the credit at 60 to the £ before leaving here & find some method of getting money through my new friends, whoever they may be (I have met the <u>Times</u> correspondent at Valencia).⁴⁸

---

⁴⁵ Eileen is teasing Orwell about his refusal to feel better.

⁴⁶ Orwell has decided to leave the POUM and join the Stalinist forces in Madrid.

⁴⁷ Eileen is upset by this change of events, which will prevent her from being near Orwell.

⁴⁸ Part of her concern is that it might be impossible for her to receive money from the bank if she leaves Barcelona. None of this concerns Orwell, of course, since he leaves all financial concerns to Eileen. Eileen's parenthetical note about meeting a *Times* correspondence is interesting as the correspondent in Valencia at that time was Kim Philby, who was later unmasked as one of Cambridge spy ring.

The other business is the cottage. I gather & hear from Mrs Blair that the aunt is not only tiring but tired,[49] & I have written to her suggesting evacuation with all the arrangements under headings. You take over in a manner of speaking. If she shows you the letter it may alarm you, but twenty minutes will settle most of the problems. There are several things to be paid, but they're all matters of shillings & the shop may have— should have—a few pounds in hand. The shop will be closed. I've said you can buy any perishables. It is not of course suggested that you should pay for these, except in the aunt's eyes, but she will never give anything away so you might dump doubtful stuff in the car & dispose of it anyhow you like.[50] If Mother is at Greenwich she might perhaps go over after the aunt is out & see that there is nothing to attract mice.[51] There is a chance that Arthur Clinton, who was wounded, may go & recuperate in the cottage. He is perhaps the nicest man in the world & I hope he may be able to use it. He'll return to England unfit, ineligible for dole & penniless. If he wants the cottage he'll ask you about it of course.

We shall owe you money. We have money in our sense of the word, but I haven't much fancy for sending cheques if they get lost in the post.

I must take this to the office now—one of the contingent is going home tomorrow & will take it. I have in progress an immense letter to mother, started two or three weeks ago, which will arrive in due course. I am very well.[52]

About the L.C.C. pay I fully agree that there must be no sessional payment—it is a vicious system.[53]

---

[49] This is another example of Eileen's word play, which we have seen her develop over the years.

[50] Again, Eileen completely expects her brother to do whatever she asks of him.

[51] Eileen also expects her mother to do whatever she asks.

[52] Eileen mentions her own health as an aside.

[53] The LCC is London County Council. Eileen is sympathising with the perceived unfairness of a system that paid a fee for each session worked instead of at an annual rate. The unfairness stemmed from the fact that a doctor could be booked for a session, but this could be cancelled at short notice; therefore time would have been set aside with no financial recompense. In pre-NHS medicine in the UK, this was one of the common problems medical practitioners faced.

My love to Gwen. By the way, I gather from the correspondence that she isn't coming. If this is wrong & she is coming of course I'll wait in Barcelona.[54]

Yours

Eileen.

For the bank's information my name is Eileen Maud Blair & my passport number 174234.

I really am sorry for you—but what can I do?

During his leave, Orwell has asked Eileen to arrange for him to meet John Dos Passos, who was also in Barcelona at that time. This was accomplished in the lobby of the Hotel Continental. After the meeting, Orwell sent Eileen with a message of thanks for meeting: "Eric wants me to thank you from the bottom of his heart. He asked me to thank you for him, because he knows he can't talk" (Orr 1984 p 8).

This hints at the inarticulate nature of Orwell's social interactional skills that others had noticed and contrasted with Eileen's gregariousness. It may also be linked to the topics covered by Orwell and Dos Passos, both of whom were starting to see cracks in the anti-fascist fighting forces. Orwell had noticed this when he returned to Barcelona on leave, where skirmishes in the street were becoming more common. At one point, Orwell was stationed on the roof of a cinema in central Barcelona for three days, unsure whom or what he was supposed to be protecting. There were rumours circulating in Barcelona that Russia was about to eliminate the POUM, referring to them disparagingly as Trotskyists who were supporting Franco. Orwell had considered resigning from the POUM and joining the International Brigade, but this trip to Barcelona showed him an unpleasant side to the Communist supporters, and so at the end of his leave on 10 May he returned to the Front to fight with the POUM.

In the midst of Orwell's leave, Eileen received a letter from Mrs. Blair informing her that Aunt Nellie was determined to leave the cottage, and so alternative arrangements for the care of that and the animals needed

---

[54] Gwen never did visit Barcelona.

to be found. Eileen quickly wrote a series of letters to her family and, as with an already established pattern of the expectation of being bailed out by them, new arrangements were made for various others to be caretakers of the cottage and animals.

Ten days after returning to the Front, whilst entertaining his fellow fighters with stories of his exploits, Orwell stood up in the trench to make a more dramatic point—and was hit in the neck by a sniper's bullet.

News of Orwell's injury reached Eileen in Barcelona. With Kopp's help, she was able to reach him around fifty hours after he had been shot. By that time, he had been through several field hospitals and had reached a larger hospital in Lerida. Eileen's organising skills, admired by all who saw her running the ILP office in Barcelona, swung into action, and soon Orwell had been transferred to a hospital closer to Barcelona where there were more expert doctors to treat him. The bullet had grazed Orwell's trachea, just missing his carotid artery, and had left him unable to speak beyond a whisper. More importantly, Eileen's actions in moving him to more advanced care also removed him from the danger of infection that lurked in less sophisticated hospitals. When she telegraphed his parents, she was able to downplay the seriousness of the injury, as any sensible and considerate person would do, once the immediate danger was over.

ERIC SLIGHTLY WOUNDED PROGRESS EXCELLENT SENDS LOVE NO NEED FOR ANXIETY EILEEN

This brief message reassured the Blairs and implied that Orwell was conscious, lucid and in good spirits (it was Orwell who "sends love", not Eileen).

Towards the end of May, Eileen arranged for Orwell to be transferred to the Sanatorium Maurin on the outskirts of Barcelona. The plan was to return to England for specialist treatment as soon as Orwell was well enough to travel. Whilst his voice continued to strengthen, he was still complaining of pains in his right arm. The doctors at Sanatorium Maurin prescribed electrotherapy. So it was that on their first wedding anniversary, 9 June, Eileen and Orwell were in the less than romantic surroundings of a hospital.

The following is one of the few existing letters that Eileen wrote to her brother at this time, but it does confirm that a great deal of correspondence travelled between London and Barcelona.

[Handwritten]

Undated, but around 10 June.

Dear Eric,

Ten days ago George Kopp wrote you an account of the medical investigations & reports on Eric[55], & I wrote letters to you & Mrs Blair & the aunt. As we wanted you all to get the correspondence quickly we gave them to a man who was crossing into France, to be sent Air Mail from there. Today we hear that he lost the whole packet. So everyone will be feeling bitterly neglected, including me as I had expected a reassuring cable.[56] I've written at least three letters & four postcards each to the three addresses since, but I don't know which have arrived or when. You might ask mother to telephone Mrs Blair & write [to the] aunt—or better telephone yourself & give a medical opinion.[57]

Eric is I think much better, though he cannot be brought to admit any improvement.[58] His voice certainly improves very slowly, but he uses his arm much more freely though it is still very painful at times. He eats as much as anyone else & can walk about & do any ordinary thing quite effectively for a short time. He is violently depressed, which I think encouraging.[59] I have now agreed to spend two or three days on the Mediterranean (in France) on the way home—probably at Port Vendre.[60] In any case we shall probably have to wait somewhere for money. The discharge is not through but I think we can leave next week, wire you for money when we arrive at Port-Vendre or other resting place, go on to Paris & spend there two nights & the day between, & then get the morning train to England. I do not altogether like this protracted travel,

---

[55] Eileen referred to Orwell as Eric in this letter.

[56] Some more of Eileen's wonderful understated humour.

[57] Again, Eileen is asking her brother for help, which he never objects to.

[58] Eileen always teases Orwell about his stubbornness.

[59] Eileen's humour subverts the expectations of "depression" being a cause for concern with her optimism that this is an improvement on whatever preceded it.

[60] Of course, as we know, they barely managed to escape safely from Spain. But they did spend a few days on the shores of the Mediterranean after they finally arrived in France.

but no urgent complication seems possible now, & he has an overwhelming desire to follow this programme—anyway it has overwhelmed me.[61]

Give my love to everyone. I now realise I haven't explained that the enclosed letter from G.K. is a copy of the one that was lost.

Thank you very much for the liniment & the things for Lois, which I collected today.

Eileen.

Did you get £20 from Fenner Brockway?

Orwell's recovery continued, and Eileen wrote hopefully of a return to England by the end of June, offering her brother an account of Orwell's desire to prolong the journey by having a few days' break in France en route. As Orwell continued to return to health, his pride overtook any caution. If he was discharged from the POUM straight from hospital, he believed the notation would be that he was "declared useless" rather than "honourably discharged". To achieve this, he needed papers signed by serving officers, and this necessitated a precarious trip back up to the Front. This trip, which he undertook from 15 to 20 June, was undertaken without Eileen, who remained in Barcelona. On 16 June, POUM was declared unlawful by the Communists, and the leaders realised they were about to be arrested. Eileen went to dinner with the Orrs and Kopp that evening, and Lois reported a frustrating meal where the very pressing topic of politics was totally avoided in their conversation. The next day, the Orrs and Kopp were arrested. Eileen was not arrested, but instead she believed that she was being used as bait for Orwell, who would be arrested on his return to Barcelona. Her paranoia is not without foundation: later research by Marc Wildemeersch (2013), making use of access to KGB files, reveals that David Crook had been explicitly tasked with spying on Orwell and Kopp for the Communist Party. Specifically, a report for the "Tribunal for Espionage and High Treason" listed Eileen and Orwell as "rabid Trotskyists" and detailed more than enough evidence to justify their arrest.

---

[61] Eileen always gives in to Orwell's strong desires, here partly masked by her usual word play.

At this point, Richard Rees arrived in Barcelona, seemingly unaware of the deteriorating situation. He found Eileen "absent-minded, preoccupied and dazed" (1962 p119), and was hurt when she refused his offer to join her for lunch. She had to explain to him that she was afraid he would be seen with her, and thus risk arrest. Her paranoia and fear of being watched was noticed by Rees, who reported, "In Eileen Blair I had seen for the first time the symptoms of a human being living under a political Terror" (ibid).

Eileen had in fact also been subjected to a late-night visit by six policemen. They had entered her hotel room whilst she was sleeping. In the middle of this terrifying invasion of her privacy, Eileen remained calm and feigned lack of concern as the men ransacked her room, taking away the papers and diaries she and Orwell had been collecting for his next work. However, Eileen's reason for remaining in bed was not an insouciance but instead a ploy to stop the men from discovering her and Orwell's passports and cheque book, which she had placed under her in the bed for safekeeping. Eileen had gambled on the men not being so uncouth as to order a woman out of bed.

Completely unaware of the turmoil in Barcelona, Orwell returned on 20 June. He entered the Hotel Continental, where he was accosted by Eileen in the lobby. Orwell later wrote in *Homage to Catalonia*: "She got up and came towards me in what struck me as a very unconcerned manner; then she put an arm around my neck and, with a sweet smile for the benefit of the other people in the lounge, hissed in my ear: 'Get out!'" (1952 p 204). The fact that Orwell had served in the POUM militia was enough to get him arrested, and Eileen made him destroy his militiaman's card, which was evidence that he had served with the POUM.

Curiously, despite a war going on and political turmoil in the heart of Barcelona, it was still a popular tourist destination. Eileen and Orwell managed to evade capture by mingling with these tourists by day. By night, they decided it was prudent for Eileen to continue the pretence of being on her own, and so she stayed in the Hotel Continental whilst Orwell slept rough around the city. Again, Eileen's organisational skills came to the fore, and she spent three long, anxious days obtaining travel papers from the British Consulate. Both she and Orwell also managed to visit Kopp in prison, risking their own lives in the process.

On 22 June, Orwell, Eileen, McNair and 18-year-old Stafford Cottman, who had served with Orwell, arranged to arrive separately at the station to board a train north to France. However, when they arrived at the station, they found the train had actually left ahead of schedule. They were all forced back into hiding for another night before eventually boarding a train on the morning of 23 June. The four of them posed as English tourists. Eileen had somehow managed to salvage some of her beloved poetry books after the ransacking of her hotel room. She used these as props for Orwell and Cottman, who took up position in the dining carriage, assuming great interest in Wordsworth and Masefield. The use of a book for Orwell to read had the advantage of ensuring he was not tempted to stand up or wander around, and thus reveal his remarkable height. Eileen's organisational skills and quick-thinking made sure Orwell was able to escape from Spain and not suffer the fate of other volunteers such as Federica Garcia Lorca.

By 1939, at the end of Spanish Civil War, it has been estimated nearly one million people had died in it, more than half of these being through malnutrition rather than violent death (Payne, 2011). This pales into insignificance when we look at what happened with the next war against fascism: the Second World War, but it shows that the conditions of civilians in Spain deteriorated rapidly after Eileen and Orwell left in the summer of 1937. This exciting and terrifying period of their early married life shows us a clear instance of Eileen saving Orwell's life. However, it is not just in wartime that this action was needed: as noted earlier, Orwell was not a well man at times, and shortly after returning to England in the late summer of 1937, Eileen found herself again called on to act quickly and decisively.

Eileen and Orwell landed back in England at the end of June 1937. They were both exhausted, mentally and physically, and in Orwell's case he was still recovering from his throat wound as well as a longer-term injury to his right arm, sustained in the early weeks of his time at the Front. They must have had a sense of dread at what awaited them back in Wallington, so they spent a few days in the luxury of Eric O'Shaughnessy's house in London before venturing home. Orwell was already planning to write a book about the "truth" of the Spanish Civil War. The British newspapers had largely taken a pro-Communist stance, and so the wider issues of in-fighting, imprisonment and executions were largely absent from the press coverage. This was one of the reasons why tourists were still travelling to Spain, and, paradoxically, afforded the couple a viable cover story on their escape from Catalonia. However, Orwell was now determined to write about the reality of life in Spain.

But, before he could start on that, there was the problem of the state of the house and gardens at Wallington. The house had been overrun with mice, and the crops, so carefully planted in the autumn, had run to seed. Many of the animals had escaped or else been adopted by other villagers. The most pressing issue facing the couple was a need to generate income. They decided very quickly not to re-open the shop, which had not been profitable when compared with the huge effort to maintain it. This gave them an extra room in their tiny cottage, which they turned into a very serviceable dining room. They also set about planting fresh vegetables and replenishing their stock of animals that could provide them with food: hens for eggs; goats for milk. They also acquired a new dog: a poodle cross they called Marx. Marx becomes a topic for many amusing anecdotes in Eileen's letters.

Meanwhile, Orwell was trying to find a publisher for his yet-to-be-written book about the Spanish Civil War. His usual publisher, Victor Gollancz, rejected it as it did not fit with the pro-Communist ethos of the Left at this time. After several other failed attempts, in December 1937 Orwell signed a contract for the book with Secker and Warburg. However, a problem remained in that all of the notes he had made during his time in Spain had been confiscated in the raid on Eileen's hotel room. Fortunately, Eileen had typed up these notes and had retained some knowledge of their content. Thus Orwell's *Homage to Catalonia* was produced as a collaboration with Eileen, whose "emendations" to the drafts she typed from his notes back in the cottage show clearly how integral she was to this book's production.

While Orwell was working with Eileen on *Homage to Catalonia*, he was also trying to earn a more regular income through writing book reviews and short journalistic articles. In fact, Orwell was turning himself into a journalist more than a creative writer as he tried to generate an income to sustain their frugal lifestyle at the cottage.

The couple's thoughts often returned to their comrades in Spain. In early August, they visited Bristol (after borrowing Eric O'Shaughnessy's car) to attend a rally in support of Stafford Cottman, the young man whom they had helped escape from Spain two months earlier. He was being hounded by members of the Young Communist League who were accusing him of being a traitor, an "enemy of the working class".

Then there was Georges Kopp, who was still in prison in Spain. He was managing to communicate with Eileen by letters, sent to her via her brother, although not all of these reached Eileen. In these letters, he pleaded for help in publicising his incarceration without trial. He was also complaining of dwindling funds and the fact that he had to share a cell with 18 other people, ranging from political prisoners such as himself to thieves, fraudsters and homosexuals. Eileen copied part of one of these letters in a message to McNair, pleading with him to help expedite Kopp's release.

29 July 1937

[Typewritten; carbon copy]

The Stores,

Wallington,

Near Baldock, Herts.

Dear John,

Herewith two enclosures. Number 1 is a copy of an ultimatum sent by George Kopp to the Chief of Police in Barcelona, together with the letter which accompanied it to my brother. Number 2 is an extract from a letter written by George Kopp to me, which is to some extent repetition of Number 1 but which gives more details of the conditions of imprisonment and will interest you personally by its reference to individuals.[62]

You will see that the important facts emerging from all the documents are that George intended to go on hunger strike on the 9th or 10th July unless he obtained some satisfaction from the Chief of Police and that he wishes his action to be given publicity. Partly because you know the conditions in Spain, I think you will be best able to decide the manner of this publicity—there is of course a strong possibility that George will be made to suffer for it however it is done, but he will have considered that

---

[62] Eileen is very concerned about the fate of Georges Kopp, whom she and Orwell were unable to free from jail when they left Barcelona. The chaotic nature of the postal service at this point, as well as the peripatetic nature of Eileen and Orwell's existence, meant that Kopp was using Eileen's brother's address to send letters to her. He also used Eileen's brother's address for personal letters meant for Eileen only. In threatening to go on a hunger strike to gain publicity, Kopp is copying the strategies used by suffragettes a quarter of a century earlier.

himself; the main doubt appears to be whether his name should be given or not.

It seems almost certain that the hunger strike has occurred, but actually these letters, although written on the 7th and 8th of July, only reached me this morning. In any case, if there is no further news before the next issue of the New Leader, we may assume that he is on strike and unable to communicate. As for publicity outside the New Leader, you and Fenner will know better than we what hope there is. Judging from Eric's experiences in attempting to publish the most conservative truth, we shall not find the English press at least enthusiastic.

Jock Branthwaite[63] proposed to come over to Letchworth on Monday on a bicycle to hear you speak and to see you. We only have one bicycle; so he will represent the whole party on that day, but you could perhaps tell him what you think. Apparently George Tioli[64] is still being helpful, which is really a magnificent gesture.

I hope to see you myself some time during next week—indeed I hope to see you here. Apart from all the sentimental considerations, there are a few hundred things I want to know.

Yours ever,

[Unsigned]

I forgot to say that the two earlier letters to which George refers never arrived.

In the midst of all of the activities regarding maintaining the cottage, writing and rewriting the manuscript for *Homage to Catalonia*, and Orwell's journalistic writing, the couple also hosted an incessant stream of visitors throughout the summer and early autumn of 1937, as the above letter to McNair hints.

Eileen and Orwell spent Christmas 1937 in the luxury of her brother's house. They returned to the cottage for the new year, and Eileen wrote

---

[63] Jock Branthwaite was the son of a miner and served with Orwell in Spain.

[64] A man Eileen befriended in Barcelona and who was suspected of being a communist spy.

a delightful letter to Norah on New Year's Day, 1938. Since The Stores had no electricity, this letter, which was typed by the light of a candle that towards the end was guttering, had a small number of typographical errors, which Peter Davison silently corrected.

New Year's Day 1938

The Stores, Wallington

[no salutation]

You see I have no pen, no ink, no glasses[65] and the prospect of no light, because the pens, the inks, the glasses and the candles are all in the room where George is working and if I disturb him again it will be for the fifteenth time tonight.[66] But full of determined ingenuity I found a typewriter, and blind people are said to type in their dark.

I have also to write to a woman who has suddenly sent me a Christmas present (I think it may be intended for a wedding present after an estrangement of five or ten years, and in looking to see whether I had any clues to her address I found a bit of a letter to you, a very odd hysterical little letter, much more like Spain than any I can have written in that country. So here it is.[67] The difficulty about the Spanish war is that it still dominates our lives in a most unreasonable manner because Eric George (or do you call him Eric?) is just finishing the book about it and I give him typescripts the reverse sides of which are covered with manuscript emendations that he can't read, and he is always having to speak about it[68] and I have returned to complete pacifism and joined the P.P.U.[69] partly because of it. (Incidentally, you must join the P.P.U. too. War is fun so far as the shooting

---

[65] Although rarely photographed wearing her glasses, Eileen was short-sighted and needed these for reading. Her expertise in touch-typing meant she could get by without her glasses, even if she had had a light to see by.

[66] Eileen's love of exaggeration here perhaps could be translated at interrupting Orwell far fewer times.

[67] It's not clear whether Eileen enclosed the letter she found, or is just copying it.

[68] Orwell takes her emendations very seriously, asking her to explain the ones he can't understand. This shows us very clearly that Eileen had a great deal of input to his writing.

[69] Peace Pledge Union. This is one of the oldest pacifist organisations in the UK, having been founded in 1934. Peter Davison explains that there is no record of Orwell having joined this organisation although there is a record of receipts for pamphlets in

goes and much less alarming than an aeroplane in a shop window,[70] but it does appalling things to people normally quite sane and intelligent—some make desperate efforts to retain some kind of integrity and others like Langdon-Davies[71] make no efforts at all but hardly anyone can stay reasonable, let alone honest.) The Georges Kopp[72] situation is now more Dellian[73] than ever. He is still in jail but has somehow managed to get several letters out to me, one of which George opened and read because I was away. He is very fond of Georges, who indeed cherished him with real tenderness in Spain and anyway is admirable as a soldier because of his quite remarkable courage, and he[74] is extraordinarily magnanimous about the whole business—just as Georges was extraordinarily magnanimous.[75] Indeed they went about saving each other's lives or trying to in a way that was almost horrible to me, though George had not then noticed that Georges was more than 'a bit gone on' me. I sometimes think no one ever had such a sense of guilt before. It was always understood that I wasn't what they call in love with Georges[76]—our association progressed in little leaps, each leap immediately preceding some attack or operation in which he would almost inevitably be killed, but the last time I saw him

---

Eileen's name in the Orwell Archive. It may therefore be Eileen who joined the PPU at this time.

[70] Eileen might be referring here to Orwell's experience with the POUM in Spain.

[71] John Eric Langdon-Davies MBE (18 March 1897–5 December 1971) was a British author and journalist. He was a war correspondent during the Spanish Civil War.

[72] There has been much speculation and disagreement amongst Orwell scholars as to whether Eileen had an affair with Kopp. She was deeply in love with Orwell, but he wasn't a romantic lover. In fact, he's on record complaining that women wanted more sex than he was willing to indulge in (although his own behaviour would indicate that this was not a real problem for him). Kopp, on the other hand, was a flirtatious seductive man, as can be seen in his letters to Eileen. He has also been described as attractive. Eileen seemed even more concerned than Orwell about getting Kopp out of jail. Orwell is on record saying he didn't suffer from jealousy. And, as Eileen said, he was very magnanimous about her feelings for Kopp. Kopp later married a relative of Eileen's, and the two couples lived close to each other in London. Their friendship continued throughout the rest of her life, and it was Kopp who took Eileen to the train station after her last visit to London.

[73] Peter Davison said that one interpretation of Dellian referred to the "Greek island of Delos, home of an oracle who posed obscure and convoluted responses to questions put to it".

[74] Orwell.

[75] Orwell seemed to accept the fact that Eileen did have a flirtation with Kopp, here euphemised by Eileen with typical word play.

[76] Eileen seems to be admitting that she had flirted with Kopp, but never considered leaving Orwell.

he was in jail waiting, as we were both confident, to be shot, and I simply couldn't explain to him again as a kind of farewell that he could never be a rival to George.[77] So he has rotted in a filthy prison for more than six months with nothing to do but remember me in my most pliant moments. If he never gets out, which is indeed most probable, it's good that he has managed to have some thoughts in a way pleasant, but if he does get out I don't know how one reminds a man immediately he is a free man again that one has only once missed the cue for saying that nothing on earth would induce one to marry him.[78] Being in prison in Spain means living in a room with a number of others (about fifteen to twenty in a room the size of your sitting-room) and never getting out of it; if the window has steel shutters, as many have, never seeing daylight, never having a letter; never being charged, let alone tried; never knowing whether you will be shot tomorrow or released, in either case without explanation; when your money runs out never eating anything but a bowl of the worst imaginable soup and a bit of bread at 3 p.m. and at 11 p.m.[79]

On the whole it's a pity I found that letter because Spain doesn't really dominate us as much as all that. We have nineteen hens now—eighteen deliberately and the other by accident because we bought some ducklings and a hen escorted them. We thought we ought to boil her this autumn so we took it in turns to watch the nesting boxes to see whether she laid an egg to justify a longer life, and she did. And she is a good mother, so she is to have children in the spring. This afternoon we built a new henhouse—that is we put the sections together—and that is the nucleus of the breeding pen. There is probably no question on poultry-keeping that I am not able and very ready to answer. Perhaps you would like to have a battery (say three units) in the bathroom so that you could benefit from my advice. It would be a touching thing to collect an egg just before brushing one's teeth and eat it just after.[80] Which reminds me that since we got back from Southwold, where we spent an incredibly family Christmas with

---

[77] Eileen admits that she lied to Kopp while he was in jail, giving him some hope that they would be together when he was released.

[78] Eileen dreads the moment that Kopp might be released, at which point she would have to tell him the truth. She goes out of her way to empathise with Kopp's situation in jail by way of excusing her action of giving him something to hope for when all hope seemed lost.

[79] This lengthy passage where Eileen seems to take on the point of view of the hopeless prisoner can be read as her self-vindication for the flirtation with Kopp.

[80] A lovely fantasy about one of Eileen and Orwell's main chores at the cottage: counting eggs.

the Blairs, we have eaten boiled eggs almost all the time. Before we had only one eggcup from Woolworths'—no two from Woolworths' and one that I gave George with an Easter egg in it before we were married (that cost threepence with egg). So it was a Happy Thought dear, and they are such a nice shape and match your mother's butter dish and breadboard, giving tone to the table.[81]

We also have a poodle puppy. We called him Marx to remind us that we had never read Marx and now we have read a little and taken so strong a personal dislike to the man that we can't look the dog in the face when we speak to him.[82] He, the dog, is a French poodle, supposed to be miniature and of prize-winning stock, with silver hair. So far he has black and white hair, greying at the temples, and at four and a half months is rather larger than his mother. We think however he may take a prize as the largest miniature. He is very appealing and has a remarkable digestion. I am proud of this. He has never been sick, although almost daily he finds in the garden bones that no eye can have seen these twenty years and has eaten several rugs and a number of chairs and stools.[83] We weren't going to clip him, but he has a lot of hairs which are literally dripping mud on the driest day—he rolls on every cushion in turn and then drips right through my lap—so we thought we would clip him a little. But now we shall never get him symmetrical till we shave him. Laurence[84] (it is a dreadful thing that you have never seen Laurence) bears with him in a remarkable way and has never scratched even his nose.

I went to stay with Mary[85]. You will have heard about the domestic changes. She went to stay with that pregnant cousin and read a book on infant feeding, from which she discovered that everything Nanny did was

---

[81] This appears to be a touch of irony, considering the situation at the cottage. The notion of "tone" to interior décor is archaic, but would chime with Eileen's love of English Literature.

[82] This melodramatic approach to their dog appears to show a joint sense of humour in admitting to their political vacillations.

[83] A remarkable digestion for sure!

[84] Davison suggests that this would be Eileen's brother, since the son, Laurence, wasn't born yet. It could be another animal, given their habit of naming animals after people. Eileen's brother was known as Eric by all the family, so it is unlikely to be her brother that she was referring to.

[85] This is presumably Bertha Mary Wardell, who graduated with Eileen and Norah.

wrong. So of course she had to come home and tell her so, because otherwise she would have killed the children[86]. Now they have a Norwegian nurse. I think she is better but it's bad luck for David who was hopelessly spoilt by fat Nanny and is not approved of by the Norwegian—who never raises her voice but puts him in the corner. Mary herself has become a good mother—when the children are there, I mean. She is perfectly reasonable with them. I don't know what happened. David is very intelligent and makes me slightly jealous because I should like a son and we don't have one.[87] Mary and I summed up human history in a dreadful way when I was there—I was in the throes of pre-plague pains[88], which had happened so late that I was wondering whether I could persuade myself that I felt as though I were not going to have them, and Mary wasn't having any pre-plague pains at all and was in a fever and going to the chemist to try to buy some ergot or other corrective. We had two parties—we went to see Phyl Guimaraens[89] and the MAMMETT CAME TO TEA[90]. She might just as well have been in Girl Guide uniform but now she organises play-readings, when all the old St. Hugh's girls go to her house and read Julius Caesar. Mary went once but she thought they would be given something to eat and they weren't, not even a bun or a cup of tea, so she is embittered and not being a good old girl any more. David and the Mammett had a nice conversation. David had told me earlier in the day that she was coming to tea and he knew her very well, so I repeated this to her and she was delighted. When he was brought into the room this happened:

'Well little David (holding out the hand), and do you think you know who I am?'

'Yes—you're granny' (with complete confidence, allowing his hand to be held and stroked).

'No (ever so kindly), I'm not granny.'

---

[86] Again, Eileen's sense of humour is evident in her use of melodrama.

[87] Eileen and Orwell badly wanted a child.

[88] This is Eileen's term for menstrual pain, which she was troubled with throughout her life.

[89] Phyl is another fellow graduate of St Hugh's.

[90] The Mammet was a tutor when Eileen was at Oxford, and organised Old Girls events.

'Oh? What are you then?'[91]

Phyl is just the same as she used to be in her most charming moments. It was fun seeing her again. I think perhaps we might have a proper reunion some day. Couldn't you come and stay with her and while she is at the office eat potato crisps at the Criterion (Mary and I did this as much for old times' sake as because it was cold)? It seems to me superlatively clever for anyone to keep herself on the Stock Exchange, as she says she does. I wonder about it all the time I'm with her.[92]

The last candle is guttering, and there isn't any good way out of this letter. But perhaps it has broken a spell. Does yours mean that June[93] is at Oxford? I just didn't know. Anyway she can't be more than fifteen. Norman?[94] John? Elisabeth? Jean? Ruth? Your mother? Your father? I don't think I want any news of you and Quartus[95] because I am quite sure I know all about you and it would be so dreadful to hear something quite different. The only thing I can do is to come and see. I am supposed to be having a holiday when the book is finished, as it will be this month, only we sha'n't have any money at all, and we were so rich[96]. When are you coming to the sales[97]? Or are you? I don't know whether I can get away even for a day because the book is late and the typescript of the final draft is not begun[98] and Eric[99] is writing a book in collaboration with a

---

[91] This would appear to be a private but rather cruel shared joke between Eileen and Norah, at the expense of an older former tutor who appears to be less affluent (she didn't provide refreshments for an Old Girls event) but is keen to keep a network of Old Girls going. We could see this an example of Eileen's sometimes wicked sense of humour.

[92] This might be a critique of someone betting on the Stock Market, since Eileen was a socialist.

[93] Presumably Norah's eldest child.

[94] Presumably Norah's other children.

[95] Norah's husband.

[96] The irony here is rooted in the intermittent feast-and-famine of the jobbing writer. Specifically here it could refer to the royalties that Orwell received from the Left Book Club for their edition of *Road to Wigan Pier*.

[97] This would be the traditional post-Christmas sales that department stores held every year.

[98] Eileen would be typing this when it was ready.

[99] Eileen's brother, Eric O'Shaughnessy, for whom Eileen was also doing typing and editing. Davison mistakenly believed that this referred to Orwell, and he was confused by what Eileen might be referring to.

number of people including a German and I keep getting his manuscript to revise and not being able to understand anything at all in it—but if you were coming to the sales these things would all be less important to

Pig.

Did I wish you a happy new year?

Please wish all your family a happy new year from me.

Eric (I mean George) has just come in to say that the light is out (he had the Aladdin lamp because he was Working[100]) and is there any oil (such a question) and I can't type in this light (which may be true, but I can't read it) and he is hungry and wants some cocoa and some biscuits and it is after midnight and Marx is eating a bone and has left pieces in each chair and which shall he sit on now.[101]

The manuscript for *Homage to Catalonia* was finally delivered to the publisher in January 1938. This was shortly before both Eileen and Orwell fell ill with seasonal influenza. Eileen's health problems were only occasionally hinted at in her letters (as with "pre-plague pains" in the letter to Norah), and never treated with any seriousness. Orwell, never a well man, was particularly susceptible to heavy colds which settled on his chest and caused coughing fits. This time, though, having retreated to his bed with a chest infection on 8 March, he started coughing violently and haemorrhaging from his mouth. This was not unknown for him, but it was the first time it had happened since their marriage. The bleeding eventually stopped, and Eileen was able to contact her brother, since the couple had recently acquired a telephone, and he arranged a chest x-ray. For unknown reasons, this was not set for another week, and Orwell started planning visits to friends and colleagues to coincide with the trip to the hospital for the x-ray.

On 14 March, in the middle of the night, Orwell started haemorrhaging again, but this time it didn't cease. Eileen, in her panic, called

---

[100] She is teasing Orwell with that capital W, implying a level of extreme importance that merits an initial capital..

[101] Eileen manages to type this long section without answering Orwell's needs, but she was an amazingly fast typist. That she can make a joke of this is another example of her not taking life too seriously.

the only neighbour she knew who had a telephone—Jack Common. Common, however, lived six miles away and only had a bike. Whilst he was on his way, Eileen called her brother Eric. He was able to give Eileen instructions, such as which ambulance to call (in pre-1948 Social Welfare days, all such care was private and there was no emergency service for her to call), and how to manage the haemorrhaging in the meantime. His calming words, along with Orwell's previous reassurances that this was not an uncommon occurrence and so he would be alright in the end, helped sustain Eileen's courage during this very alarming incident. Whilst it was Eric O'Shaughnessy's advice and help that ultimately saved Orwell, had it not been for Eileen's presence of mind, he might well have died that night.

Eileen wrote to Jack Common kindly thanking him, even though he wasn't able to help her.

Monday [and Tuesday, 14-15 March 1938]

24 Croom's Hill

Greenwich

Dear Jack,

You'll probably have heard about the drama of yesterday. I only hope you didn't get soaked to the skin in discovering it. The bleeding seemed prepared to go on for ever & on Sunday everyone agreed that Eric must be taken somewhere where really active steps could be taken if necessary—artificial pneumothorax to stop the blood or transfusion to replace it. They got on to a specialist who visits a smallish voluntary hospital near here & who's very good at this kind of thing & he also advised removal, so it happened in an ambulance like a very luxurious bedroom on wheels[102]. The journey had no ill-effects, they found his blood pressure still more or less normal— & they've stopped the bleeding, without the artificial pneumothorax. So it was worth while. Everyone was nervous of being responsible for the immediate risk of the journey, but we supported each other. Eric's a bit depressed about being in an institution devised for murder, but otherwise

---

[102] Even in the midst of this very distressing event, Eileen is finding time to add humour to her surroundings.

remarkably well. He needn't stay long they say,[103] but the specialist has a sort of hope that he may be able to identify the actual site of haemorrhage and control it for the future.

This was really to thank you for being so neighbourly from such a distance, & in such weather. One gets hysterical with no one to speak to except the village who are not what you could call soothing.

I'll let you know what happens next. I have fearful letters to write to relations.[104]

Love to Mary & Peter.[105]

Eileen

The time that the letters in this chapter cover–just twelve months–show how Eileen had saved her husband's life twice in this short period. Their first full year of marriage had been fractured by their political engagement that had led to Orwell and then Eileen travelling to a battle zone. Also, we can see their lives vacillated between the privations of their poverty-stricken lives in the cottage in Wallington and the cosseted luxury of stays in Eileen's brother's house in London. Money is mentioned in most of Eileen's letters, and this is a constant theme that occupies them for the whole of their married life. But it is Orwell's health that is their main concern, and the perilous state of their finances is softened by their families' and friends' willingness to help them. This is something we will see again in the next chapter, where Orwell's health again dictates their lives.

REFERENCES

Diggins, John P. (1975), *Up from Communism: Conservative odysseys in American intellectual history*, Columbia University Press, New York.
Fussell, Paul (1975), *The Great War and Modern Memory*, Oxford University Press, Oxford.
Orr, Charles A. (1984), *Homage to Orwell–as I knew him in Catalonia*, Unpublished pamphlet.

[103] Orwell stayed in the sanatorium until 1 September.

[104] As usual, Eileen has taken on the duty of informing all of Orwell's relatives.

[105] Jack Common's wife and son.

Orwell, George (1952), *Homage to Catalonia,* Harcourt Brace, New York.
Payne, Stanley G. (2011), *The Franco Republic* (1936–1975), University of Wisconsin Press, Madison.
Rees, Richard (1962), *George Orwell: Fugitive from the Camp of Victory*, Southern Illinois University Press, Carbondale.
Wildemeersch, Marc (2013), *George Orwell's Commander in Spain: the enigma of Georges Kopp,* Thames River Press, London.

CHAPTER 6

To Marrakesh (1938-1939)

It would be useful to begin this chapter with a brief discussion of the diagnosis and treatment of tuberculosis, and with an overview of health care in Britain in the 1930s. This will help us understand more clearly what is behind the letters that we will be looking at.

To begin with, tuberculosis had been the greatest single cause of mortality in adults for centuries. Throughout the nineteenth and into the early part of the twentieth century, it was listed as the main cause of a quarter of all adult deaths (Charlton and Murphy, 1997). This, however, would mask the deaths from other diseases with similar symptoms (coughing blood, loss of weight, fatigue), particularly lung cancer. In the UK, public health records show very, very few cases of deaths from lung cancer in this period, whilst the combination of unfiltered cigarette smoking, pipe smoking, and general air pollution would all have proved causal to a much greater degree (ibid). Tuberculosis has been around for centuries under different names. The Ancient Greeks referred to it as "phthisis", whilst the Ancient Romans called it "schachepheth". In English, it was referred to as "the white plague" in the eighteenth century, and from then on as "consumption", even after Johann Schonlein had coined the term "tuberculosis" in 1834. It was only in 1921 that an effective vaccine was developed by French scientists Albert Calmette and Jean-Marie Camille Guérin. The Baccile Calmette-Guérin (BCG) vaccine became widely used globally as health care systems developed through the twentieth century, given largely to children to prevent them from contracting the disease. For those who could afford it, treatment was restricted to warmth, rest and good food before the discovery of antibiotics. The effective antibiotic treatment was developed in 1943 when Selman Waksman, Elizabeth Bugie and Albert Schatz developed streptomycin (Charlton and Murphy, 1997).

So, for anyone born at the turn of the twentieth century, there would have been no vaccination, and for anyone contracting tuberculosis in adulthood, there was no effective treatment beyond palliative care. In Britain at this time, there was an emergent welfare state, starting in 1911 with National Insurance Committees, whereby employees would be automatically docked a part of their wages to fund primary health care (through general practitioners, or GPs); access to unemployment and sickness pay; and a pension in old age. Secondary care, as in care from hospital specialists, would be available only to those who could afford it, or else resort to the public hospitals attached to work houses. By 1937, social welfare had developed in Britain in terms of care in the community, such as through community nursing and child welfare clinics, but it was still another 11 years before there would be a fully national health service. For people like Eileen and Orwell, choosing to live in a self-sufficient way, there was no regular income from which they could pay National Insurance, and no spare money to spend on specialist health care. When Orwell fell ill in late 1937, it is likely that Eileen's brother stepped in to provide the private health care that Orwell so badly needed. But, even then, the level of treatment for someone diagnosed as having tuberculosis was very limited.

By the late 1930s, treatment of tuberculosis and other associated lung diseases was developing rapidly, particularly through the work of Dr Eric O'Shaughnessy. However, there was still no effective cure, and wealthier patients would be prescribed fresh air, preferably dry fresh air. 1938 had started badly for Eileen, with George in hospital following his serious bout of haemorrhaging. Whilst Eric O'Shaughnessy could pay for the treatment Orwell received, the couple continued to live in their dilapidated cottage at Wallington. The conditions in the cottage were hardly conducive to good health, with the constantly smoking chimney, the flooding kitchen, the freezing bedroom, and the poisonous gas lanterns. The outside toilet was also at best inconvenient, and the work the couple did around the house was largely out of doors, irrespective of the weather. Whilst Orwell was convalescing, Eileen was responsible for running the cottage, its garden and the various animals they kept. She did make some money by selling eggs, in addition to her longer-standing income from typing manuscripts.

Once a fortnight, she would endure the tedious journey by bus, Underground, train and bus to visit Orwell in hospital. In addition to all of this, Eileen was also managing the publication of *Homage to Catalonia*, which was finally released on 25 April 1938. The book was very well received, with critics lauding it as the best thing Orwell had written so far. However, it did not sell well, with only 683 copies being sold, despite the critical praise. It was only after Orwell's death that the book received far-reaching acclaim.

During this time, Eileen was handling the business of distribution with Orwell's agent, Leonard Moore, and she wrote two letters to him near the end of May 1938. The first of these is very short:

24 May 1938
[Handwritten]
Wallington,
Near Baldock, Herts.
Dear Mr Moore,
Eric would like two more copies of "Homage to Catalonia", if possible, one to be sent here & one direct to him. I hope I am right in asking you for these—I'm not sure.
I ought to have written to you before but the future remains very vague. However, I think some plan will be settled this week & then I will write to you again.
Yours sincerely, Eileen Blair.

The second letter from Eileen gives us a greater insight into the confusion around Orwell's health. She also repeats her requests for money owed.

[Typewritten]
30 May 1938
Wallington, Near Baldock, Herts.
Dear Mr. Moore,
I promised Eric I would write and tell you the news about him, which is that he is to go abroad for the winter, staying at Preston Hall until he

leaves England—that is, probably until August or September.[1] After that we hope he will be able to come home, though not to this house. We think of trying to find somewhere to live in Dorset.[2] All this does not of course mean that he is worse, but only that the position has been made clearer to him.[3] As a matter of fact, the original diagnosis was wrong: he had bronchiectasis and probably no phthisis. Apparently there is no point in treating bronchiectasis by the absolute rest that sometimes cures phthisis, and I think he is going to be allowed up as soon as the weather is reasonable. He ought also to be able to do some gentle work on the novel in July or August. Of course it's not easy to work in a sanatorium, where people actually walk about and impose a timetable that probably interferes with the work timetable, but the book seethes in his head and he is very anxious to get on with it.[4] I ought to have written to you some time ago about this novel, when Eric first realised that he couldn't finish it by October, but he then wanted Gollancz to be told that it would be ready anyway before Christmas. Now he thinks that it will be ready in the spring and this seems quite probable.[5] I should be very grateful if you could give Gollancz a message about it in whatever terms you think proper.

I hear there is a wonderful review of Homage to Catalonia in the Observer, but I haven't seen it yet. On the whole the reviews have really been very good don't you think? It's interesting that the C.P. have decided not to be rude—and extremely clever of them to be reticent in the definitely Communist press and to say their little piece anonymously in the T.L.S. and the Listener.[6] By the way, do you know when Warburg proposes to

---

[1] Eric O'Shaughnessy has managed to convince Orwell that he must be somewhere warm over the winter.

[2] Orwell had very reluctantly agreed to look for somewhere warmer in England for the couple to live the following spring. However, he later changed his mind, and they moved back to the cottage.

[3] Eileen believed that she had made this move clear to Orwell. However, she was wrong.

[4] It seems likely that Eileen was taking shorthand notes during her visits and then bringing back typed pages for Orwell to work on.

[5] *Homage* was eventually published in April 1938.

[6] Eileen's use of abbreviations here perhaps needs explaining. CP is Communist Party. Her comment relating to this reflects their experiences in Barcelona, which Orwell had been critical of in *Homage*. The TLS is the *Times Literary Supplement,* which started its weekly publication in 1902 and continues to be regarded as one of the leading publications of its type. Reviews in the TLS were anonymous by default until 1974. *The Listener* was another cultural weekly magazine, published by the BBC from 1930 until 1991. Another

pay an advance? We thought he was to pay £75 in January and £75 on publication, but perhaps that's wrong.[7]
Eric is still being extraordinarily amenable and placid about everything, and everyone is delighted with his general condition.[8]
Yours sincerely,
Eileen Blair

During the four months Orwell was in the sanatorium, he continued to publish book reviews and journal articles, as well as sending formal letters rebutting some points made in negative reviews of *Homage to Catalonia*. As he was not allowed a typewriter in his hospital, it must have been Eileen who took shorthand dictation from him and then typed up the material when she returned home. One of the best-known articles he wrote at this time was "Why I Join the I.L.P.".

However, selling eggs was hardly bringing in a fortune, and it fell to Eileen to try and find other sources of income. She borrowed money from a friend, Denys King-Farlow[9], whilst waiting for the advance payment for *Homage to Catalonia*. She also chased up royalty payments from his publishers, and negotiated a revised deadline for the next novel. Orwell, on the other hand, had been repeatedly warned by his doctors not to exert himself, and was banned from "literary work", only allowed bed rest with a little light crossword solving. By early June, Orwell was allowed out of bed for one, then three hours a day, but he was still largely confined to rest.

The following letter to Leonard Moore shows Eileen's concern for her husband's well-being, but it's also chatty and informal. It's clear that Eileen was still operating the open-house policy that she and Orwell had established when they first arrived at the cottage, with guests welcome even when inconvenient. This letter also establishes that Eileen was doing paid typing to increase the couple's income.

---

highly regarded source of literary criticism and reviews, it was also noted for its apolitical stance.

[7] As usual, Eileen was dealing with their money problems.

[8] Eileen's mischievous humour is shown again, as she feigns delighted surprise in the reviews from sources she suspected might not have been sympathetic.

[9] An old Etonian friend of Orwell's.

7 June 1938
[Handwritten]
Wallington,
Near Baldock, Herts.
Dear Mr Moore,
One of my weekend guests tells me that he lost a letter to you that he was going to post for me. So I write again to thank you for the cheque; possibly you will have two acknowledgments but indeed you have earned many. I did not expect to see the second half of the advance for a long time.
I am extremely sorry about Miss Perriam. That business is hell I know. But I also know a woman who had a series of similar operations about eight years ago & has since had no further trouble, so I do hope Miss Perriam may go on resembling her.[10]
You must be terribly overworked. I suppose the summer is your easier time but of course on the other hand it's almost intolerable (to me anyway) to be in London throughout the hot weather.
I am busy too—typing a novel about the Afghan frontier, complete with a "man-child" being reared to avenge his dead father by a devoted mother & a half-blind grandmother. The grammar is as original as the plot & the punctuation perhaps unique. Does it not surprise you to see what books are completed?[11]
Eric has been allowed up & is very pleased with himself.[12]
With many thanks,
Yours sincerely,
Eileen Blair

When Eileen missed the post with her letter of June 7, she added the following on June 8.

I missed the postman this morning so have opened this to thank you for the book & letter brought by him. I had to write an almost unintelligible letter to Warburg which did convey I hope the idea that he should stop asking Eric to write blurbs. He persists in doing this & Eric hates getting the books but there is some suggestion (to Eric anyway) that if he doesn't write the blurb he is letting someone down. So I was to tell Warburg that

[10] There is no information about Miss Perriam's illness.

[11] We have no record of how many books Eileen typed, or how often she did this kind of work, in order to earn more money.

[12] Another example of Eileen's humour, here at the expense of her husband.

he is not going to write any more "bits".[13] Probably he will though. He always enjoys doing things for the New English Weekly[14] as Mairet will print anything he writes & never presses him. I think it's quite good for him to write short articles when he feels like it; it's the compulsion that is exhausting, not the writing. As for the correspondence in the Times Lit. Supp. that you may have seen, it has been a delight.

I'm sorry you've had so hard a time with Warburg. I believe the book ought to sell quite well but I wish he had more money for publicity. The Time & Tide, New Statesman & Observer reviews really warrant a splash. If you are ever in the direction of Maidstone, Eric would be delighted to see you of course—the place is on the London road about 2½ miles from Maidstone & there are no special visiting hours.[15]

Yours sincerely,
Eileen Blair

The novel that Eileen was renegotiating would be *Coming Up for Air*. Orwell had started to write an outline for this whilst in the sanatorium, but he was unable to do much more because of the enforced bed rest. However, by the end of July, Orwell was able to get up and go for long walks around the grounds of the sanatorium, occasionally taking a bus to a nearby lake and indulging in fishing.

The sanatorium was within easy reach of London, and Orwell had lots of visitors aside from Eileen. Eileen herself had asked her good friend, Lydia Jackson, to visit Orwell whilst he was convalescing. From Lydia's recollections, she records that they went for a walk around the park and, when resting on the grass, Orwell embraced her. She writes:

> It was an awkward situation. He did not attract me as a man and his ill health even aroused in me a slight feeling of revulsion. At the same time, the fact that he was a sick man, starved of intimacy with his wife, made it difficult for me to repulse him. I did not want to behave like a prude, or to treat the incident as a serious matter. (Jackson, 1976 p 429).

---

[13] Orwell had asked Eileen to make this request.

[14] The New English Weekly was established in 1932 as a review of public affairs, literature and the arts. The founding editor, Alfred Orage, died suddenly in 1934 and was replaced by Philip Mairet.

[15] Eileen asked a number of people to visit Orwell, including Lydia.

She tries to justify her compliance: "Why should I push him away if kissing me gave him a few minutes of pleasure? I was convinced that he was very fond of Eileen and that I was in no sense a rival to her" (ibid).

Given this all took place just over a month after Eileen and Orwell's second wedding anniversary, it reflects rather badly on both Orwell and Lydia. Lydia rationalises her actions of compliance by treating this as not being "serious", and not hurting Eileen. What Orwell was thinking is not known, but with Eileen visiting once a fortnight, he was hardly "starved of intimacy". This relationship between Orwell and Lydia would become more complex, as we shall see, and as Topp (2020) discovered from Lydia's diaries, Lydia believed Orwell would have left Eileen for her if Lydia has asked him to.

Eileen, meanwhile, was still managing Orwell's publishing affairs and the general maintenance of the cottage. She also kept their friend Denys King-Farlow informed.

[Handwritten]
22 June 1938
Wallington
Dear Denys,
When I told you on the telephone that I was more or less writing to you it was quite true. But I was also having flu, although at that time incredulously because the time even of this year seems so odd.
I hadn't forgotten this money: indeed I have thought of it often with growing appreciation as the "advance" on the Spanish book went on not coming.[16] Eventually it was extracted by instalments! Poor man—I mean poor publisher. I hope it was time that you didn't need. As a matter of fact I shouldn't have kept the cheque if I'd had any doubt about repaying it almost at once. Or I think not.[17]
Eric isn't so ill as they thought, as you'll have gathered. He of course has never believed that he was "ill", but for the first two months or so he appeared to have phthisis in both lungs which could have been pretty hopeless. Now it turns out to be bronchiectasis, which people do go on having more or less indefinitely under really favourable conditions.[18] I suppose he told you that we can probably go abroad for the winter together instead of his going to a sanatorium, & after that we have to find a perfect cottage

---

[16] Eileen is referring to the money she borrowed from King-Farlow.

[17] Another example of Eileen's humour.

[18] Eileen is the one who keeps all their relatives and friends updated on their plans.

in one of the southern counties at an inclusive rental of about 7/6.[19] I shall come back early to do this—They even think that he might leave Preston Hall in August & spend a month or so under normal conditions in England—he must of course be very "careful" but the treatment really only consists in resting a great deal & eating a lot. We might perhaps stay on a farm somewhere.[20] By that time this cottage will be handed over either to the landlord or to an unfortunate old uncle of Eric's who is suggested as a tenant.[21]

I'm so glad you went to see Eric & took him out. I think it's really more depressing for him to be in this semi-confinement than to be in bed, & he loved having a party.[22] It was particularly nice of you to send that money instead of offering to.

With many thanks,
Yours sincerely,
Eileen Blair

As we can see, Eileen was working on plans to remove Orwell from the damp Wallington cottage for the winter, preferably abroad. She was also determined not to return to Wallington, and made plans to look for a place that would be warmer and drier, focusing on Dorset. Her initial plans were to spend the winter in the South of France, but her brother Eric intervened and insisted that they go to French Morocco, on the grounds that the climate there was warmer and drier. Eric was working on what would become an authoritative textbook on tuberculosis, and had told his sister and her husband that Orwell had tuberculosis "in both lungs which could have been pretty hopeless" (in Davison, 2000 p 242). This diagnosis, it later transpired, was changed to bronchiectasis, which would not require the same level of extended bed rest that tuberculosis did. Bronchiectasis is a chronic disease where there is a permanent enlargement of the airways of the lungs, leading to a greatly increased susceptibility to lung infections. In more severe cases, such as Orwell's, this would be associated with wheezing, chest pain, weight loss, and coughing up blood. These are all symptoms that could be confused with tuberculosis, although this would be unlikely in the case of a diagnosis by

---

[19] Again, Eileen is dreaming that she can convince Orwell to give up the cottage in the spring and move to a warmer part of England.

[20] This dream never happened.

[21] In fact, the couple never did give up the cottage.

[22] This was most likely a celebration of Orwell's upcoming 35th birthday.

a specialist such as Eric O'Shaughnessy. There is much room for speculation as to why he would have misdiagnosed Orwell, but perhaps the most likely is that he wanted to enforce bed rest on someone who was clearly not looking after himself. That said, the effect on Eileen was to make her exhausted, which is hardly what a beloved brother would wish.

After all this, Eileen and Orwell did decide to spend the winter in Morocco. How they were to finance this was not clear. Whilst they had managed to live in a self-sustainable way, it was taking its toll. Orwell's health, however, took priority, and when a friend offered them the money for the trip, they accepted it. Whilst the offer was made on condition of anonymity, Eileen and Orwell insisted on treating this as a loan. Meanwhile, Eileen was left with the task of sorting out the cottage and its menagerie. This process seems to have been underway from early June, as Denys King-Farlow records visiting the cottage and finding Eileen had sold the geese, the goats and the chickens, and was there packing the place up. By July, Orwell was helping by writing to Jack Common to ask him to look after the cottage during their absence, implying that there was no clear plan to dispose of the cottage and move to Dorset on their return from Morocco. Orwell definitely did not want to give up the cottage. Eileen also wrote to Jack Common with her advice about how to deal with the cottage and the animals. The goats and chickens would appear not to have been sold, as Orwell wrote detailed instructions for their care.

Before the details of their trip to Morocco were finalised, Eileen went to spend two weeks alone at a guest house by Lake Windermere in the Lake District. Her guest house, Chapel Ridding, was very respectable and quite up-market compared with the Wallington cottage. How she could afford such a holiday, and why she was there on her own, are not known. However, Orwell mentioned her absence in passing in several letters at this time, and it may be that this holiday had been long planned for both of them to have a break together. But with Orwell still in the sanatorium, Eileen went on her own. She had been ill at various times, and perhaps the luxury of time in the location associated with some of her beloved Romantic poets would act as a tonic. Topp (2020) discovered some possible reasons for Eileen's visit to Windermere, suggesting that this was a planned solo holiday for Eileen to be in the vicinity of her beloved Lakeland poets, and the trip was at least partly paid for by her former Oxford tutor, Ernest de Selincourt. De Selincourt was in the Lake District at exactly this time to speak at the opening of Wordsworth's birthplace in nearby Cockermouth, following its acquisition by the National

Trust. Eileen's continuing links with Oxford could well have meant she was still in touch with some of her former tutors. Davison appreciated Topp's suggestions about this confusing visit. We have a fascinating letter from Eileen, written to Common whilst she was at Chapel Ridding, where she details the layout and content of the cottage in delightful detail.

Eileen Blair to Jack Common
20 July 1938
[Handwritten]
Chapel Ridding
Windermere
Westmorland
Dear Jack Common,
I suppose you have or soon will have my wild telegram. I hope I'll have one from you long before you get this letter but we'll just have to play a peculiarly complicated cat's-cradle for a few days because posts leave here practically never & then at strange hours like 3.30. I haven't yet heard about my letters being delivered anywhere else. Perhaps they aren't. Using the telephone, we can't hear the local exchange, so don't try that.[23]
If you do want the cottage, it's a pity I didn't know last week because you could perfectly well have had it—I really hoped to pack it up one way or the other before coming away. But the difference between packing it up for store & for lending is considerable—e.g. one fills the drawers to store them & empties them to lend—so I couldn't do anything constructive or much destructive.[24] I suppose you, & more importantly your wife, know what the cottage is like—that it hasn't got a bathroom or any hot water, that it frequently absorbs water like a sponge (perhaps very frequently; in some mysterious way the wind seems responsible), that it's 3½ miles from a shop, that the sitting-room chimney is not manageable by me though it may be by someone efficient. That's all I can think of at the moment, except that we never bought any furniture for it. But you saw yourself what it looked like. On the other hand it is habitable & it won't cost money. The goat still has her kid because I like goats & don't like goat's milk, but if you don't like killing kids a man will do it & you'll then have about 2½ - 3 pints of milk for about 1½d. a day. I didn't stock the garden for the winter because I thought no one would be there, but we can still put in some greens & there are potatoes, parsnips & onions, & a few trench &

---

[23] Eileen was attempting to make arrangements in advance without knowing whether Common would want to live in the cottage over the winter or not.

[24] Eileen can't resist adding humour wherever possible.

runner beans; also a good crop of cooking apples on one tree & quite a few plums.[25]

If you can transport them you could bring things like tools & wheelbarrows—very usefully, because Eric made a wheelbarrow which is permanently in the field as its wheel developed a split personality & I can't persuade it all to go home together.[26] I don't know what Eric has told you about the place. It has the sitting-room you'll remember, a kind of passage-room with a fireplace that we used to have as a sitting-room when we kept the shop, an ill-designed kitchen with a sink & cold water, a Calor-gas oven (this is very convenient for quick heating but the cylinders are expensive & I've always been meaning to combine it with an oil cooker—there is an old Rippingill & a couple of Beatrices[27] that are good for slow boiling); upstairs a square landing we use as a dining-room, which is actually very warm & can be heated enough in any weather by one of the Beatrices, & two bedrooms opening off it, one with a double bed & one with a single bed.[28] The place isn't over-furnished & you could probably bring anything special, such as an easy chair or/and a chest of drawers etc. I did mean to buy it a number of things but again thinking it would be empty I haven't done so. Heaven knows I don't want to put you off—from my point of view your coming has every advantage.[29] If you wire that you want the place & I hear nothing more I'll be in the cottage on Monday to hand it over. If you could arrive in the afternoon or early evening I could demonstrate the creatures. Goats are not difficult to manage but there are some growing chickens who need special food for a few more weeks. You could send a postcard to Wallington with any last minute alterations—I'll actually arrive some time on Saturday or Sunday morning. A letter posted to me here after Thursday will miss me.

I must say I hope you are strong-minded enough to take Wallington on.[30]

Yours sincerely
Eileen Blair

---

[25] Orwell also sent Common a long letter listing these same problems with the cottage.

[26] This is a wonderful example of how Eileen could tease Orwell.

[27] Rippingill and Beatrices are types of portable cookers.

[28] The ceiling in the upstairs rooms of the cottage was high enough for Orwell to stand up straight, while in the downstairs rooms he was forced to walk while stooped over.

[29] Eileen wanted to be honest about the cottage while at the same time hoping Common would choose to stay there for the winter.

[30] Eileen again emphasised her wish for the Commons to take over the cottage.

Eileen returned to Wallington at the start of August, just a few days before Common was expected to move in. She then moved to her brother's house in London, the plan being to take Marx to be looked after by Orwell's sister, Marjorie, in Bristol, with both Eileen and Orwell visiting his parents in Southwold *en route* in the middle of August. Eileen was particularly keen on this idea as her good friend, Norah, also lived in Bristol. However, Eric intervened and insisted that Orwell was not strong enough to visit the senior Blairs and that they should only visit Marjorie, and, even then, it should be at the end of August. Thus the visit to Norah in Bristol was cancelled.

On 2 September 1938, Eileen and Orwell set sail on the *SS Stratheden* for Morocco for the winter. They planned to spend six months in the dry, warm climate of Morocco and took with them a typewriter, an Arabic phrase book, and the proofs of the French edition of *Homage to Catalonia*. Their anonymous friend had given them £300 to finance their plans. They also had a supply of Vasano, a drug meant to prevent seasickness, which Orwell was very keen to try as he had been seriously distressed by seasickness on previous voyages. Unfortunately, Eileen had booked their travel via the wrong port, and so a four-day voyage to Casablanca took twelve days, since they eventually had to take a train from Tangier to Casablanca before finally reaching Marrakesh. On arrival, most of their luggage went missing in the chaos of the station there. They stayed at the Hotel Continental, which Eileen found listed in an old copy of *Cook's Tourists' Handbook,* but it turned out to be rather rundown and used by sex workers. Eileen also had developed a fever. They both found the weather unbearably hot, but Orwell quickly found a house for them: the Villa Simont. This was about three miles away from the town, but he thought it would be conducive to productive writing. However, it was not available until 15 October, so they had about a month to wait. This gave them time to explore Marrakesh and witness the poverty of a large part of the population. They were also searching for furniture and chattels for their rented house, a task which Eileen recorded with lively detail in her letters, whilst Orwell also listed in his diary the animals they were going to buy to sustain them in their villa. In other words, they seemed to be trying to set up a house not dissimilar to that at Wallington.

The first letter we have from Eileen relates their chaotic arrival, and is written to Orwell's mother, Ida, whilst they were still staying in the Majestic Hotel.

[Handwritten]
15 September 1938
Majestic Hotel
Marrakech[31]
Dearest Mrs Blair,

I think Eric sent postcards today, explaining that I'd been "upset" as he says. We could both be said to have been upset, partly I expect by the climate & partly by the horror we conceived for this country. My additional achievement was some kind of fever, possibly from food poisoning but more probably from mosquitoes—Eric has eaten the same things but hasn't been bitten to any extent whereas I look as though I were made of brioches.[32]

The journey until we left Tangier was so pleasant that we were spoilt. It's true that we went to Gib by mistake & then got held up at Tangier because the boats to Casablanca were full, but Gib was quite interesting & Tangier enchanting. Eric's stuff for seasickness worked even on the crossing from Gib. to Tangier, which was rough (he walked round the boat with a seraphic smile watching people being sick & insisted on my going into the "Ladies' Cabin" to report on the disasters there), & the Continental Hotel in Tangier was very good indeed. If we could have come here by sea as we intended we should probably like Morocco better but we had to come by train which meant having breakfast at 5 a.m., going through endless agonies to satisfy police & customs authorities of all nations before getting into the train at all & then having more police & customs interrogations a) before the train left the International Zone, b) before entering the Spanish zone & c) before entering the French zone. The Spaniards were very pleasant & careless which was as well because at the last minute a man came round & collected the French newspapers that most people had & that were not allowed in Spanish territory. We had in our suitcases a collection of about 20 newspapers, Fascist & anti-Fascist. The French were in character, absolutely refusing to believe that we were not coming to Morocco to break the law. However, they agreed to let the Morocco police do the arresting & we got as far as the junction where we were to change into a train with a restaurant car.[33] By this time it should have been 11 a.m. & was 11.45. Everyone fled across the station surrounded by hordes of Arab porters, aged 10-70, & the train started before we were

---

[31] The spelling of Marrakech that Eileen uses is now largely obsolete, with the more usual spelling now being Marrakesh.

[32] Eileen always underplayed her health issues, as did Orwell his.

[33] Crossing these borders in 1938 was quite difficult for everyone.

well in it. Our junior porter, who was about 3'6", had not unnaturally put the two cases he was carrying down on the platform so that he could catch us to get his tip (he said they were in the dining-car), but to establish this took us hours & to get the cases at Casablanca took two days.[34] Then we came to Marrakech, again leaving at 7 a.m., & went to the Hotel Continental which had been recommended to us & which may have been quite good once. Lately it has changed hands & is obviously a brothel. I haven't much direct knowledge of brothels but as they offer a special service they can probably all afford to be dirty & without any other conveniences. However we stayed for one day, partly because Eric didn't notice anything odd about it until he tried to live in it[35] & partly because my temperature was by that time going up about one degree an hour[36] & I only wanted to lie down, which was easy enough, & to get drinks, which were brought me by a limitless variety of street Arabs who looked murderous but were very kind. Eric of course ate out & this is very expensive in Morocco so we moved here as soon as possible. This is the second most expensive hotel in Marrakech but it's much cheaper to have full pension here (95 fr. a day for two) than to go to restaurants.

Sunday. Eric made me go to bed at that point,[37] & since then we've been busy. He has written to you this morning while I unpacked, so you'll know about Mme Vellat & the villa in prospect. I think the villa will be fun from our point of view. It's entirely isolated except for a few Arabs who live in the outbuildings to tend the orange grove that surrounds it. We're going to buy enough furniture to camp with. As it will be the cheapest French furniture obtainable the aesthetic effect may be unfortunate, but we hope to get some decent rugs as we want them to take home. There is a large sitting room, two bedrooms, a bathroom & a kitchen. No provision for cooking but we'll have some little pots with charcoal in them & a Primus. The country is practically desert but may look different after the rains. Anyway we can have a goat & Eric will really get the benefit of the climate. In Marrakech itself he couldn't. The European quarter is intolerable with a second-rate respectability, & very expensive. The native quarter is "picturesque" but the smells are only rivalled by the noises. Eric was so depressed that I thought we should have to come home but he is now

---

[34] Eileen is barely able to hide her anger at all the unnecessary trouble they were put through.

[35] Orwell was known for his absence of this kind of judgement.

[36] Eileen might be exaggerating a bit here, but she was obviously quite sick.

[37] So it seems that Orwell did, at times, notice Eileen's health.

quite excited about the villa & I think will be happy there.[38] According to Dr. Diot (who was recommended by a friend of my brother's in Paris) the climate is ideal for him, or will be in a few weeks when it's cooler. And the villa has a sort of observatory on its roof which will be good to work in.

The second bedroom is of course Avril's when she wants it. If she went to Tangier by sea the fare would be about £12 return. At Tangier one can stay at the Continental for 10/- a day all in. The fare from Tangier to Marrakech by train is 155 fr. second class. Unfortunately the train gets into Casablanca at 3 p.m. or so & the next one to Marrakech leaves at 8 & takes all night. It would be better to stay one night at Casablanca, which I suppose would cost another 10/- altogether, & get the morning train here. It only takes 4 hours & one sees the country such as it is. We loathed it but that was largely because we were sentenced to live in it for six months.[39] As one approaches Marrakech camels become more & more common until they're as ordinary as donkeys, & the native villages are extraordinary collections of little thatched huts about 5 feet square (but generally round), sometimes surrounded by a kind of hedge of dead wood or possibly a mud wall. We don't know what the walls are for; they aren't strong enough or high enough to keep anything out. Marrakech itself was largely built of mud & has enormous mud ramparts. The earth dries a reddish colour which is very beautiful <u>in earth</u> but unfortunate when approximately reproduced in paint by the French, who like to call Marrakech "la rouge". Some of the native products are lovely, especially the earthenware pots & jugs they use.

Dr. Diot hasn't really examined Eric yet but intends to. He is not particularly sympathetic but he must be a good doctor[40] & through him we'll be able to know that the chest really is reacting properly.

Please give my love to Mr Blair & Avril. I do hope Mr Blair is getting out & that Avril will get out as far as Morocco. It's said to be a wonderful light here for photography. From her point of view it might have been more interesting to stay in Marrakech but one can walk one way (about 3 miles) in cooler weather & a taxi will cost about 2/6 I think. She might be able to hire a car if she liked to do her International driving test before coming. Anyway there are buses from Marrakech to all the other places.[41]

---

[38] In this instance, Orwell was searching for a place for them to live, while Eileen usually took care of this kind of detail.

[39] Eileen acknowledges that Morocco does have some attractions.

[40] Eileen trusts her brother's recommendation completely.

[41] Avril never did visit them in Morocco.

With love
Eileen

The villa had two bedrooms, and Eileen and Orwell's letters home are peppered with offers of their spare room to any guests. However, unlike the spare room at Wallington, no one risked the trip to Morocco. Added to this, the self-sufficiency they had enjoyed at Wallington was not to be replicated in Morocco. The chickens took so long to lay the first egg that both Eileen and Orwell included commentaries of this in their letters home. The goat was also rather reluctant to be milked, despite Orwell's experience of milking Muriel at Wallington.

In the background, through all of this, was the approaching war in Europe. In late 1938, in Morocco, there was an increasing fear of another conflict. Throughout the 1930s, the British government had hoped to avoid war by ignoring Hitler's expansion plans across to the east of Europe. In 1936, these expansionist plans had become clear when Hitler's army entered the Rhineland, and two years later he annexed Austria. In September 1938, just as Eileen and Orwell were setting off for the Moroccan adventure, the Munich Conference brought together the leading nations of Europe. At the end of conference, British prime minister Neville Chamberlain appeared to have averted war by agreeing that Germany could occupy the Sudetenland, which was the German-speaking part of Czechoslovakia. This became known as the Munich Agreement. It was greeted with widespread approval in Britain, and Chamberlain infamously returned to Britain waving the agreement, which he said promised "peace in our time". Orwell, along with 148 others, had signed an anti-war manifesto, "If War Comes, We Shall Resist", which was published in the *New Leader* on 30 September 1938. His letters home were full of entreaties to his friends to continue as "anti-war and anti-fascist". However, despite the written assurance of "no more territorial demands in Europe", in March 1939, Germany occupied the rest of Czechoslovakia.

Eileen and Orwell's letters are full of references to the threat of war at this time. The letters they received must have been similarly preoccupied, as both Eileen and Orwell refer to gas masks and digging air raid shelters. As this letter from Eileen to Marjorie Dakin shows, the threat of war was very much in their minds.

[Handwritten]
27 September 1938[42]
Chez Mme Vellat
rue Edmond Doutte Medina
Marrakech
French Morocco
My dear Marjorie,

We've just had our first letter—from Mrs Blair. It was full of good news. I'm so glad you have a well family & that Marx appreciates his good fortune. I only hope he behaves as they say.

Yesterday we were rather hysterically writing semi-business letters in the hope that they'd be delivered before war broke out. Today the papers are somewhat calmer, but it's maddening to see none except those published in Morocco (we can get others but 4 to 8 days late & those at the moment might as well be years old).[43] The extraordinary thing is that no one here seems interested. We were in a cafe when the evening paper arrived yesterday & only one other person bought one & he didn't open it. Yet there are many young Frenchmen here who would be mobilised for service in France I suppose. The general idea is that Morocco would be very safe, anyway inland. The Arabs don't seem ripe to make trouble & if they did make it the poor wretches would have 15,000 regular troops to contend with in Marrakech alone, complete with artillery & all. So long as we're allowed to stay here, & that will probably be as long as we have any money, we probably have a better chance than most of keeping alive. Though what we should be keeping alive for God knows. It seems very unlikely that Eric will publish another book after the outbreak of war.[44] I was rather cheered to hear about Humphrey's[45] dugout. Eric has been on the point of constructing one for two years, though the plans received rather a check after he did construct one in Spain & it fell down on his & his companions' heads two days later, not under any kind of bombardment but just from the force of gravity.[46] But the dugout has generally been by way of light relief; his specialities are concentration camps & the famine.[47]

He buried some potatoes against the famine & they might have been very useful if they hadn't gone mouldy at once. To my surprise he does intend

---

[42] Eileen is using their future address.

[43] Eileen repeats some of their activities to different members of their families.

[44] By this time, Eileen has completely dedicated her life to Orwell and his writing.

[45] This would be Margery's husband, Humphrey Dakin.

[46] Eileen is again making fun of Orwell's construction ability.

[47] Again making fun of Orwell's worries, though Eileen must have been worried about these things also.

to stay here whatever happens. In theory this seems too reasonable & even comfortable to be in character[48]; in practice perhaps it wouldn't be so comfortable. Anyway I am thankful we got here. If we'd been in England I suppose he must have been in jail by now & I've had the most solemn warnings against this from all the doctors though they don't tell me how I could prevent it. Whatever the solution I do still desperately hope that there won't be war, which I'm sure would be much worse for the Czechs. After all political oppression, though it gets so much publicity, can make miserable only a small proportion of a whole nation because a political regime, especially a dictatorship, has to be popular.[49] We keep seeing & being exasperated by pictures of London crowds "demonstrating" when we don't know what they're demonstrating for, & there are occasional references to "extremists" who are arrested but whether the extremists are Communists demonstrating against Chamberlain's moderation or Fascists or socialists or pacifists we don't know.[50] Eric, who retains an extraordinary political simplicity in spite of everything, wants to hear what he calls the voice of the people. He thinks this might stop a war, but I'm sure that the voice would only say that it didn't want a war but of course would have to fight if the Government declared war.[51] It's very odd to feel that Chamberlain is our only hope, but I do believe he doesn't want war either at the moment & certainly the man has courage. But it's fantastic & horrifying to think that you may all be trying on gas masks at this moment.

You'll probably have heard that we don't like Marrakech. It's interesting, but at first anyway seemed dreadful to live in. There are beautiful arches with vile smells coming out of them & adorable children covered in ringworm & flies. I found an open space to watch the sunset from & too late realised that part of the ground to the west of us was a graveyard; I really couldn't bear Eric's conversation about the view as dominated by

---

[48] Yet more teasing at her husband's expense.

[49] This comment reflects the philosophy of "divide and rule; unite and conquer", whereby anyone seeking to rule a large population needs to have their consent to do so. Antonio Gramsci (1971) refers to this as "hegemony", whereby the populus allow themselves to be dominated and oppressed because it appears to be "common sense" that the ruling classes should be in charge. All the ruling classes have to do is to convince the populus that this is in their best interests.

[50] There were a lot of demonstrations in London and other cities at this time, promoting causes such as the anti-communists and communists; anti-fascists and fascists; pro-war and anti-war.

[51] Eileen seems very cynical here, reflecting her pacifist stance in the immediate aftermath of the First World War.

invisible worms & we had to go away without seeing the sunset.[52] On the whole, however, I get acclimatised & I thought Eric was moving in the same direction, but he says he isn't.[53] But when we have our villa (we move in on the 15th) he is going to be happy. He is even buying things for the house, including a copper tray four feet across that will dominate us for the rest of our lives. We also have two doves. Here they live in a cage but at the villa they are to go free. One can't have any tame animals because on the whole they have dreadful lives here & six months' spoiling would only make the future worse for them. Otherwise we'd have some donkeys—you can buy a donkey for 100 francs.

I expect you can't read a word of this. We only have one table & Eric is typing diary notes on it.[54] He sends his love to everyone, including Marx. So do I.

Eileen

If there is a war I don't know what Bristol, or indeed anywhere, will be like. But if at any time you wanted some place more remote for the children it's quite possible that the cottage will be empty. I don't know what the Commons would do but we've suggested to my brother that the cottage might anyway be kept in statu quo. It could be almost as safe as anywhere in England, & comparatively self-supporting, so we thought someone might be glad of it.[55] Of course the Commons may all stay. Someone at my brother's house (24 Croom's Hill, S.E.10) will know. My brother himself would be mobilised at once I suppose as he's in the RAMC.[56]

[At top of letter] There's no actual news yet about E's health. The doctor says we must allow 3 or 4 weeks for "acclimatisation" before expecting much.

During all of this time, both Orwell and Eileen seem to have been ill almost continuously. Aside from the ailments that would seem to have been brought on by the change in their diets, Orwell was still suffering from bouts of chest problems. Eileen was also suffering from a recurrence of her undisclosed illness, which became such a problem she spent money

---

[52] We can speculate on whether Orwell was just giving Eileen a hard time or whether he was upset by this thought himself.

[53] Orwell insists that he is still unhappy.

[54] And of course Orwell's needs come first.

[55] Many people made use of the cottage during the war years.

[56] RAMC is Royal Army Medical Corps. Unbeknownst to Eileen at the time, her brother's enlisting at this time will lead to his early death.

on a taxi to Marrakesh (rather than cycling) to get an X-ray. The X-ray did not show anything amiss, so no treatment was offered. In her letters, she again downplays her own health problems and instead engages in lively and chatty descriptions of their life in Marrakesh.

Something of this turmoil and disruption is set out in Eileen's typically chatty and humorous letter to Geoffrey Gorer.

4 October 1938
Chez Mme Vellat
Marrakech
Dear Geoffrey,
Your letter has just arrived. Of course we are blameworthy. I thought Eric had written to you & now I see he can't have done so. For myself I don't remember the last few weeks in England except that they were spent almost entirely in trains. People had to be said good-bye to & things (including Eric) collected from all over the country & the cottage had to be handed over furnished but nakedly to the Commons who are spending the winter there & mustering the goats etc. We were thrust out of England very hurriedly partly in case war broke out & partly because Eric was getting rebellious & I had rebelled.[57] As it turns out this was rather a pity. Marrakech is the <u>dernier cri</u> of fashionable medicine. Certainly it is dry. They've had three years' drought, including 17 months entirely without rain. But the climate doesn't get tolerable in any year until the end of September & this year the hot weather still persists. We are both choosing our shrouds (the Arabs favour bright green & don't have coffins which is nice on funeral days for the flies who leave even a restaurant for a few minutes to sample a passing corpse)[58], but have now chosen instead a villa. It's in the middle of an orange-grove in the palm-tree country at the foot of the Atlas from which the good air comes. I think Eric really will benefit when we get there but it isn't available until the 15th. We've bought the furniture—for about £10. I've only seen the place once for five minutes & I wasn't allowed to open the shutters & there was no artificial light, but I believe it could be very attractive. Garnished with us & our ten pounds' worth it may be odd to the eye but will be comforting to the spirit. We shall even have goats who will be physically as well as

---

[57] This most likely refers to her brother, Eric, who was insisting that the couple leave England as soon as possible.

[58] First, Eileen jokes that both she and Orwell might die soon. But, also, she writes a description of the flies at a funeral, and some believe her version is superior to the way Orwell himself described this scene (in *New Writing*, December 1939).

emotionally important because fresh milk is otherwise unobtainable.[59] It's five kilometres from Marrakech.

Do you know Morocco? We found it a most desolate country—miles & miles of ground that is not technically desert, i.e. it could be cultivated if it were irrigated but without water is simply earth & stones in about equal proportions with not even a weed growing. We got all excited the other day because we found a dock. The villa is in one of the more fertile bits. Marrakech itself is beautiful in bits. It has ramparts & a lot of buildings made of earth dug up about five feet below ground level. This dries a soft reddish colour so the French call Marrakech "la rouge" & paint everything that isn't earth a dreadful salmon-beige.[60] The best thing is the native pottery.

Unfortunately it generally isn't glazed (except some bits painted in frightful designs for the tourist trade) but we're trying to get some things made watertight. There are exquisite white clay mugs with a very simple black design inside. They cost a franc & it seems to us that people here generally earn about a franc to two francs an hour.

Eric is going to write to you & I shall leave him the crisis. I am determined to be pleased with Chamberlain because I want a rest.[61] Anyway Czecho-Slovakia ought to be pleased with him; it seems geographically certain that that country would be ravaged at the beginning of any war fought in its defence.[62] But of course the English Left is always Spartan; they're fighting Franco to the last Spaniard too[63].

I hope the old book & the new go well.[64] Are you going to America? If you happen to come to the south of Europe, call on us. It isn't very difficult—indeed there's an air service from Tangier—& we have a spare room (quite spare I should say, not even furniture in it) & we could go & look at the country on donkeys & possibly at the desert on camels, & we should enjoy it very much.[65]

---

[59] Orwell always wanted to own a goat or two. He was ahead of his time in valuing goat's milk.

[60] Eileen does manage to come up with different ways to describe Marrakesh and their villa to their different friends.

[61] Orwell is more upset than Eileen pretends to be by pre-war conditions in Europe.

[62] Eileen is of course right about this.

[63] Eileen's long-held pacifist leanings are clear here, as is her continued political engagement.

[64] The names of Gorer's books can only be speculated on.

[65] Again, both Eileen and Orwell would have welcomed visitors, but no one did manage to visit them.

I'd better send love from us both in case Eric's letter gets delayed. He has begun his novel[66] & is also carpentering—there is a box for the goats to eat out of & a hutch for the chickens though we have no goat yet & no chickens.[67]

Yours ever
Eileen.

The villa is not in any postal district & I think we have to have a "box". We'll let you know the proper address when we discover it.

By December 1938, Eileen and Orwell were preparing to spend Christmas at their villa in Marrakesh. Eileen's lively letter to Mary Common is full of details about their chaotic shopping trips and the general topsy turvy nature of their life in the villa. What is also interesting is the ease with which Eileen and Orwell have slipped into a sort of middle-class existence, engaging staff to look after them when shopping or at home.

[Typewritten]
5 December 1938
Boîte Postale 48
Marrakech
Dear Mary,

We have just got back from a Christmas shopping. It began by my bicycle having a puncture. The next stage was my arrival in Marrakech, entirely penniless, two minutes after the bank had shut. By the time Eric arrived for lunch I had scoured the town (in which we know no one) for succour and had succeeded in cashing a cheque and in collecting a retinue of guides, porters etc., all of whom had most charmingly waited for money so long that they might be said to have earned it.[68] After lunch we began to shop and we went on for two and a half hours, surrounded by as many as twenty men and boys, all shouting and many of them weeping. If either of us tried to speak, long before we had mentioned what we were talking about everyone present cried 'Yes, yes. I understand. The others don't understand.' We bought a lot of things in one shop because the people there will post to England—at least so they say. The things are being sent

---

[66] *Coming Up for Air*.

[67] Eileen's word play is in evidence, used here to emphasise the ridiculousness of their situation.

[68] Eileen is often not good at organizing her time, but here creates a humorous chronology at her own expense.

in three lots, to three key recipients who are to distribute them.⁶⁹ You are a key recipient, and you ought to get a dish for Mrs. Hatchett, a brass tray for Mrs. Anderson,⁷⁰ and a 'couverture' for yourself (and Jack). You may of course get something quite different, or nothing at all. A porter is engaged if he succeeds in laying hands on any piece of property, and as I put each thing on its appropriate pile it was instantly seized by one to four helpers and put somewhere else, or the pieces in several different places.⁷¹ Supposing you do get something, there may be duty to pay. I don't think it can be more than three or four shillings and I hope it will be nothing. We have sent a few things home already without trouble (by which I mean paying money) and they should be kind at Christmas, but it is perfectly probable that they put on for Christmas a special staff to be unkind. Anyway if there is duty of course we'll refund it when we get back or before by proxy, but meanwhile we can't think of any better arrangement than that Peter⁷² should pay it. Peter, like all our younger friends, is having money for Christmas because we can't get anything here for children unless we pay about thirty francs for something that Woolworth makes better. Money means 5/-. I hope that will arrive, but naturally we are doing all this much too late. We should have done it too late in any case, but in fact Eric was ill and in bed for more than a week and as soon as he was better I had an illness I'd actually started before his but had necessarily postponed.⁷³ I enjoyed the illness: I had to do all the cooking as usual but I did it in a dressing-gown and firmly carried my tray back to bed.⁷⁴ Now we are both very well, or I remember thinking that we were very well last night. This evening we are literally swaying on our feet and the menu for supper, which once included things like a mushroom sauce and a souffle,⁷⁵ has been revised to read: Boiled eggs, bread, butter, cheese; bread, jam, cream; raw fruit. The servant⁷⁶ goes home after lunch. He was supposed to sleep here in a kind of stable, but he prefers to cycle

⁶⁹ But this arrangement seems to be a good idea.

⁷⁰ Two of their neighbours at the cottage.

⁷¹ Eileen is clearly exaggerating, but it's not clear just how much.

⁷² Mary and Jack Common's son. This is another joke, since Peter is just a boy.

⁷³ This self-sacrificing humour is clearly Eileen's attempt to make light of her own illness. It is highly unlikely anyone can postpone the onset of an illness, so her humour relies on this being widely known.

⁷⁴ Again, Eileen's humour is making light of what must have been a very stressful situation.

⁷⁵ Was Eileen indeed making such fancy dinners in their villa?

⁷⁶ Even in the villa they had a servant.

the five or six miles to Marrakech morning and evening. I like it much better. There is nothing for him to do in the evening except wash up the supper things, and until they were dirty he used to sit on the kitchen step, often in tears, getting up every ten minutes or so to tidy the kitchen and put away (generally in the cellar) the things I was just about to use for the cooking. It is customary, among the French as well as among the Arabs, to get up at five o'clock at the latest, and he arrives here about seven with fresh bread and milk for breakfast. It is early enough for us. We come to understand each other fairly well, though I seldom know whether he is speaking French or Arabic and often talk to him myself in English. The weather has got quite cold, which is delightful. Indeed it's a good climate now and I think we sha'n't die of it, which until recently seemed probable in my case and certain in Eric's.[77] His illness was a sort of necessary stage in getting better; he has been worse here than I've ever seen him.[78] The country is, or was anyway, almost intolerably depressing, just not desert. Now it's better because a few things are growing, and according to the guide books by February or so the whole land will be covered with a carpet of wild flowers. We found a wild flower the other day with great excitement and as it was a kind of lilyish thing without any stalk we suppose it was the first shred of the carpet.[79] In our own garden we have had heartrending experiences. I suppose we have sowed about twenty packets of seed and the result is a few nasturtiums, a very few marigolds and some sweet peas. They take about three or four weeks to germinate and either grow at the same pace or don't grow higher than half an inch. But generally of course they don't germinate.[80] The two goats are more satisfactory now because they went right out of milk and that saves trouble.[81] Until recently they were milked twice a day, with Mahjroub[82] holding head and hind leg, Eric milking and me responding to cries of agony while some good cows' milk boiled over; and the total yield of the two per day was well under half a pint. The hens however have become very productive—they've laid ten eggs in four days. We started with twelve hens but four died immediately, so if you like you can do the sum I was thinking of doing but find too difficult.[83] I hope all those great hens at Wallington will be ashamed. They

---

[77] Apparently, they were both quite ill until the weather cooled down.

[78] Eileen implies that Orwell had to be very sick before he could get better.

[79] But they were mistaken: it wasn't a flower at all.

[80] The soil is not proper for the kind of garden they wished to have.

[81] More humour, as Eileen's dislike of milking the goats is well established.

[82] The servant.

[83] But clearly not as many eggs as they hoped.

really ought to be laying pretty well (i.e. about four each a week) now. Last Christmas[84] we had great numbers of eggs and sent quite a lot away, with the result that all the lucky recipients got letters from the P.M.G.[85] who regretted that a parcel addressed to them had had to be destroyed because it was offensive.[86] I must write some Christmas letters, which is why I go on typing this.[87] I get intolerably melancholy if I have to say exactly the same thing twice, so at about the tenth or fifteenth Christmas letter I am sending people the most surprising greetings,[88] but by the twentieth I am resigned to intolerable melancholy and wish the rest a happy Christmas. That's what I wish you, and a bright New Year of course. And Eric, I am sure, does the same. And we both send our love.
Yours,
Eileen

Eileen's Christmas letter to Norah is decidedly more indiscreet in terms of her personal views of people, but again gives us more information about their life in Marrakesh, including details of Eileen's own ill health that is otherwise glossed over in her other letters.

[Handwritten]
14-17 Dec 1938
Boîte Postale 48
Marrakech
[no salutation]
I know my dear girl will receive a New Year Gift just as gladly as she would have done a Xmas Present.[89] Whether she will guess what to do with it afterwards I do not know. They say it's to put money in & indeed if one does that it sits erect in an appealing way. But that's just as you like dear. Only I would like to hope that it will be full of money all through 1939 & that you will have other riches too, the better kind.

---

[84] When they were at the cottage.

[85] Postmaster-General; the government minister responsible for the postal system in the UK.

[86] Surely they did a better job of packaging the eggs than Eileen implies here.

[87] Making fun of her own procrastination.

[88] Eileen implies that she can send repetitive letters to friends about 20 times before she runs out of energy.

[89] Eileen's excuse for being late for Christmas.

The news is that I feel very happy now.[90] So far as I can judge the happiness is the direct result of yesterday's news, which was a) that Mr Blair is dying of cancer, b) that Gwen's baby Laurence had to be taken to Great Ormond Street (he is 4½ weeks old, or 5), c) that George Kopp proposes to come & stay with us in Morocco (he has no money & we had heard the day before by cable that he was out of jail & Spain; Eric's reaction to the cable was that George must stay with us & his reaction to George's letter announcing his arrival is that he must not stay with us, but I think the solution may be that George won't find anyone to lend him the necessary money). Eric however is better. I protested a lot about coming here at the beginning of September & I like to be right but I did feel too right.[91] The weather was practically intolerable. I had a temperature of 102 before I'd been in the place twenty-four hours & Eric, without any actual crisis, lost 9lbs in the first month & coughed all day & particularly all night so that we didn't get thirty minutes' consecutive rest until November. He has put on about five of the pounds again now & doesn't cough much (though still more than in England) so I think he may not be much worse at the end of the winter abroad than he was at the beginning.[92] I expect his life has been shortened by another year or two but all the totalitarians make that irrelevant.[93] One reason for my unwillingness to come when we did was that I'd made all the arrangements to come to Bristol, bringing Marx the poodle (who is wintering with Eric's sister there) but staying with you. Of course you hadn't heard but you know how pleased you would have been. We were hurled out of the country largely because Eric defied brother Eric to the extent of going to see his father who was already ill though cancer hadn't been thought of. Brother Eric was unable to think of any more lies about the disease (they'd kept him in Preston Hall on a firm and constantly repeated diagnosis of phthisis for two months after they knew he hadn't got it & I discovered in the end that on the very first X-rays the best opinions were against even a provisional diagnosis of phthisis) so turned his attention to Morocco.[94] Of course we were silly to come but I found it impossible to refuse & Eric felt that he was under an

---

[90] Eileen is using a type of gallows humour here, where she is trying to defend herself from sorrow by making jokes.

[91] At first Eileen had worried that the move to Morocco was a mistake.

[92] And she still doesn't think the move will be beneficial for Orwell.

[93] Again, Eileen is implying that Orwell won't be able to write again while there's a threat of war.

[94] Eileen is repeating the details of why they went to Morocco for the winter.

obligation though he constantly & justly complains that by a quite deliberate campaign of lying he is in debt for the first time in his life & has wasted practically a year out of the very few in which he can expect to function. However, now that we're hardened to the general frightfulness of the country we're quite enjoying it & Eric is writing a book that pleases both of us very much. And in a way I have forgiven Brother Eric who can't help being a Nature's Fascist & indeed is upset by this fact which he realises.[95]

If you would like some news about Morocco I'll send you a picture postcard. The markets are fascinating if you smoke (preferably a cigar) all the time & never look down. At first we lived in Marrakech itself, <u>en pension</u> (after the first night which we spent in a brothel owing to Cooks' lists being a bit out of date). Marrakech crawls with disease of every kind, the ringworm group, the tuberculosis group, the dysentery group; & if you lunch in a restaurant the flies only show themselves as flies as distinct from black masses when they hurry out for a moment to taste a corpse on its way to the cemetery.[96] Now we live in a villa several kilometres out. It is furnished with grass & willow chairs made to order for six francs (armchairs they are, rather comfortable), two rugs & a praying mat, several copper trays, a bed & several camel-hair 'couvertures', three whitewood tables, two charcoal braziers for cooking, about a third of the absolutely essential crockery & some chessmen.[97] It looks rather attractive.[98] The house stands in an orange grove & everything belongs to a butcher who cultivates the orange-grove but prefers to live with his meat. The only neighbours are the Arabs who look after the oranges. We have an Arab too, called Mahjroub. His life history is 'Moy dix ans et dooje ans avec Francais—soldat.' He says a lot of good things, sort of biblical. 'Dire gaz' means 'If you put oil in the methylated spirits cup of a Primus it make fumes'—which you could hardly tell apart from Mizpah.[99] He has been worried lately because he never can remember the French for fish but this week he's really learnt it—it's oiseau. We understand each other very nicely now (he often calls me Mon vieux Madame) though I seldom know

---

[95] This statement about her brother is often quoted and analysed.

[96] Another version of the flies at a funeral. Shelden (p302, 1991) comments that many think that Eileen's description is better than Orwell's.

[97] This is one of the rare mentions implying that she and Orwell played chess.

[98] Eileen makes the villa sound very attractive.

[99] Davison explains this as: A Palestinian place-name referred to in Genesis 31:49 and used as a word or token expressing close association: "The Lord watch between me and thee", often inscribed on brooches or rings exchanged between lovers.

whether he is talking French or Arabic & myself often speak English. He does the shopping & pumps the water & washes the floors (Moy porty sack chitton) & I do the cooking & curiously enough the washing. The laundries are very expensive (10 francs for a sheet, 11 francs for a shirt, 14 francs for a dress) & generally take two or three weeks. I think probably no one uses them except me so they have to engage a staff every time I send anything. We have two goats who used to give half a pint a day between them at two milkings (the milking being done by Eric while Mahjroub holds head & hind leg) but now their yield has fallen off. Our hens however lay very well. We bought 12, 4 died immediately & the remainder have laid 10 eggs in three days; the answer is a Record for a Moroccan Hen. We have people at the back door wanting to buy them. We also have two doves. They don't lay eggs but if they think of it will doubtless nest in our pillows as they spend most of the day <u>walking</u> about the house—one behind the other.

A thing I must remember is Eric's sister. I was going to Put you in Touch during that weekend. They only came to Bristol about July. Their name is Dacombe[100]: Marjorie <u>at</u> 40, Humphrey rather older I suppose, Jane 15, Henry 10, Lucy 7. They live in St. Michael's Hill—166 I think. Deep in my heart I dislike Marjorie who isn't honest but I always enjoy seeing her.[101] We all spent Christmas together & Humphrey wanted to tell me a story that wasn't fit for the children. It was a very long story, lasting through every passage & always converging on the larder which was colder than any place I remember. I never knew what the story was about, though the children explained several bits to me, but it was a good story.[102] The children are nice children. If you were to call on them it would be kind & you might like them. Humph rather reminds me of Frank Gardner but it's libellous because he hasn't the same habits.[103] I'm really fond of him. If you don't call the meeting shall take place when I fetch Marx in the spring but the call would be better for my reputation. The whole family by the way is generally in a state of absolute penury. Of course the <u>nicest</u> Blair is

---

[100] Their last name was actually Dakin.

[101] This is a detail Eileen has only shared with Norah.

[102] Eileen implies that the children actually know the story that Humphrey is trying to keep private.

[103] Davison was unable to identify this man.

Mr Blair[104] who's dying but the poor old man is 82 & he doesn't have any pain which is something.
Choosing your mother's Christmas card is always one of my treats but this year I've missed it. Partly because of the Christmas cards. Partly because a fortnight ago I suddenly got violent neuralgia & a fever. Normally I go into Marrakech on a red bicycle made in Japan for someone with very short legs & the biggest hands in the world, but for this occasion I had a taxi to go for an X-ray. It seemed obvious that I had another cyst—indeed I even packed a bag in case I had to go into hospital again[105]. There was nothing whatever the matter with my jaws & the fever just went away two or three days ago & today I went out for the first time with a handkerchief round my head. I sent off two parcels & filled in 12 forms & paid more for the postage than I had for the contents. But it's too late for Christmas cards so give your mother my love instead for the moment, & your father, & Ruth, Jean, Billy, Maurice, June, Norman, John, Elizabeth[106]. Even Quartus, & yet uniquely Norah is loved by
Pig.

Despite this chaos and ill-health, Orwell was still managing to write what would become *Coming Up for Air*. Perhaps helped by a distance from England, he was able to write a book that is embedded in the English countryside. He also wrote nine very lengthy, detailed letters of instructions to Common. These also included great plans for the future of the cottage, showing that he was ignoring Eileen's wish to move to Dorset.

In early February, however, he wrote that Eileen was going to look for their new house when they returned to England. This was rescinded in a letter of 5 March, when he wrote, "After much thought we've decided to go on living in the cottage for the rest of the summer and not move till the autumn". The "much thought" possibly masks long, heated discussions between them about their future residence, with Eileen arguing for the move and Orwell eventually victorious, as he usually was, in arguing to remain at Wallington.

---

[104] Eileen's obvious affection for Mr Blair Snr is in contrast with Jacintha Biddicum's recollection of him as an authoritarian bore in her memoir of her childhood friendship with Orwell.

[105] Eileen gives details of what could have been the main illness she suffered from when in Marrakesh.

[106] Norah did not have eight children. This list probably includes other family members.

In late January, Eileen and Orwell went for a week's trip to the Atlas Mountains. This trip is notable for the rather disturbing actions of Orwell. On arrival in their Taddert hotel, Orwell had become fascinated by the local women who were offering sex to visitors. According to various letters and other accounts, he begged Eileen's permission to visit one. Eileen leaves no record of this herself, but as Tosco Fyvel recalls, "Eileen agreed and so he had his Arab girl" (1982 p 109). Eileen was very unwell herself, although this is not mentioned in any detail, so perhaps she had not the energy to argue. Orwell himself claimed bragging rights for this and repeated the story of his night with what has been assumed was an Arab sex worker, with added embellishment, over the years, to two of his friends[107]. However, a Moroccan woman explained to Topp that it would have been the custom for the hotel owner to offer either his wife or his daughter to a male guest such as Orwell, thus making the exceptionalism Orwell claims slightly less remarkable. The couple's return to Marrakesh on 27 January saw Orwell take to his bed, too ill to even write in his many diaries for three weeks. Somehow, by the middle of March, Eileen and Orwell were back in a Marrakesh hotel, packed up and trying to find a passage back to England. Eileen was busy typing the manuscript for *Coming Up for Air* at this time, including during the ship voyage back to England.

Around this time, Georges Kopp had re-entered their lives. He had been released from prison in Spain in December 1938 and Eileen had urged her brother to give him a room in the house at Greenwich. He was still there, three months later, and it may have been that the extended stay was proving just too much for Gwen O'Shaughnessy, who also had a newborn child to look after. So Eileen and Orwell contacted Jack Common to ask that he find Kopp somewhere to stay in Wallington, saying that this would be paid for, along with money to cover the cost of food, by Gwen. However, with the growing sense of doom about the coming war, Kopp left Greenwich and set off for France to join an anti-fascist unit.

As Eileen and Orwell were making plans to return to England, they sent many letters to family and friends. One of these, from Orwell, was an attempt to set up an assignation with Lydia Jackson. He wrote:

---

[107] See Fylvel, 1982 p109.

So looking forward to seeing you! So try & keep a date or two open for a few a days after 1st of April [...] I have thought of you so often—have you thought about me, I wonder? [...] I know it's indiscreet to write such things in letters, but you'll be clever & burn this, won't you? (Davison, 2000 vol 11 p 336)

Orwell ended up sending three separate notes to Lydia, which she of course kept, after he arrived back in London. In her book, Lydia recalls this in negative terms: "His masculine conceit annoyed me" (Jackson 1976 p 430).

The trip back to England was much less problematic than the voyage out. They were at sea for only four days, arriving in London on 30 March. The manuscript for *Coming Up for Air* was delivered on time to the publisher, perhaps the only positive outcome of their time in Morocco. Eileen and Orwell returned to the Wallington cottage, but this was only for two short months , as the event they so feared had finally happened: war with Germany.

REFERENCES

Charlton, John and Murphy, Mike (1997), *The Health of Adult Britain 1841-1994, Vol 2, Infecton in England and Wales 1838-1993,* Chapter 13, Office for National Statistics, London.

Davison, Peter (ed) (2000), *The Complete Works of George Orwell. Vol 11.* Secker & Warburg, London.

Fyvel, Tosco. (1982) *George Orwell: A personal memoir.* Weidenfeld and Nicholson, London.

Gramsci, Antonio (1971) *Selections form the Prison Notebooks,* trans Quentin Hoare and Geoffrey Nowell Smith. Lawrence & Wishart, London.

Jackson, Lydia (1976) *A Russian's England.* Paul Gordon Books, Warwick.

Shelden, Michael (1991), *Orwell: the authorized biography.* Harper Collins, New York.

CHAPTER 7

At War (April 1939–April 1941)

Following Germany's invasion of Czechoslovakia in March 1939, in direct contravention of the Munich Agreement, the whole of Europe started to prepare for the worst. As the letters Eileen sent from Morocco show, these fears and resigned preparations had been going on for several months. By the spring of 1939, even the most optimistic of people found themselves queuing for gas masks and digging air raid shelters in the garden. Jan Struther's "Mrs Miniver" column in *The Times*, which ran from 1937 to 1939, recorded the minutia of everyday life for a middle-class woman in London. What connects the fictional Mrs Miniver with Eileen is her optimism and general zest for life. Even Mrs Miniver, in the spring of 1939, is shown lying awake at night fearful of the future. In her column written to coincide with the arrival of war preparations in the spring of 1938, Mrs Miniver wrote about taking her children and live-in servants (cook and housemaid) to be fitted with gas masks. She muses: "[…] there are no tangible gas masks to defend us in war-time against its slow, yellow, drifting corruption of the mind" (Struther, 2001, p. 65). As Britain started the long preparations for war, Eileen and Orwell returned from Morocco.

When Eileen and Orwell landed in England on 30 March 1939, they had with them the complete typed manuscript for *Coming Up for Air*. Orwell took this to his publisher on April 1 whilst Eileen stayed at her brother's house in Greenwich. Unbeknownst to her, Orwell was intent on keeping to the arrangement to meet Lydia Jackson that he had proposed earlier. However, when he turned up, Lydia wasn't there. He left a note to express his disappointment, and then wrote that "if clever I may be able to look in for an hour tomorrow morning, so try & stay at home in the morning, will you?" (Davison 2010, p. 167). It seems he did manage to be sufficiently devious to slip away from Eileen the following day, but, once again, Lydia was not at home. Both Eileen and Orwell then travelled to Southwold to stay with his parents and to collect Marx from Bristol. Eileen had no notion that her husband was planning an affair with one of her closest friends. In her account of this, Lydia is both defensive of Eileen and seemingly willing to comply with Orwell's desires: "I was annoyed by his assuming that I would conceal our meetings from Eileen", then "I wanted to avoid meeting him when I was in that hostile mood, capable of pushing him away if he tried to embrace me" (Jackson 1976, p. 431). In later reminiscences, Lydia muses that, as an older woman, she was perhaps flattered by the attention Orwell paid her.

Any further pursuit of Lydia seems to have been curtailed by another bout of illness. When Eileen returned to Southwold after picking up Marx, she found both his parents unwell and also her husband. Eileen herself was ill, but, even so, she was looking after three people now.

Eileen and Orwell had planned to return to the Wallington cottage by 5 April, and the Commons had arranged to leave by then. However, with the debilitating illness Orwell had developed, their return was delayed. Eileen's mother had to step in to go to the cottage and look after the animals and the garden until Eileen and Orwell were fit enough to travel, and they finally arrived home on 12 April. They found the garden was overgrown and a tangle of weeds, so their first task was to make it ready for planting. However, the exertion and on-going illness took its toll on Orwell, and from 25 April to 9 May he was very ill, going to convalesce in a sanatorium. This may have been Miller General Hospital, which is in Greenwich. Thus Eileen was once again splitting her time between visiting her husband and tending the garden and animals at Wallington. It is not clear how long Orwell was in hospital, but he was back at Wallington, making notes in his nature diary, by the start of June.

Coming up for Air was accepted by Victor Gollancz and went into print with remarkable speed. By the start of June, Orwell was already asking for extra copies. It was very well received, with critics remarking on the well-rounded hero that was a much more developed character than Orwell had previously created. This is the first book that had been written with Eileen present throughout the process of creation, and there are touches of fun and whimsy in the book that had not previously been seen in Orwell's work, and which could well have come from Eileen's influence. Orwell's father's illness progressed to its final stages around this time. Orwell always felt that he had not lived up to his father's expectations, but the very positive reviews of *Coming Up for Air* reached his father just before he died at the end of June.

When Orwell returned to the cottage, his daily routine of keeping the garden and animals in hand resumed. By the summer of 1939, they had improved the cottage enough to have running water indoors, electric lights, and a better stove, as well as a telephone. However, the roof was still corrugated iron, and incessant damp was still in evidence. With war on the horizon, Orwell was obsessively stock-piling food to keep them going in case of shortages.

Despite his repeated illnesses, Orwell was also now visiting Lydia in London quite frequently. How far this affair progressed is unclear, but Lydia's story recounts physical intimacy tinged with guilt that her close friend was being betrayed. Orwell had never been an advocate for monogamy, and Eileen understood this. Perhaps she weighed this against her own fleeting dalliance with Georges Kopp. Lydia eventually ended the affair with Orwell, but only after Eileen had arrived at her house in a fury of suspicions that Orwell was having a secret affair. However, the "other woman" was thought to be Brenda Salkeld, whom, as Eileen knew, Orwell had been pursuing for years, even before his marriage. Given Eileen's reported reaction to Orwell's visit to a sex worker in Morocco, it seems that Eileen was more upset at the secrecy of any affair than at the actual affair itself. However, what Lydia then realised was that she was not "special" to Orwell, but one of a series of females he pursued. Lydia's decision to call a halt to the affair was successful in that Orwell didn't write to her again until April 1945, when he was informing her of Eileen's death.

Meanwhile, Orwell was behind in writing his next book: *Inside the Whale*. The essay on Dickens was finished, with Eileen's help, at the end of August 1939. The couple left Wallington on 24 August, fearing war was imminent. Eileen went to stay with her brother in Greenwich whilst Orwell went to stay with L. H. Myers in Hampshire before joining the family at Greenwich around 3 September. Myers was the friend who had given Eileen and Orwell the loan for the trip to Morocco, although this was not known by Orwell until 1946. Eileen wrote to Orwell from

London whilst he was staying with Myers, but, unfortunately, as we know, he didn't save her letters. On 1 September, Germany invaded Poland. Britain had pledged to defend Poland, and so was left with no choice but to declare war with Germany (Whyte and Hannant 2011). After listening to Chamberlain's sombre announcement of the start of war at 11:15 a.m. on 3 September, Orwell returned to the Wallington cottage, but Eileen stayed in London.

From September 1939 to May 1940, there was very little military action across Europe. In contrast with the rapid German invasion of Poland, the war was relatively static at this time. The war plans of the British and French were fundamentally defensive, with an Allied naval blockade of Germany. On the home front, Britain braced itself for a rapid German invasion in the manner of the blitzkrieg Poland had experienced. Civil defence plans were put into effect immediately. In particular, there was a great fear of arial attack and so air raid precautions were rigorously imposed. The British government issued a host of new laws as part of the Defence of the Realm legislation, including conscription, limited rationing of food, and prioritising the use of public transport for military purposes (Todman 2016).

Eric O'Shaughnessy had enlisted in the Royal Army Medical Corps (RAMC) in September 1939 and had volunteered for overseas service. He was due to depart for France in the middle of September, leaving Gwen with their infant son, Laurence. Before he left, he made Eileen promise that she would be on hand to comfort Gwen whilst he was away. This suited Eileen well, as she was tired of the drudgery of the cottage and had decided not to spend another winter in the cold, damp hovel. Lydia suggested that Eileen was actually in need of adventure, and the chance of being in London and thus in danger appealed to her.

On a more practical basis, Eileen was able to get a job in London, which would greatly help the couple's finances, as there had been very little income since the spring. The first job she got was in the Press and Censorship Bureau of the Ministry of Information, which was the central government department responsible for publicity and propaganda during the war. With her excellent connections from Oxford, she was able to present herself as more than a shorthand typist. Whilst the exact nature of her work there is unknown, it is clear that she was able to feed back to Orwell sufficiently juicy information about the geography and architecture of the Ministry for him to develop what would become *Nineteen Eighty-four*.

Eileen managed to travel up to Wallington every second weekend, and was able to help Orwell manage the garden and animals whilst there. She was, of course, still typing his manuscripts and the typed version of *Inside the Whale* was delivered to the publisher, two months late, in October. They spent Christmas 1939 at Greenwich. The winter of 1939–1940 was one of the coldest on record and the cottage at Wallington was almost impossibly frigid. Orwell returned to the cottage early in January, but when Eileen eventually managed to join him, she found the cottage so frozen that she insisted Orwell return to London with her. On 30 January, they battled through snowdrifts to the station, where further delays were caused by the restrictions on travel for non-military purposes. Orwell stayed at Greenwich for about six weeks, most of the time being in bed ill. He then returned to Wallington, leaving Eileen in London earning the wage that allowed them to continue living in some sort of comfort.

As spring arrived, Orwell arranged to move to London. Managing the Wallington cottage on his own must have proved too much, and the pressure he was putting himself under to write book reviews whilst also managing the garden and animals, coupled with being apart from Eileen, doubtless were major factors. He got work as a theatre and film critic at *Time & Tide*,[1] where Lettice Cooper was associate editor. Orwell was also now a sergeant in the Home Guard and had a tailor-made uniform to fit his exceptionally tall frame.

Eileen and Orwell also moved out of the family home in Greenwich and into a small top-floor flat on Chagford Street, Westminster. For those who were not fortunate enough to have a garden where they could dig their own air raid shelter, community air raid shelters were constructed. These could be in the basements of buildings, or infamously within the London Underground system. For Eileen and Orwell, the shelter would have been a few minutes' walk from their flat, perhaps in the Baker Street Underground Station that was close by. There were also shelters in Whitehall where Eileen could have gone in the case of day-time raids.

In the spring of 1940, Germany launched attacks against the Scandinavian countries and across Western Europe. Norway in particular was targeted for its strategic location as both a land bridge and with west-facing ports. It was attacked by sea and air on 9 April 1940. A month

---

[1] Time & Tide was a British weekly political and literary review magazine, founded by Lady Rhondda in 1920. It was a strong supporter of feminist causes and left-wing politics in this early period of publication.

later, on 10 May, Germany launched attacks on France, Belgium, Luxembourg, and the Netherlands. However, London in the spring of 1940 was strangely quiet. Whilst war raged across Europe, Britain had instituted blackouts, meaning all externally visible lights had to be extinguished or hidden by a specified time each day. The population was in a state of readiness, with gas-masks strung across shoulders when out and about, and sign-posts removed in anticipation of invasion. But no invasion came. This period, stretching back to September 1939, earned the label "the phoney war". But by the end of May 1940, the German army had largely conquered France and was close to the ports. This was the end of the phoney war.

In Britain, there were also great political changes. On 8 May, the House of Commons debated the disaster that had befallen Norway, which the British navy had pledged to defend. Neville Chamberlain was targeted for particular criticism and he was forced to resign. On 10 May, Winston Churchill succeeded him as prime minister.

After Germany invaded Scandinavia and advanced across Western Europe through to the channel ports in May 1940, the war could be said to have truly begun for Britain. The British army, known as the British Expeditionary Force (BEF), was pushed back to the French port of Dunkirk, along with French and Belgian troops. One of the new prime minister Winston Churchill's first tasks was to organise the evacuation of these troops from Dunkirk. This was easier said than done. The beach at Dunkirk was gently shelving, meaning that large warships could only pick up troops from the sea wall, or East Mole, which extended into deep water. A more complex evacuation was needed. This was given the code name Operation Dynamo, the name coming from the offices of Admiral Bertram Ramsay, who was based in a room deep in the Dover cliffs that had once contained a dynamo (Didley 2010). Operation Dynamo organised the vanguard cover for the retreating troops, whilst also calling on the owners of smaller boats to join in the exercise, as they would be better able to reach the shallow waters. These boats became known as the "little ships".

This operation began on 26 May, with 800 naval vessels of all shapes and sizes deployed to help evacuate the troops from the beach. A staggering number of men needed to be evacuated—more than 400,000—and, as Ramsay reported to Churchill, it could be expected that only 20,000 to 30,000 could be saved. But, after eight days, 338,226 men had been rescued, an astonishing number. This meant that the British could believe that this was not a major defeat, but instead a miraculous victory. To this day, the phrase "Dunkirk spirit" is used to refer to optimism in the face of defeat.

However, not all the men who were on the beach and in the towns of Dunkirk and Lille made it out. Nearly 40,000 prisoners of war were captured by the Germans, most of these being the remnants of the French army that had delayed the advancing German army long enough for the Dunkirk evacuation to take place (Gelb 1990). A further 68,000 died in the fighting that went on whilst waiting to be rescued. Operation Dynamo was completed on 4 June 1940, and on the same day Churchill went to the House of Commons and gave what was to become one of his most famous speeches, known as the "We shall fight them on the beaches" speech. His great skill with rhetoric became a feature of the wartime audio landscape that Eileen and Orwell consumed via the nine o'clock news bulletins on the radio.

In the chaos of evacuated troops pouring into London in June 1940, news of Eric O'Shaughnessy was anxiously awaited. Troops from all the Allied nations were part of that evacuation. In London, Eileen was frantic with worry. Orwell wrote in his diary on 1 June that he went to "Waterloo and Victoria to see whether I could get any news of [Eric]. Quite impossible, of course. The men who have been repatriated have orders not to speak to civilians and are in any case removed from the railway stations as promptly as possible. Actually I saw very few British soldiers" (Davison 2001c, p. 174).

Lydia was with Eileen for some of this time and described her anguish: "Eileen paced up and down the room, smoking one cigarette after another. 'I just don't know what we shall do with Mother', she was saying. 'I'm sure Eric is dead'" (Jackson 1960, p. 122). Eric had, in fact, died on 27 May, before Operation Dynamo had begun. He had been killed in the fighting in Dunkirk, his body never recovered. In researching her biography of Eileen, Topp discovered the privately published diaries of a fellow doctor who had encountered Eric at Dunkirk; George McNab. In personal correspondence with his son, Richard, he told her how the diary recorded the terror of the aerial bombing of the retreating army of which he and Eric were a part. His diary records how he came across Eric, sitting in a café in Dunkirk during a bombing raid, but that Eric refused the urging of his colleagues to take cover in a cellar. The café received a direct hit, killing Eric instantly.

Eileen had lost her heroic older brother, the person whom she had competed against to be the cleverest, and the person who had rescued her repeatedly from the poverty of life at Wallington. Although there are no letters from Eileen at this time, other accounts of her grief show her being profoundly depressed for well over a year after Eric's death. Tosco Fyvel, for example, recalls Eileen and Orwell visiting his house outside of London in the summer of 1940:

> We all noticed a profound change in [Eileen]. She seemed to sit in the garden sunk in unmoving silence while we talked. Mary, my wife, observed that Eileen not only looked tired and drawn but was drably and untidily dressed [...] she was completely withdrawn. (Fyvel 1982, p. 105)

In London, Eileen and Orwell walked the streets together, finishing their day in their local pub listening to the nine o'clock news on the radio. This news often included an address by Churchill. Orwell reported Eileen's view on this:

> [She] believed that uneducated people are often moved by a speech in solemn language which they don't actually understand but feel to be impressive (Davison 2001c, p. 197).

Orwell's 37th birthday on 25 June that year is marked by a letter he wrote to Brenda Salkeld. In it, he lamented the non-consummation of their long-running affair, and seemed to imply that Eileen had given him permission to attempt to pick up on this affair as a "birthday treat". He wrote:

> Today is my birthday & Eileen said I was to give myself a birthday treat [...] I've been longing for months to write to you & compelling myself not to [...] Eileen said she wishes I could sleep with you abt twice a year, just to keep me happy. (Bowker, 2003, p. 266)

Brenda, of course, continued to refuse Orwell's advance, which probably meant that this relationship continued for many years more than it would have if they had actually slept together even once.

Eileen received a letter from Georges Kopp in September 1940. Written to her before he had heard the news of Eric's death, the letter announced Kopp's escape from a German field hospital with the help of various French civilians. He went on to recall the beauty of the Catalonian countryside in the sort of detail that must have struck a chord with Eileen. In all the hundreds of letters she must have received over the years, this is one of the very few that she kept. However, it seems she did not answer it, and a year later, Kopp was writing to other acquaintances desperately trying to find news of Eileen.

When the first air raids did come to London, in June 1940, Eileen and Orwell treated them with a general insouciance. However, it would be September before the nightly bombing raids would start in earnest. Hitler's plan had been to destroy British miliary forces in anticipation of a land invasion. However, this strategy for air superiority was won by the British in what became known as the Battle of Britain throughout the summer of 1940. Germany's tactic changed to be one of destroying morale by bombing towns and cities. The first raid took place on 7 September 1940. This raid on London left 430 dead and more than 1,600 injured. The day became known as "Black Saturday" and marked the start of 57 consecutive nights of bombing, with some raids during the day as well (Ziegler 2002).

Whilst London was the most heavily bombed, other port cities and industrial towns also suffered greatly. Birmingham, Coventry, Bristol, Liverpool, and Sunderland all were regularly targeted. The effect of the Blitz on civilians was intended to be demoralising through disrupted sleep, fear, and destruction of homes and civic buildings. More than 40,000 civilians were killed across the UK in these raids, almost half of them in London, where more than a million houses were lost. Orwell wrote of the intensity of the raids that made the whole house shake and rattle, but, as the raids continued, he and Eileen stopped going to the shelter and instead just tried to get back to sleep.

Eileen was continuing to work at the Ministry for Information but loathed her job. She and Orwell would try to get away from London and go to the Wallington cottage at least once a month, and on 15 October they were both able to get a week there, not planned as a break but enforced owing to Orwell having an infected arm. However tempting the peace and relative safety of Wallington might have been, both Eileen and Orwell felt it their duty to stay in London and brazen it out along with everyone else. Orwell commented, "You can't leave when people are being bombed to hell" (Symons in Shelden 1991, p. 329). Whilst at Wallington, however, Orwell was still an active member of the Home Guard, where he carried the rank of sergeant. His poor health had excluded him from the regular army and his guilt at this exemption perhaps contributed to his desire to return to London and at least show solidarity with those in greatest danger in Britain.

Eileen was still not well. The combination of grief, lack of sleep, and overwork were all wearing her down. Lydia reported that, "whenever I pleaded with her for wisdom in taking reasonable care of herself, she replied that it was George's health, not hers, that was valuable" (Jackson 1960, p. 123). Orwell was often laid up in their flat in Chagford Street with recurrent bouts of illness. Eileen continued to neglect her own health to such a degree that, in November 1940, she had to take a whole month off work to recuperate. Both Eileen and Gwen had pressed Orwell to go to Canada for safety, perhaps to join his nephew, Gwen and Eric's son Laurence, who had been sent there earlier in 1940. Orwell rejected this, reasoning:

> Better to die if necessary, and maybe even as propaganda one's death might achieve more than going abroad [...] not that I want to die; I have so much to live for, in spite of poor health and having no children. (Davison2001c, p. 197)

Ever generous and hospitable, Eileen and Orwell would often welcome friends for dinner, then have to offer them overnight accommodation on a camp bed if they were caught in an air raid. In all of this, Orwell was still writing and Eileen was still typing for him, even though writing his manuscripts was curtailed by the inconveniences of wartime. However, this period of Orwell's creativity includes one of his best-known essays, "The Lion and the Unicorn".

In December of 1940, Eileen wrote a short letter to Norah. Her humour is back to something like its normal level, with frequent forays into self-deprecation at the expense of her own health.

[handwritten]
c. 5 December 1940
24 Croom's Hill SE 10
[*no salutation*]
This is to accompany a Charming Gift but I don't know what the gift is yet because it will be bought this afternoon. Or so I hope. I have been ILL. Ever so ill. Bedridden for 4 weeks & still <u>weak</u>. You know or Quartus[2] does

---

[2] Norah's husband.

perhaps though it's more than all my local doctors do. They diagnosed cystitis and then they diagnosed nephrolithiasis & then they diagnosed Malta fever[3] with ovarian complications & then they went all hush-hush while they diagnosed a tuberculous infection so that I couldn't possibly guess what they were testing for. They haven't yet diagnosed cancer or G.P.I.[4] but I expect they will shortly.[5] They're in a great worry[6] because nothing can be found wrong with my heart as that was assumed to be giving out very soon. Meanwhile a perfectly sweet little pathologist like a wren did an ordinary blood count & found the haemoglobin down to 57%. This is much despised by the clinicians but in fact they can find nothing else.[7] So now I hear I'll be cured when I weigh 9 stone. As my present weight is 7st 12. with my clothes on I think perhaps they'll lose interest before the cure is complete.[8] I went to Norfolk for a fortnight's convalescence and wanted to start work on Monday as all this is just silly, but I can't go back without a health certificate & the wretched man won't sign one. However I am now allowed to go shopping on medical grounds though the financial ones aren't so good.[9]

How is your paint?[10] I hope for a Word at Christmas. Marjorie (née Blair) says they're quite O.K. but I don't know where S. Michael's Hill is &

---

[3] Malta fever is another name for brucellosis, which is caused by the ingestion of unpasteurised milk from infected animals. Symptoms include fever, loss of appetite, fatigue, joint and muscle pain and headaches.

[4] GPI is the common abbreviation for "general paralysis of the insane".

[5] As usual, Eileen is joking about her own constant illnesses.

[6] Eileen displaces her own concerns for her health completely here, with only the doctors appearing to be worried.

[7] This is a puzzling statistic. Haemoglobin is not usually measured in percentages, although on occasion it could be and a woman's normal haemoglobin range would be between 36 and 48%. A haemoglobin of 57% would be cause for great concern and, in someone like Eileen who was prone to heavy menstruation and was generally unwell with fatigue, this is not likely. Instead, we might speculate that she is pointing to 57% of the normal measure, which would be in keeping with her on-going medical problems.

[8] The normal healthy weight for a woman of Eileen's height would indeed be much greater than she offers as her actual weight. Being underweight can have multiple causes, and can also lead to a wide range of health problems, such as irregular menstruation; reduced immunity; fatigue.

[9] Eileen and Orwell always complained about their constant money problems.

[10] An obscure question, but perhaps relates to a comment by Norah in a previous letter to Eileen.

have no inside information about the Bristol blitz[11]. I may give up this job for a bit anyway & perhaps see for myself after all. I had arranged a long weekend (which I was going to spend with <u>you</u>) because the pain was worse but then it got a lot worse & the long weekend was merged in sick leave.[12]

George has written a little book, no. I in the Searchlight Books[13] (Secker & Warburg 2/-), out next month, which please note. Explaining how to be a Socialist though Tory.[14] It was going to cost 1/-, which would have been better, but Warburg changed at the last minute & the book had to have another 10,000 words inserted to give value for twice the money. Some of the later ones look like being good.

I hope you have a tolerable Christmas. We're having the Dinner on Boxing Day, theoretically for lonely soldiers but they are so lonely that we don't know them yet. Mother is still away of course. Now I shall go and shop. But can you send on an envelope to Mary, of whose address I have no idea[?] I also don't know whether she got any further news about Teddy though he was posted Missing in the <u>Times</u> months after the <u>Glorious</u> went down. She was really magnificent about that. I have been assuming that it was hopeless but of course it's possible that he was taken prisoner. George Kopp, whom I had also assumed dead, was captured with two bullets in his chest & part of his left hand shot off. Later he escaped to unoccupied France & he's now trying to get here but his letters take about two months to come so one can't know much of what is happening.[15]

By the way, where is Norman? I hope not in Egypt[16].

Now I must go shopping being as ever a Devoted Pig.

---

[11] Eileen's ignorance of the bombing raids in other parts of the country is not unusual. To preserve moral, it was government policy to release few details.

[12] Eileen was still hoping to be able to visit Norah in Bristol.

[13] A series of longer essays published as hardback books to be edited by Orwell and Fyvel, of which Orwell's *The Lion and the Unicorn* was the first. Whilst the series had been planned around an initial estimate of 17 titles, only ten were actually published as the printer's sock paper was destroyed in the Blitz.

[14] This ironic description of Orwell has been reprinted numerous times.

[15] Kopp did eventually arrive back in England for a short time.

[16] The German offensive across Africa was at its height, with Egypt being the focus of Rommel's attention at this time.

Having walked twelve or fourteen miles to find mother <u>soft</u> slippers <u>with</u> heels, I had to buy everyone else hcfs[17] in a horrible shop. Last year's gift was identical I believe but you will have a nice stock of white hcfs for the cold days.

Eileen's mother had moved into a nursing home in St Leonards-on-Sea on the south coast some time before war was declared. By March 1941, she was back in London in hospital at Greenwich, fading fast, and she died on 21 March of heart failure. It was Orwell who went to register the death, not Eileen, perhaps indicating that she was too exhausted by the events of the previous year to carry out this morbid task. Eileen inherited her mother's meagre estate, which included the house at Hillingdon. Eileen chose to retain this house and its small rental income.

The next letter we have by Eileen is again to Norah, probably written in March 1941. The light touch of her self-depreciating approach to her health in the letter she had sent at Christmas is still there, but the whole tone in darker. Eileen had lost her brother and her mother in quick succession, and with Gwen's decision to send her son to Canada for safety, there was no need for Eileen to help out at the Greenwich house any longer. Added to that, there was the steady grind of frequent air raids and the encroaching gloom of the blackouts. Although there is no evidence to suggest there had been bomb damage to Chagford House, it seems Eileen and Orwell were looking to move again. Eileen's letter hints at this. The flat they moved to was not far from their old one, but in a more modern building, Langford Court. This was a popular area for European refugees since the 1930s, and so it was into this cosmopolitan environment that Eileen and Orwell would eventually move.

[handwritten]
c. March 1941
[*no salutation*]

---

[17] Handkerchiefs would seem be a very unglamorous gift at this point in the war, but giving Christmas presents, no matter how mundane, seemed to be always important to Eileen.

The semi crest means that the paper was waste[18] before it Flowered. The same is true of my time as a government servant.[19] There is not much paper[20], so to sum up:

Physical condition—much improved by air raids, possibly because I now sleep several hours a night longer than ever in my life;

Mental condition—temporarily improved by air raids which were a change, degenerating again now that air raids threaten to become monotonous;

Events since the war—daily work of inconceivable dullness; weekly efforts to leave Greenwich always frustrated; monthly visits to the cottage which is still as it was only dirtier[21];

Future plans—imaginings of the possibility of leaving a furnished flat ('chambers') that we have at Baker Street & taking an unfurnished flat north of Baker Street to remain in George's Home Guard district, with the idea that we might both live in this flat[22]—probably to be frustrated by continued lack of five shillings to spend & increasing scarcity of undemolished flats & perhaps by our ceasing to live anywhere.[23] But the last is unlikely because a shorter & no less accurate summing up would be
NOTHING EVER HAPPENS TO
Pig.

Please write a letter. The difficulty is that I am too profoundly depressed to write a letter. I have many times half thought I could come to Bristol but it is literally years since a weekend belonged to me & George would have a haemorrhage.[24] I suppose London is not a place to come to really

---

[18] Eileen seems to be using off-cuts of paper that is used elsewhere in the Ministry (hence the refence to crest).

[19] Eileen left her job at the Ministry of Information, but she resumed working for the Ministry of Food in early 1942.

[20] By early 1941, paper shortages were starting to be very noticeable.

[21] Eileen's usually charming ironic humour is missing in this letter. Instead, we have her attempting humour through a parody of a news report, possibly the shipping forecast, with its regimented sections and abbreviated grammar.

[22] The couple did move from Chagford St. to an apartment on the top floor at 111 Langford Court. This apartment was reimagined, in *Nineteen Eighty-Four*, as Winston's walk-up apartment, since the elevators didn't always work.

[23] Eileen's rather grim humour here is noticeably different from her other letters. However, she can't resist a more optimistic closing salutation, reassuring her good friend that she is unlikely to perish in an air raid as her life is uneventful.

[24] Eileen now realised how dependent Orwell was on her, hinting that it might even be the case that he could create a health problem of his own whenever she had a chance for a break.

but if you do ring NATIONAL 3318.[25] My departmental head is almost as frightened of me as he is of taking any decision on his own & I can get Time off.[26] Meanwhile give my love to everyone. E.

The couple moved house in April 1941, making a fresh start in an unfurnished flat. Perhaps this helped Eileen cope better with the personal losses she had suffered in the previous year, as the fresh start meant there were fewer memories to contend with. Outside, the war continued. Heavy bombing of British cities wrought destruction on an unprecedented scale. The focus of the war also shifted to German advances around the Mediterranean and in North Africa. Rommel's army entered Egypt on 26 April and Greece surrendered on 27 April. The war was not going well for the Allies.

References

Bowker, Gordon (2003) *Inside George Orwell*. Palgrave Macmillan, New York.
Davison, Peter (2001c), *The Complete Works of George Orwell*. Vol 12: A patriot after all, 1940–1941. Secker & Warburg, London.
Davison, Peter (2010) *Orwell: A life in letters*. Random House, London.
Didley, Douglas (2010) *Dunkirk 1940: Operation Dynamo*. Osprey, London.
Fyvel, T. R. (1982) *George Orwell: A personal memoir*. Weidenfeld and Nicholson, London.
Gelb, Norman (1990). *Dunkirk: the incredible escape*. Michael Joseph, London.
Jackson, Lydia (1960) 'George Orwell's First Wife', *The Twentieth Century Magazine*. Vol 168, August 1960.
Jackson, Lydia (writing as Elisaveta Fen) (1976) *A Russian's England*. Paul Gordon Books, Warwick.
Shelden, Michael (1991) *Orwell: the authorized biography*. Harper Collins, New York.
Struther, Jan (1939, 2001) *Mrs Miniver*. Virago, London.
Todman, Daniel (2016) *Britain's War: Into Battle, 1937-1941*. Oxford University Press, Oxford.
Whyte, Bert and Hannant, Larry (2011) *Champagne and Meatballs: Adventures of a Canadian Communist*. Athabasca University Press, Edmonton.
Ziegler, Philip (2002) *London at War, 1939-1945*. Pimlico, London.

---

[25] This would be Eileen's office phone, accessed via a switchboard.
[26] At least Eileen realised how persuasive she could be when she wanted to be.

CHAPTER 8

Eileen at the Ministry of Food (1941–1944)

This chapter covers an intense period of challenges, both in terms of Eileen and Orwell's lives, but also the exterior world of the Second World War. The length of this chapter is explained by the fact it contains 35 letters by Eileen that are held in the BBC Written Archive. As such, it is a rich repository of more letters by Eileen than exist anywhere else. These letters show a different side to Eileen: her professional voice, which is tempered by the playfulness that is a hallmark of her personal letters. The chapter also looks at the creative exchanges between Eileen and Orwell at this time, which end up in the novel, *Animal Farm*.

On April 1, Eileen and Orwell moved out of the Chagford Road flat, possibly because of minor damage such as broken windows or damaged roof, and into a larger flat: 111 Langford Court, just round the corner from Abbey Road in St John's Wood. This was a much more solidly-built house, and had a lift to take them up their top-floor flat. The other flats in the building were occupied by a mix of European refugees.

The blitz continued around them, but their air of insouciance continued as they generally refused to have their rest disturbed, despite the noise of the bombs falling and detonating close by. On 10 May, there was a raid that included bombs dropping very close to Langford Court. Orwell's diary notes that this caused quite a stir, with a huge fire close by. This prompted the couple to take the situation a bit more seriously than they usually did: "We slipped on some clothes, grabbed a few things and went out [...] actually, all that had happened was that the bomb had set fire to the garage and burned out the cars that were in it" (Davison 2001c, pp. 495–6).

However, the general insouciance exhibited by Eileen and Orwell was surely an act of bravado. One friend, Mark Benney, recalls an evening when Eileen and Orwell had been to the Benneys' for dinner during an air raid. A bomb fell just 50 yards from the flat, lifting the four diners out of their seats. Benney reports that Orwell tried to pass this off with a comment about their luck at being in a well-constructed home, whereas Eileen cried, "No, no—not *again*!" (Benney 1966, p. 166). It seems Eileen's nerves were shot to pieces by the incessant bombing, which was hard for her to bear after the grief of the past year. There was widespread anxiety and even feelings of hopelessness amongst the population at this time, as recorded in the Mass Observation diaries (see Sheridan 1990 for a fuller account), but any public demonstration of this was censored by the government as it battled to keep moral up on the home front.

Despite this, Hitler's plans for destroying civilian moral were more or less failing, and through a huge propaganda campaign, the British believed that this was true. Censorship included blocking publication of the reports of widespread bombing across the country, and reports of looting and mob violence only appeared many years after the war ended. Eileen had been working in the Censorship Department of the Ministry for Information, but found the work futile and exasperating. Coinciding with the end of the blitz came Eileen's decision to leave the Ministry. Lydia recalls Eileen "seemed to have less energy. Less sparkle. She seemed to me always tired. She neglected her health" (Jackson in Wadhams 1984, p. 68). From July 1941 to early 1942, Eileen had no paid job. The cessation of the blitz meant a good night's sleep was possible, and there was no stress involved in a job she loathed.

Since moving to London, Orwell had been working not only as a theatre and film critic for *Time & Tide*, but also as a broadcaster for the BBC. He was engaged full-time by them as Talks Assistant for the BBC's Eastern Service, where it was hoped his radio output would counter the generally positive reception of German propaganda in India. Orwell produced stimulating radio programmes from writers such as E. M. Forster, Rebecca West, and T. S. Eliot. He also devised a "magazine programme" around literature. Desmond Avery, author of *Orwell at the BBC in 1942*, commented to Topp, "I felt sure Eileen must have helped with at least some of them... Orwell always conspicuously needed help", from amongst others Richard Rees, Mabel Fierz, and his sister Avril, but "probably from Eileen most of all" (Topp 2020, p. 313). As well as producing huge amounts of content for the BBC, Orwell was still writing book reviews, which were duly typed by Eileen. This burst of energetic production took its toll and Orwell was often off work for weeks at a time with a recurrence of his lung problems. Again, it was Eileen who looked after him, but now it was without the support of her beloved brother.

Women were conscripted into war service in December 1941, and in early 1942 Eileen must have felt well enough to "do her bit". She began working in the public relations department of the Ministry of Food, a job which she thoroughly enjoyed, as it allowed her to engage in the sort of editing and creative scriptwriting where she so excelled. Food rationing had been introduced in January 1940 to ensure a fair share for everyone in a time of national shortage. The Ministry of Food was responsible for overseeing rationing, and every citizen was given their own ration book with coupons that they could use to buy the rationed goods, and householders had to register with particular retailers. Basic foodstuffs, such as sugar, meat, fats and cheese, were the first to be rationed. Not all food was rationed: bread, fruit and vegetables were often in short supply, but never rationed. (Sitwell 2016). As part of the Ministry's strategies to distribute information and knowledge about food and rationing, there was a five-minute radio programme broadcast every morning after the 8 am news bulletin. This programme, *The Kitchen Front*, had started in June 1940 and was a mixture of recipes, general cooking and nutritional advice. The programme had initially been broadcast only once a week, but by May 1941 it had expanded to six mornings, and included a regular rota of speakers. Lord Woolton, Minister for Food, was keen to develop the programme. In early 1942, he appointed Howard Marshall, an established broadcaster, who became Director of Public Relations, and at the same time, he employed Eileen as a second officer to work alongside Marshall's assistant, Robert Westerby. Harman Grisewood was someone Eileen had known since they were both at Oxford. His biographer mentions that they may have been in a relationship at some point during that time (Bowker 2003, p. 284). Eileen would meet him again through her wartime work with the BBC, and also his cousin, Freddy Grisewood.[1] Eileen also came

---

[1] Freddy's name is sometimes spelled Freddie. In all of her letters, Eileen uses the Freddy spelling, and that is the one he uses in his autobiography. We will continue this format. Eileen's use of his first name in her correspondence, rather than referring to him

across the novelist Lettice Cooper, who was working for the Ministry of Food's Public Relations Division. (Cooper's novel, *Black Bethlehem*, was published in 1947 and was inspired by her war work. The character of Ann is now thought to be based on Eileen.)

For reasons we can only speculate about, when working with the BBC, Eileen referred to herself as "Emily". All her colleagues knew her by that name, and she signed all her letters with that name. Topp suggests this was a name she adopted from playing a character in a Mrs Buggins radio script. Eileen had been aware of the Buggins programme since its conception and she might have been the person who suggested using that programme as part of the Kitchen Front content. Alternatively, given the similarity of the names "Eileen" and "Emily" (which are sometimes indecipherable in her signature), it may be that someone misread her name and used "Emily" in error. As we saw earlier, even at school her name was confused when she appeared on one occasion in the school magazine as "Elsie". Given Eileen's sense of humour, it is not beyond possibility that she adopted this name as a joke, just as she had with "Pig", and retained it. In any case, perhaps she was playfully teasing her husband whose own name was blurred between "Eric Blair" and "George Orwell".

Many of the letters Eileen wrote whilst in this job show a tension between the BBC and the Ministry of Food, with both organisations seemingly booking speakers and contributors for the Kitchen Front without fully collaborating with the other. It was Eileen's job to try and resolve these disputes.

Eileen was initially employed to act as liaison between the Ministry of Food, where recipes were developed and tested, and the BBC. A letter in the Crick archive from a Mrs A. Nilson who worked with Eileen gives us more information about her role:

> People invited to broadcast on The Kitchen Front submitted scripts and recipes and Eileen had to see that the final version was in a form that satisfied both the BBC and the Ministry of Food [...] It was not an easy job but she did it with great skill and tact. (Crick Archive)

Once approved, it would be Eileen's job to make sure the scripts were appropriate for the five-minute slot. Some of these scripts came from a

---

as "Mr Grisewood" or just "Grisewood" reflects to the fact that there were two people with that surname working with Eileen.

format developed before Eileen joined the team, and related to a comic scenario involving the character Mrs Buggins, played by Mabel Constanduros. In addition, along with Lettice, Eileen would interview would-be speakers who might be selected to appear both on the Kitchen Front and at Food Meetings that they arranged in public locations around London.

The first extant letter on file, held in the BBC Written Archive, is dated 28 February 1942, and is from Eileen (writing as Emily) to Jean Rowntree, a producer at the BBC. As was the custom at this time, women would refer to one another by their marital title and surname except in the most intimate of friendships.

> Ministry of Food (official letterhead)[2]
> 28 February 1942.
> Dear Miss Rowntree,
> I am returning the two scripts from Mr. Hopkin. Mrs. Horton will not hear of them so I am afraid that is that.
> I am also enclosing two sets of recipes from a Miss Pamela Pain. I don't know whether she might possibly be of some use to you for Wise Housekeeping. I think she cooks very attractively but our people feel that she is altogether too fancy. She may have some interesting ideas because she has apparently quite a collection of old cookery books that she uses and, in spite of the Kitchen's qualms, she is, in fact, a practical housekeeper cooking ordinary rations.
> Yours sincerely,
> [signed]
> [handwritten PS] Also enclosed—a letter about a Wise Housekeeping broadcast.

The close working relationship between the Ministry of Food and the BBC at this time is clear from these letters. This is shown in the next letter we have, sent on 20 March, in response to one from Miss Rowntree, who suggested an additional speaker and recipe for Kitchen Front. As with all the recipes included in the programme, this one reflected wartime rationing and the need to experiment with ingredients that might have been overlooked prior to the war.

---

[2] Reproduced courtesy of BBC Written Archives Centre, R51/285/2.

Ministry of Food (official letterhead)[3]
20 March, 1942
Dear Miss Rowntree,
I am returning Mrs. Turnbull's letter and the sheep's head script.
I quite agree about the hints and gadgets,[4] but I'm not quite clear whether Mrs. Turnbull wants to produce a script that will be <u>hers</u> although she won't read it, or whether she would let us pick her brains as convenient. We have a lot of odd suggestions sent in by different people and I think the Food Reporter[5] might profitably devote some time to them. He might do this as a kind of features perhaps, instead of mentioning every week that Warrington and Doncaster share with every town in England a plentiful supply of salt cod and a dearth of green vegetables.
Miss Kennedy's script Can you use this? The difficulty on the Kitchen Front at the moment is that we have Friday speakers booked so far ahead—if Miss Grossbard[6] speaks on April 24, we have no free date before May—and I am nervous of arranging a broadcast on a rare commodity (though this may seem an odd description of a sheep's head) much in advance. These things have a habit of disappearing from the shops for no apparent reason, and our policy people[7] might well approve the script one month and stamp on it the next. On the other hand, your Regional people[8] probably won't like the decision to be held over for weeks. I do think it is a good recipe.
Yours sincerely,
[signed]
Emily Blair
Public Relations Division

---

[3] Reproduced courtesy of BBC Written Archives Centre, R51/285/2.

[4] As well as promoting recipes, the Kitchen Front series includes tips on cooking and preparing food.

[5] The Food Reporter was a regular feature on the Kitchen Front.

[6] This may be Berthe Grossbard, who arrived in Britain in the late 1930s as a Jewish refugee from Austria. She had given talks about Austrian culture on BBC radio in the late 1930s. One report in *Radio Review* (13 May 1936) welcomed her "romantic talk in a romantic way" and complimented her "attractive accent". In 1941, she wrote, with Carl Brinitzer, *German Versus Hun*, a book which explored German identities through writings from a wide range of authors.

[7] Each Kitchen Front script, although produced by the BBC, was approved by the Ministry of Food.

[8] The national reach of the BBC's output meant the regional offices were sources of local enquiry and input. It seems that, in Mrs Turnbull's case, she had contacted a regional office, who in turn had handed this to the central team in London.

The regular correspondence between the Ministry and the BBC shows the collaborative nature of their work on the Kitchen Front. The need to be as clear and accurate as possible for the listeners was paramount, and Eileen's letter shows her own attention to this, as she is wary of using the sheep's head recipe too far into the future when such an ingredient may not be easily obtainable.

In the next letter we have, from 8 April 1942, the close working relationship between the Ministry and the BBC is shown to be a cause of some confusion to the listeners, who were unclear whom to contact following a broadcast. In this letter, too, we can enjoy Eileen's chatty, colloquial writing style. She playfully refers to scripts by their food topic rather than writer, and shows her frustration with the rapid turnover of scripts, which still required extensive checking by the Ministry (for recipes, this was in terms of compliance with current rationing as well as in terms of nutritional value, aside from the need to test the recipes in the Ministry's kitchens).

> Ministry of Food (official letter)[9]
> 8 April 1942
> Dear Miss Rowntree,
> Herewith your noodles script. I see nothing against it. You have our macaroni script (Miss Buxhoeveden[10]) now, so you'll see the approach is quite different. Madame Kowalska[11] can't broadcast for us again for a couple of months anyway, and I think her speciality is eggless 'pasta'.[12]
> By the way, our Food Advice Division want to know whether they might have copies of the Wise Housekeeping[13] broadcasts. They constantly get enquiries that turn out to be based on your broadcasts and are difficult to understand without the scripts. The great public, of course, are quite unable to distinguish between Ministry of Food and B.B.C. talks on food—that is probably a bitter pill for you but has to be swallowed! Can you

---

[9] Reproduced courtesy of BBC Written Archives Centre, R51/285/2.

[10] A contributor to the Kitchen Front.

[11] A regular contributor to the Kitchen Front.

[12] Eileen's use of scare quotes for "pasta" here reflects the fact that eggs are usually a vital ingredient in the production of pasta. But, in wartime, fresh eggs were in short supply, hence the need for an eggless version.

[13] Wise Housekeeping was another wartime programme, broadcast later in the morning. This was a magazine programme for women, and dealt with all aspects of running a household in wartime.

arrange for the scripts to be sent over or is there some contra-regulation? They don't, of course, need them in advance and they would be properly appreciative.
Yours sincerely
[signed]
Emily Blair
Public Relations Division
P.S. I'm sorry about the gin and cocoa contretemps, but as you know I couldn't help it. From my point of view it may be useful as I've been trying for weeks to get Dr. Hill's script earlier. It never arrives until Tuesday, and is more difficult to get out than the others as it has to be passed by our doctors.[14] On the other hand Dr. Hill is, of course, our star turn—the one broadcaster whom everyone likes.

This sense of constant flux and no little rising panic continues in the following letter of 9 April. However, it also appears Miss Rowntree has come up with a workable solution in the form of a typed schedule that would be shared between the BBC and the Ministry.

Ministry of Food (official letterhead)[15]
9 April 1942
Dear Miss Rowntree,
Here is a schedule. Freddy Grisewood has now agreed to give the Dish of the Week a send-off as they say. Miss Park has agreed to her two revised dates. I have written to Mrs. Webb[16] cancelling her broadcast for April 27 and Mr. Westerby has done the same for Mrs. Buggins on the 20th. I am fairly sure neither of them will mind, and the only thing that is still disturbing me about the business is your end of it. I mean your sufferings. Seeing this typed schedule, I think it would help all of us if we had one like it for each month. One gets a clearer picture than the Ministry of Food's conception of a diary can give. Anyway, by one means or another I hope the crises will become less frequent.
Yours sincerely,
[signed]

---

[14] The Ministry of Food employed dieticians and medics to ensure the advice given to listeners was beneficial.

[15] Reproduced courtesy of BBC Written Archives Centre, R51/285/2.

[16] This is Mrs Arthur Webb, who had started broadcasting her own programme on the BBC, "Making the Most of a Wartime Larder", in September 1939. This was eventually replaced by the Kitchen Front, and Mrs Webb continued to contribute recipes.

Emily Blair
Public Relations Division

It seems to have become quite clear that typed letters were not quite the most efficient means of communication, and this was particularly the case by this point in the war, as paper shortages were being keenly felt. Even in the official letterhead paper of the Ministry we can see economies being made in the size of the paper. As the war progressed, the paper quality diminished and scraps of paper were employed for official letter writing at times. In the case of the BBC, many of their letters and memos actually appear on the backs of old radio scripts.

In Eileen's letter of 13 April, she arranges to see Miss Rowntree in person to discuss the programming over lunch.

Ministry of Food (official letterhead)[17]
13 April 1942
Dear Miss Rowntree,
Here at last is our list of suggestions for the Kitchen Front Pool. Now that Your Idea[18] has gone, the Pool principle ought to be quite workable. Of course we shall be putting up additions to the list, I expect, but we ought always to give reasonable notice. Indeed, unless it means a lot of extra work for you, I promise to submit new speakers' names to you as soon as we make our first contact with them. This will probably mean that you have the trouble of looking up the records, if any, of a certain number of people who in fact will never broadcast for us at all. But the alternative system, by which we would establish the suitability of a speaker from our point of view before referring the name to you, is difficult to operate without involving ourselves in moral obligations. What do you think?
It also occurred to me that "special" scripts—on this new Schedule the Friday and Saturday talks—might be sent across to you for a sort of preliminary viewing in their natural state before we have actually accepted them all. I'm not sure whether this would simplify or complicate our lives. I am in fact just beginning to see how this combined programme doesn't work. Could you have lunch with me one day next week—say Wednesday

---

[17] Reproduced courtesy of BBC Written Archives Centre, R51/285/2.

[18] This is not mentioned in any previous letters, but may have been something they discussed over lunch. Eileen's use of initial capitals gives this a sense of importance, but whatever Rowntree's plan for the recruitment and rotation of speakers was is lost to us.

or Thursday? There is a pub called Shelley's in Albermarle Street[19] which has large English meals and large tables on which we could spread the documentation and so clarify my mind.
Yours sincerely,
[signed]
Emily Blair
Public Relations Division.

The decision to meet over lunch must have led to a more regular arrangement, and certainly one that suited both Eileen and her BBC colleagues. However, at this stage at least, there are still letters which show a productive relationship that continued to be frantically busy as they worked as a team to come up with new and refreshing ideas for the Kitchen Front broadcasts.

One element of the broadcasts that appears to have been discussed over lunch is the inclusion of a wider range of regional accents. The BBC was, and still is, strongly associated with the Received Pronunciation (RP) accent of English; so much so that it is also known as BBC English. However, at the start of the war, the BBC had realised there was a need to broadcast voices beyond the authoritarian RP accent's regionless but class-bound significance. Early experiments using the popular Lancashire-born broadcaster Wilfred Pickles to read the news had met with huge resistance from listeners, who wrote in to the BBC complaining that they couldn't trust a news reader whose accent was not RP. However, for the more homely ethos of the Kitchen Front, which already had the long-standing inclusion of Mrs Buggins and her Cockney accent, regional accents were considered a very positive addition. In a letter to Eileen dated 14 April, Mrs Rowntree offers a new speaker, a Mrs Brook, who she describes as having "a strong Lancashire accent" and would "be a most refreshing speaker on the Kitchen Front".

In following up Eileen's letter of 13 April, Mrs Rowntree also sent a memo to her colleague, Miss Quigley, attaching Eileen's letter. She is more direct in highlighting the problems of working with the Ministry of Food, mostly pointing out the confusion that has arisen in terms of which agency should be issuing invitations to speakers. As the memo states, she is trying to set up a system "to safe-guard [...] against the Ministry's habit

---

[19] Shelley's is now called the King's Head. Topp reports that the large tables were still there on a recent visit.

of making overtures to speakers before we have had a chance of checking their broadcasting records".[20] In attaching Eileen's letter, she adds that she "finds her very easy to co-operate with, [as she] sees the problems on both side". The memo includes a list of possible additions to the Pool, but notes that this list excludes Ambrose Heath, as the Ministry "practically refuse to use him". Heath was a well-known journalist and food writer. He had embraced the wartime rationing system and was producing a range of cookery books, so he would seem to be a suitable contributor. It may be that there were unspoken reasons for his exclusion, perhaps personal animosity.

Eileen next wrote on 17 April, in response to the BBC's sending two scripts for approval (as per the system that was well-established by this point). Part of wartime rationing included a strict limit on how much fat could be purchased each week. As Eileen's letter indicates, the recipe-testing kitchen had used more fat than they should have, and Eileen volunteers that these were "delicious", but then the guilty pleasure of the treat is apologetically glossed over as being visible in greasy marks on the script. The letter is largely made up of a summary of the Ministry's notes on the script, again focusing on rationing and nutrition.

Ministry of Food (official letterhead)[21]
17 April 1942.
Dear Miss Rowntree,
Here are your two scripts. I am sorry they have been held up, but we have had that kind of week.
The Helen Burke one is quite all right. The other I must apologise for. The Kitchen made some of the recipes (the date flapjacks were delicious) and were a bit free with their fat apparently. You'll find it on the paper.[22]
Miss Macleod also made some pencil notes on this script. The points she wanted to make are:-

---

[20] Reproduced courtesy of BBC Written Archives Centre, R51/285/2. Miss Rowntree to Miss Quigley, 15 April 1942.

[21] Reproduced courtesy of BBC Written Archives Centre, R51/285/2.

[22] Even in her business correspondence, Eileen couldn't help but use her sense of humour.

1. (Page 1.) Steamed puddings are good for children.[23]—I expect you will rub this out.
2. (Page 2.) Sardines and the oily fishes are very valuable in children's diet.—This has two aspects. I don't think we have any rights, as it were, over your dietetics, but Miss Mcleod is right. On the other hand, please don't accept her amendment as it stands, because there aren't enough sardines for the people who already wish to buy them. My own suggestion is that the comparison should be omitted altogether. In fact both the fishes and the fruits are valuable, but in this script it doesn't seem necessary to mention the fishes. The sentence could run "Some of their points should be spent on raisins and dates and prunes"—or indeed it could be left out.
3. (Page 2.) Children should have their full cheese ration. This of course is off the point. On the other hand, if you and/or your speaker want to do a bit of good propaganda for the children, she could say that her scone mixture can be flavoured with grated cheese. It is a fact that people still think cheese is bad for children,[24] whereas (vide Dr. Hill[25]), they really ought to get their full ration and it's perfectly digestible if used grated. For your information, as they say,[26] the cheese ration is not fully taken up, which is surprising. I suppose a lot of people don't much like this cheese neat and don't both to dilute it.

To repeat myself, the only alternation we really would like is the omission of sardines—and I do apologise for the unmannerly treatment of your script.

Yours sincerely,
[signed]
Emily Blair
Public Relations Division.

---

[23] The wellbeing of children had long been a government priority. Throughout the twentieth century, prior to 1948, social-welfare legislation had built up a child's health system that pre-empted the NHS. During the war, this was particularly seen as the remit of the Ministry of Food, and this letter shows Eileen developing her own interest in this area, which would build into joining with Nell Heaton at talks about child nutrition around the country as the war progressed.

[24] Cheese is a valuable source of protein and, with wartime rations restricting meat, it became a vital component of diets.

[25] Dr Hill was the resident medical advisor in the Ministry, who also appears in Kitchen Front broadcasts.

[26] This interesting aside appears in this letter to ameliorate the potential bossiness that could be implied by "for your information".

The next letter, sent on 23 April 1942, appears to be in response to a letter from Miss Rowntree, following on from another lunch meeting (hinted at in Eileen's postscript mention of "table talk"). It seems the conversation had turned to an aspirational list of potential "voices" and talents. Eileen, with her excellent connections in the literary world, here lists some starry names of her own. Her link with Ethel Mannin is also hinted at being a personal one, as she offers to contact her to persuade her to join the Kitchen Front performance team.

> Ministry of Food (official letterhead)[27]
> 23 April 1942
> Dear Miss Rowntree,
> Thank you for your additions to the Kitchen Front pool. From my point of view, the more we have to pick from the better. I am particularly glad to see another man.
> I should like to have Naomi Jacob[28]—indeed I should like a small collection of women writers. Ethel Mannin[29] wrote to the Ministry offering to 'help'. She has a remarkable personal popularity among women and I think would be a draw for us. On the other hand she has told Lettice Cooper that she does not wish to speak. I might be able to persuade her, but before making that attempt I should like to know whether she would be acceptable to you. I could get others. Women who write, like women who act, often make rather a cult of cooking. But could you some time check up on Ethel Mannin?
> We are thinking of Cicely Courtneidge[30] to alternate with Mabel Constanduros when Mrs. Webb[31] finishes. Robert Westerby says that Jeanne de

---

[27] Reproduced courtesy of BBC Written Archives Centre, R51/285/2.

[28] Naomi Jacob was a novelist who came from the North East of England, as did Eileen. She was politically active, standing for parliament as a Labour candidate, and she also used her writing to tackle issues such as antisemitism and women's rights.

[29] Ethel Mannin was a popular novelist, travel writer and political activist. Like Eileen and Orwell, she supported the anti-fascists during the Spanish Civil War. Her early links with the British Labour party developed into greater sympathies for the Soviet Union in the late 1930s.

[30] Cicely Courtneidge (Dame Esmeralda Cicely Courtneidge) was an Australian-born actor who was well known for her roles in comedies on stage and in film. During the Second World War, she was actively engaged in fund raising for the troops.

[31] Mrs Arthur Webb.

Casalis[32], who was my first pick for this, was difficult to handle—and indeed we can't use her now until her most unfortunate broadcast the other night with Howard Marshall has been forgotten.
Yours sincerely,
[signed]
Emily Blair
Public Relations Division.
[handwritten postscript]
This might have been longer the [*unintelligible*] yesterday of course, but I'm sending it as continuation of some of the table talk. [signed] Emily B.

The meetings over lunch and over the phone appear to have been very productive, but leave little written trace for us. A memo from Miss Rowntree, dated 8 May 1942, shows evidence of conversations they had had. The memo relates to the proposed change to the running time of the Kitchen Front, suggesting it be longer than five minutes. Miss Rowntree offers a compromise that the programme could be extended by a minute or a minute and a half for the Ministry to use for special announcements (largely connected with changes in rationing), on an ad hoc basis. She writes, "Mrs Blair would, I know, be satisfied with a gentleman's agreement in which she was free to ask for an extra minute or minute and a half in these special cases". This suggestion would appear to have been accepted by both the BBC and the Ministry, as it is mentioned in other correspondence later on.

Another letter to Eileen from Miss Rowntree, dated 22 May 1942, highlights a different issue that they had discussed: the content of the Kitchen Front programmes. As Miss Rowntree's letter states, listeners had been writing in to complain about the imbalance of recipes to advice, with the latter being more in demand. This probably reflects a problem that had been building around recipes, where the lack of variety in ingredients meant that several recipes were repeated after a few weeks. In particular, Miss Rowntree suggests Dr Hill be put in charge of a new programme about vegetarianism, which again links to Eileen's letter of 17 April, where she highlights the difficulty of the supply of fish, but the nutritional value of cheese. Miss Rowntree offers to visit Eileen at the Ministry, and so we have no extant letter to follow this up.

[32] Jeanne de Casalis was born in Basutoland (currently Lesotho) and, after being educated in France, she moved to London, where she became a stage and film actor in the 1930s.

As we will see, with Eileen working with the BBC through her job at the Ministry of Food, and with Orwell also working at the BBC, together they were earning a reasonable, steady income for the first time in their married lives. They were also both enjoying rare periods of good health. In the spring of 1942, they had moved to a larger flat at 10a Mortimer Crescent, Kilburn, just round the corner from their previous flat. One of their first visitors was Orwell's cousin, Henry Dakin, who stayed for a few weeks in 1942. His recollection of Eileen provides us with a vivid picture of her:

> Eileen was one of the nicest and least dressy women that I have ever known. A great deal of the time she wore her black overcoat—it was rather chilly in the flat—and chain-smoked cigarettes, letting the ash fall off the end of her cigarette and down her coat [...] Her hair, whilst rather curly, seemed in perpetual need of a comb, but through it all came the Irish charm [...] her delightful smile and her apparent interest in whatever subject was the topic [...] Eileen didn't usually make the most of herself around the house but when going out for the evening she would sometimes dress up to the point where she became quite dazzling.[33]

This flat also came with a large garden, and soon Eileen and Orwell were busy recreating some of the self-sufficiency they had enjoyed at Wallington. In particular, their flock of hens meant that they were always able to procure fresh eggs, even when most people had been made to resort to the inadequate powdered-egg substitute. The more readily available supply of fresh produce and the larger flat meant that they were better able to invite friends and acquaintances for dinner and offer them a bed for the night. This was both practical and impractical. The couple had more fresh food than some people, but they still were subjected to rationing. When it came to offering a bed for the night, this was eminently sensible, given the on-going black-out and general shortage of public transport.

Eileen seems to have taken a couple of weeks off work to facilitate the move to the flat in Mortimer Crescent. She returned to work in mid-May 1942.

It seems Miss Rowntree took extended leave in July, as letters from both Eileen and Westerby are addressed to Winifred Holmes, who was

---

[33] This is reproduced from a note given to Topp personally by Henry Dakin.

covering for Rowntree. Holmes's letters to Eileen in July are largely connected with the inclusion of a new speaker, a Mr Moana, whose Moari dishes were proving problematic in terms of the unusual ingredients. Again, it is the accent of the presenter that is highlighted as being appealing.

Ministry of Food (official letterhead)[34]
22 July 1942.
Dear Mrs Holmes,
Here are next week's arrangements:-

Monday,	July 27.	alp. F. H. Grisewood—	Fruit preserving.
Tuesday	" 28.	Mabel Constanduros—	Mrs Buggins.
Wednesday	" 29.	alp. G. E. Oake[35]—	Bread waste.
Thursday	" 30.	Nell Heaton[36]—	Cooking Dictionary.
Friday	" 31.	Mrs Hobman—	Keeping Food Cool.
Saturday,	Aug. 1.	Janet Dunbar[37]—	Questions You Ask.

The following week belongs entirely to Mrs. Ingillson for her week's catering, which Miss Rowntree billed.
Yours sincerely
[signed]
Emily Blair
Public Relations Division.
[handwritten] Miss Rowntree does know about Mr Oake. He is Deputy Director of Public Relations here & asked to be put on air after his small son was given a rabbit to be fed on toast!

This letter of 22 July is interesting as it contains the first mention (on file) of Nell Heaton. Holmes's response to Eileen's letter, in a letter dated 23 July, gives us more information about Nell, as this extract shows.

---

[34] Reproduced courtesy of BBC Written Archives Centre, R51/285/2.

[35] Deputy Director of the Ministry of Food.

[36] Nell Heaton's name appears several times in the Kitchen Front files as she appeared as a panellist on several occasions. She became very well known as a cookery writer after the war.

[37] This may be the same Janet Dunbar who edited Prosper Montagne's *New Larousse Gastronomique*. It was first published in French in 1938.

> I have seen both Miss Roberts and Miss Heaton. I liked them both personally very much indeed—Miss Roberts particularly. I don't know who found her but she really is a find with a delightful voice, and personality, and willing to take a great deal of trouble. Miss Heaton is very nice, but I do still find her rather refined[38], and I am trying to get her out of it. I gave her a rehearsal at the microphone so that she might get over her nervousness of the mike and will be less formal and more herself.[39]

As we will see in Eileen's letters of 1945, Nell came to be a good personal friend of both Eileen and Orwell. She was five years older than Eileen but was also a Sunderland Church High Old Girl. Nell had left the school before Eileen arrived, but she would have kept up with the Old Girls' network set up by Miss Ironside through the school magazine, *The Chronicle*, which Eileen also subscribed to. Nell was independently wealthy, being the only daughter of a brewer from Sunderland who had sold up and settled into gentlemanly farming at the end of the First World War. Nell never married, but in the interwar years she seems to have seized the opportunities available to a wealthy single woman and travelled extensively. She had a particular love of Central America, but this was less as a passive tourist than as a woman with the sort of enquiring mind that Miss Ironside had advocated. Like Eileen, Nell engaged in some freelance journalism when she returned to England in the late 1930s, and at the start of the Second World War she set up and ran one of the first "Cooking for Victory" advisory bureaux in Harrods department store. Through this, she ended up working for the Ministry of Food and, through her contact with Eileen, she was regularly featured as a panel member of the Kitchen Front from 1942 onwards. She also continued her food advisory work, giving talks and demonstrations in towns and villages across the country. A particular specialty was in feeding young children on the ration system, and one of her first published books—*Feeding Under Fives* (1946)—covers this, and links with the concern the Ministry and BBC had for child nutrition at this time.

Nell appears to have been popular as a broadcaster on the Kitchen Front, despite Holmes's initial concerns about the potential to alienate listeners through her "refined" accent. In a letter from Westerby to

---

[38] To refer to someone's voice as "refined" is generally to see it as being unfavourably posh, often with too-careful enunciation that sounds unnatural.

[39] Reproduced courtesy of BBC Written Archives Centre, R51/285/2.

Holmes on 23 July 1942, he requests that the BBC send mail addressed to Kitchen Front speakers over to the Ministry for them to pass on to the speakers. This process was intended to give the Ministry a better idea of the popularity of speakers. He focuses particularly on Nell Heaton:

> I gathered, during a conversation with Miss Heaton, that you had had some fan mail in reply to her talks. If this is the case we would be most interested to see it here.
> Some time ago Miss Rowntree made an unofficial arrangement[40] with Mrs. Blair to the effect that we should see personal mail and forward it to the speaker, but this arrangement never came into effect.[41]

This appears to have been a very frenetic period of letter writing between the Ministry and the BBC, as Mrs Holmes took over from Miss Rowntree and new speakers were being recruited. The next letter from Eileen continues this discussion:

> Ministry of Food (official letterhead)[42]
> 24 July 1942.
> Dear Mrs. Holmes,
> I enclose a script for Wednesday—written by our Deputy Director, G. E. Oake who is going to broadcast it. The script is rather short, but I have been warned that there should be an announcement on Wednesday arising out of the weekly Press Conference, which happens on Tuesday. Something about price lists! I hope the Announcer will be able to read this[43], because it doesn't seem to hitch on very well to Mr. Oake's cry from the heart.
> I'm also enclosing Mrs. Hobman's script for Friday. She is coming up to town on Thursday, arriving about midday, and I have asked her to make an appointment with you for a rehearsal. She is coming to see us anyway—just before lunch I think.
> By the way, Nell Heaton was delighted with her run-through at the microphone and I think it was an awfully good idea. My wireless is still not

---

[40] Holmes's response, dated 24 July, confirms the forwarding of Nell's letters to the Ministry, but also offers a reason why there might not be as much personal mail arriving. She suggests that this is because the cost of postage has increased markedly, and also people might be too busy to send personal letters of this nature.

[41] Reproduced courtesy of BBC Written Archives Centre, R51/285/2.

[42] Reproduced courtesy of BBC Written Archives Centre, R51/285/2.

[43] This shows that the system that Eileen and Miss Rowntree had put in place in May was working well.

connected, but I hear she was much better this week. Her fan-mail was produced by Harrods devotees[44], but they certainly sound pleased which is something.
Yours sincerely,
[signed]
Emily Blair
Public Relations Division.

By 30 July, Miss Rowntree was back at her desk. She apologises for the confusions and queries from Mrs Holmes during her absence, and ends her letter to Eileen, "I hope we shall continue to meet from time to time"[45]. Holmes, however, was still communicating with Eileen. In a letter of 31 July to Eileen, she raises a very difficult issue that had arisen owing to a lack of communication between the Ministry and the BBC.

> Mr. Geoffrey Smith rang up yesterday to ask whether we were going to get Mrs. Krebs to speak about edible fungi. Mrs. Krebs came to see me a few weeks ago and asked me whether she could give some talks on the Kitchen Front on this subject. I told her that our policy was not to mention this subject if possible, as it was a very dangerous one and that unless you were publishing something in pamphlet form to which it could be referred, I would rather not handle such a talk. Since then, Dr. Hill introduced the subject into his latest script and as it was too late to make any alterations we had to let it go through, though very reluctantly. Since the broadcast by Dr. Hill, two letters have come in from people who listened to the talk and say they were poisoned by eating the fungi he recommended. They both had to go to hospital. This, I think, proves our case. If you are running another campaign to get people in this country to eat different kinds of fungi from the ordinary mushroom and were publishing something on the subject, we should be glad to have talks on the subject, but without illustrations we know the danger of speaking of such things on air. I am sure that you will agree about this. As soon as I hear from you I will write to Mr. Geoffrey Smith.[46]

---

[44] It seems the fan mail was not from a very wide range of people, but, as Eileen points out, it has come from a particularly salubrious clientele who were already familiar with Nell's work through her food demonstrations at Harrods.

[45] Reproduced courtesy of BBC Written Archives Centre, R51/285/2.

[46] Reproduced courtesy of BBC Written Archives Centre, R51/285/2.

As this letter shows, Eileen was the point of contact for all manner of queries. Holmes's letter shows the difficulties faced when one broadcast demanded input from two different organisations with two different agendas. In this case, even the esteemed medical advice of Dr Hill came into question. In using the second person pronoun "you" throughout the letter, Holmes is holding Eileen directly accountable for the subsequent fallout from the lack of communication. At no point does she suggest that this "you" could be the Ministry.

By August of that year, Jean Rowntree had been replaced permanently by Winifred Holmes as the BBC producer for the Kitchen Front. Rowntree wrote to her head of department that Holmes should ensure that the dynamic between the BBC and the Ministry of Food be made absolutely clear from the start of her role, whilst also writing to Eileen in the hope that they could still meet socially.

The next letter, from 4 August, does not address Holmes's concerns in the letter of 31 July. We might begin to explain this by the move to more in-person, informal meetings when Eileen was dealing with the Kitchen Front colleagues, or else to more frequent telephone calls.

> Ministry of Food (official letterhead)[47]
> 4 August 1942.
> Dear Mrs. Holmes,
> So far as Mr. Barratt is concerned, I think you have dealt with him very nicely. Of course we couldn't ever use this script or, I should say, any from him because he always finds the answer in a tin can.
> As for Mrs. Thorne, she may of course be the answer to all our prayers—but I have no confidence in people who feel sure that we should find them useful. Do you want to follow her up?
> Yours sincerely,
> [signed]
> Emily Blair
> Public Relations Division.

Eileen's assertion in this letter that she doubts the potential usefulness of Mrs Thorne simply on the basis of this would-be participant having volunteered herself is at odds with her sentiments about Ethel Mannin

---

[47] Reproduced courtesy of BBC Written Archives Centre, R51/285/2.

in her letter of 23 April. Whether she felt other participants had let her down in the intervening months is not clear.

Eileen's next letter, dated 7 August, shows the diligence she exhibited in her liaison role.

> Ministry of Food (official letterhead)[48]
> 7 August 1942.
> Dear Mrs. Holmes,
> I gather you don't want Mrs. Jungman much, but we might as well decide about her now.
> She has virtues—the recipes when tried did turn out as she implied they should. They are very economical and practical and, given that new potatoes are used in the savoury dish, fit the supply position well. The jelly was made here with apple and I think would be very popular with children[49]. On the other hand, neither dish seems to me to belong to Foreign Flavours[50], and there is no other hold for the script. I think the decision really rests on Mrs. Jungman's power to put herself across as a personality—and you have the dope on that.
> Yours sincerely,
> [signed]
> Emily Blair
> Public Relations Division

In Holmes's response, on 12 August, she explains that Mrs Jungmann is "ineradicably" not a good broadcaster, but she would be willing to have "one not very well presented broadcast" if Eileen felt strongly about a specific recipe. On the other hand, the poor fit of the recipe into the current themed schedule might offer a way of putting her off. At the end, Holmes finishes, "I am afraid I am sending the baby back to you". There are no further mentions of Mrs Jungmann until 23 November, when she is mentioned as having submitted another script, but it is rejected by both Eileen and the BBC, so we might assume that she was not quite "put off" by Eileen.

The next letter we have from Eileen is dated 19 August, and it seems to be in response to a letter from a would-be contributor sent to the BBC about one episode of the Kitchen Front, the letter itself lost. However,

---

[48] Reproduced courtesy of BBC Written Archives Centre, R51/285/2.

[49] Again, Eileen is acutely aware of the dietary needs of children.

[50] This was a regular Kitchen Front feature.

this does show the sort of work that Eileen was required to carry out, beyond programming and scheduling (Fig. 8.1).

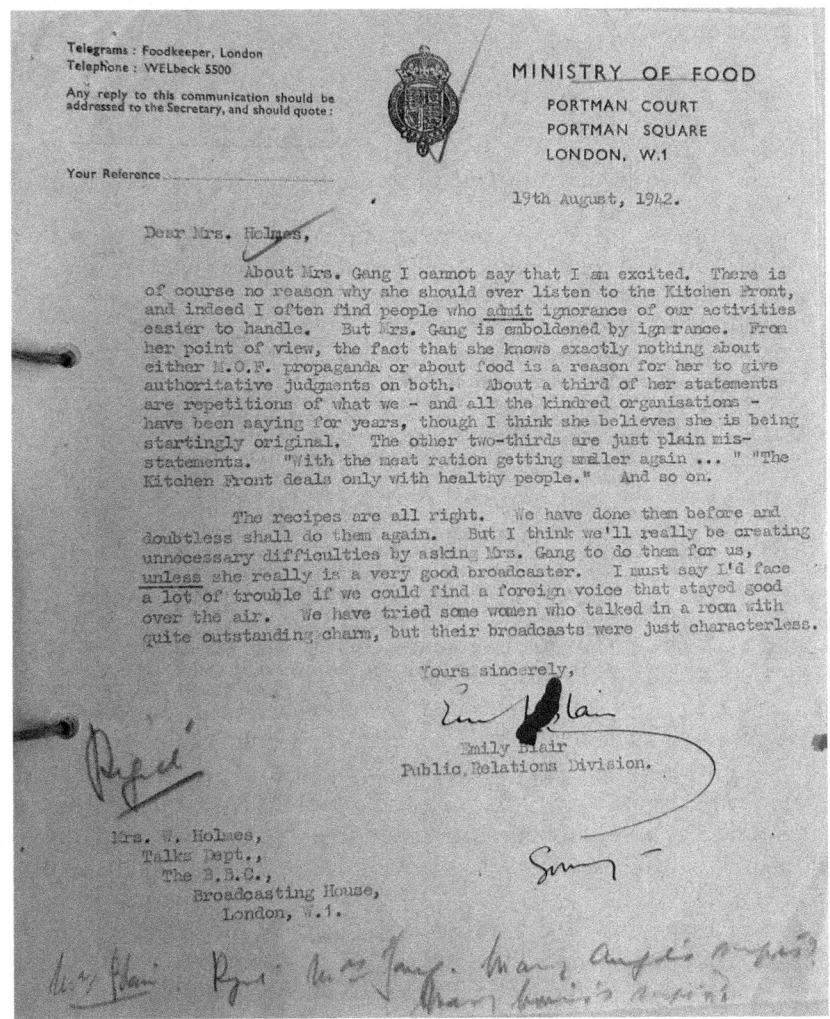

Fig. 8.1 Ministry of food letter from Eileen Blair, signed "Emily". Dated 19 August 1942. BBC written archives centre, R51/285/2

Ministry of Food (official letterhead)[51]
19 August 1942.
Dear Mrs. Holmes,
About Mrs. Gang I cannot say I am excited. There is of course no reason why she should ever listen to the Kitchen Front, and indeed I often find people who admit ignorance of our activities easier to handle. But Mrs. Gang is emboldened by ignorance. From her point of view, the fact that she knows exactly nothing about either M.O.F. propaganda or about food is a reason for her to give authoritative judgments on both. About a third of her statements are repetitions of what we—and all the kindred organisations—have been saying for years, though I think she believes she is being startlingly original. The other two-thirds are just plain misstatements. "With the meat ration getting smaller again…" "The Kitchen Front deals only with healthy people." And so on.[52]
The recipes are all right[53]. We have done them before and doubtless shall do them again. But I think we'll really be creating unnecessary difficulties by asking Mrs. Gang to do them for us, unless she really is a very good broadcaster. I must say I'd face a lot of trouble if we could find a foreign voice that stayed good over the air[54]. We have tried some women who talked in a room with quite outstanding charm, but their broadcasts were just characterless[55].
Yours sincerely,
[signed—ink splat over BLAIR][56]
Emily Blair
Public Relations Division.
[handwritten with arrow to ink splat] Sorry

---

[51] Reproduced courtesy of BBC Written Archives Centre, R51/285/2.

[52] Eileen's irritation is clear in this opening paragraph.

[53] Eileen's enthusiasm for the recipes is decidedly luke-warm, but she does not dismiss them without consideration.

[54] Eileen's meaning here is unclear. It may be a typing mistake with an omitting negation, such as "a lot less trouble" as there was a perennial problem of finding people who made for good radio, and the following sentence would appear to follow on from that.

[55] Mrs Gang's redeeming feature seems to be her "foreign voice". Many of the letters from the BBC to Eileen show a keen awareness of diversity in voices, and in particular the inclusion of refugees' voices and recipes.

[56] This letter is the only one on file that contains an ink splat, and that it comes at the end of the letter of pent-up frustration is perhaps not coincidental. Eileen's reaction to this is to apologise.

This is the only letter on file where there is an ink splat, and perhaps is reflecting the haste with which Eileen signed the letter, as well as its exasperated tone. Any notion that she was being bad-tempered is alleviated by the handwritten apology alongside the ink splat, showing she is aware that such a feature could be construed as being from a surly writer.

In a letter of 6 August from Westerby to Holmes, he starts by saying that Eileen has asked him to write. In the letter, he repeats the earlier arrangement for selecting speakers as being firstly the job of the Ministry, who will check that there is no on-paper objection to their participation, and then would request they prepare a brief which the Ministry would vet before passing on to the BBC. However, as we can see, the workload Eileen was attempting to manage was extremely high. On 18 August, Westerby wrote again to Holmes, but this time asking for a pause in soliciting contributions as "we are still absolutely snowed under". He finishes his letter:

> I hope you agree. But if you don't, a glimpse at the harassed and inundated Mrs. Blair would soften your stony heart—even if the prospect of the same emotions in myself might not do so.

Holmes responded to this letter, more or less pointing out to Westerby that it is the fault of the Ministry for setting up this system in the first place. However, she finishes:

> Certainly, I should be moved to tears if I saw Mrs. Blair snowed under with material—I will do my best to prevent that happening. She looked far from well when we lunched together on Monday.[57]

It would seem that Eileen was now meeting Winifred Holmes for lunch, as well as continuing her longer-standing engagement with Miss Rowntree.

The hectic round of selecting and approving speakers and recipes continued unabated. In her letter of 21 August, Eileen again diligently offers reasons for her decisions, and suitable flexibility within those decisions.

---

[57] Reproduced courtesy of BBC Written Archives Centre, R51/285/2.

Ministry of Food (official letterhead)[58]
21 August 1942.
Dear Mrs. Holmes,
Mrs. Norris. We think she's very good too. But where are we to put her? I think she might have a couple of Thursdays, but that wouldn't be till October by the look of things. By the way, as an administrative point, she ought to be put on the panel don't you think?
Mary Angel. I greatly fear these scripts were just forgotten. Now Robert[59] "definitely doesn't like any part of" Rations for one or Saving Ways. My Trouble[60] today is that I definitely don't like any part of anything whatever. But Treating the Troops is a good idea. I'm sending all the scripts across as I gather you haven't seen them. I can't write to Mrs. Angel myself as I haven't her address, and anyway you seem committed to a letter, but the position seems to be that we should like a Treating the Troops if she would be prepared to alter the script a good deal to accord with a changed supply position[61]. We must not in effect tell everyone to bake bread because of fuel. It is even doubtful whether we should advise large sandwich meals because of the bread position. Unrationed 'process' cheese is out, so is chocolate, and I should say sultanas. Salad on the other hand, chopped cabbage and parsley as well as lettuce, should be emphasized. But a very useful story could be told about potatoes and the increased cheese ration—potato scones, potato and cheese pastry and so on to supplement the sandwiches. They take some fat but very little. Also potato pasties can be made with any kind of filling and are really very good[62]. I don't know how difficult it would be for Mrs. Angel to come and see us, but I'm enclosing a sheet of potato recipes that you could send her if you liked as a preliminary. We seem to be giving her a good deal of work for 5 guineas, but after all she needn't do it if she doesn't want to.
Yours sincerely,
[signed]
Emily Blair
Public Relations Division.

---

[58] Reproduced courtesy of BBC Written Archives Centre, R51/285/2.

[59] This would be Robert Westerby, Eileen's colleague at the Ministry.

[60] Eileen's use of an initial capital here implies that she is aware of her frustration and is trying to make light of it.

[61] As usual, the content of the Kitchen Front was liable to changes and directions made because of wider forces at play, such as fuel shortages and flour shortages.

[62] Eileen's comment indicates that she has sampled these recipes, created in the Ministry's own recipe-testing kitchens.

Several other letters appear in the files, addressed to Eileen from Holmes, but there are no other replies from her, again indicating personal spoken communication may have been used. However, at the end of August, there is a long letter in response to a listener who had written a strongly worded complaint about one broadcast of the Kitchen Front, and this prompted Eileen to respond in a lengthy, itemised letter to Holmes. It seems that the broadcast actually occurred in the middle of the month, as indicated by a letter to Eileen from Miss Rowntree, dated 15 August, in which she mentions "enormous post" generated by Mrs Ingillson's broadcast, commenting that "it looks as though that sort of thing is what people want". She did, however, enclose Miss Michael's long letter criticising the programme. Mrs Ingillson was a regular contributor to the Kitchen Front and had been given a whole week's programming to explore menus using current rations. Eileen took two weeks to respond, possibly because, in addition to her usual workload, she had had to seek out the scripts that were in question.

Ministry of Food (official letterhead)[63]
31 August 1942.
Dear Mrs. Holmes,
I enclose the annotations on Mrs. Ingillson's week's catering that you gave me the other day. I'll deal with the points one by one.[64]

1. The catering was not for a dated week—the whole text is in the past tense[65]. The extra sugar ration applied to two weeks only in the year. [Handwritten amendment to "dated week"—"day before yesterday".]
2. 1 lb. of cheese was bought on Monday and one on Wednesday. This is quite reasonable to me.
3. The consumption of bread is below average—quite deliberately as the average consumption of bread must be decreased. In this connection:

   a. Bread is not meant to be eaten when potatoes are served, as they generally are for breakfast. And hence—

---

[63] Reproduced courtesy of BBC Written Archives Centre, R51/285/2.

[64] Eileen's annoyance with the listener's comments is clear from her rigorous refutation of most of the points raised.

[65] It seems Eileen's background in English Language is coming in useful at last.

b. Tuesday's potatoes would certainly be inadequate, and another 6 lbs. were bought on Wednesday.

4. I don't know why Miss Michael decided that the spending of points was indiscriminate. It wasn't. I agree that an analysis of the money-point-allocation would be useful, but it would mean at least one more script. We have done a certain amount on the subject of course.
5. Each lettuce supplied one salad for four and one lot of sandwiches. People who liked lettuce could almost certainly eat more—but then the salad in each case was a mixed salad.
6. See 3.
7. Old potatoes are still on sale, and the new ones in the shops generally mash quite easily.
8. See 3.
9. See 3.
10. Tea is not budgeted for[66]. People in this very low income level don't generally have afternoon tea—as a set meal anyway.
11. This series was primarily an analysis of spending money. If we had made no provision for purchases such as dried egg, which ought to be made but cannot be made every week that would have been reasonable ground for criticism.
12. There seems to be some conflict between this criticism and No. 3. Perhaps more allowance should be made for the extremely high nutritive values of herrings and cheese.

Whatever the defects of these menus, Mrs. Ingillson cannot be blamed. She merely read the scripts aloud. The material was based on actual calculating done by one of our staff, to some extent directed by the dieticians, who checked and approved the menus from a nutritional point of view[67]. It is claimed that the money—admittedly a very small sum—was spent as advantageously as possible. Such a claim must of course be open to argument, but we had for it the best authority available in this country. The

---

[66] This relates to afternoon tea, a traditional middle-class light meal, rather than the beverage. In working-class homes, "tea" may be the main meal of the day, but, as Eileen is implying, the main meal is already set in the broadcast menu, and thus afternoon tea would be an additional meal.

[67] Again, we can see that there were many hands at work in producing the Kitchen Front scripts.

general reaction was extremely good and we have had more [than] 750 requests for the shopping and menus chart[68].

In spite of an apparent lack of meekness perhaps in my reply[69], we are grateful to Miss Michael for such detailed criticism, and we should like more (on scripts generally I mean, not only on this series). With vivid recollection of the calculations we did here[70], I appreciate the trouble she took—and I am not surprised she failed to register some of the purchases. Here is a copy of the shopping and menu chart, which will make it a bit easier for her to follow our replies, if she wants to do so.

Yours sincerely,
[signed]
Emily Blair
Public Relations Division.

Rather surprisingly, the next letter, dated 2 September, comes signed by Eileen's secretary, Mrs Search.

Ministry of Food (official letterhead)[71]
2 September 1942.
Dear Mrs. Holmes,
Mrs. Blair, who is away on sick leave, asked me to send you a copy of this little book[72] which has just been published.
Yours sincerely,
[signed] K. A. Search
For Emily Blair
Public Relations Division

The key information about Eileen being on sick leave might suggest a sudden illness, but there is also a handwritten letter from Eileen to Mrs

---

[68] The implication here is that there was a very positive and interested response to the broadcast.

[69] Eileen is recognising that there is a somewhat exasperated tone to her defence.

[70] Again, we can see Eileen has been hands-on in producing the script, with great care and attention to detail.

[71] Reproduced courtesy of BBC Written Archives Centre, R51/285/2.

[72] This was probably the Ministry's own publication of recipes, called *The Kitchen Front*, which carried a cover illustration by the well-known illustrator, Forgrasse. The book cover carried the text: "122 wartime recipes broadcast by Frederick Grisewood, Mabel Constanduros and others, specially selected by the Ministry of Food". It was priced at 6d.

Holmes dated on the same day. In it, she returns to the Miss Michael letter, but also gives us a bit more information about her illness, showing that this is something that is not sudden but has been planned.

> Ministry of Food (official letterhead)[73]
> [Handwritten—2 September 1942]
> Dear Mrs Holmes,
> This particular recipe is not approved by M.A.F.[74] Most of our plans are no good—Mrs Kowalski says why one kind will do, whilst M.A.F. didn't like saying even that. But if you would like to give the author a keen glance for the future, good luck to placing. We have one for coleslaw.
> I hope you got my long long letter written at[75] Miss Michael. I genuinely would like contact, but in this case the criticisms were really frivolous excepting bread. I could see no motive making that except a very natural desire to be rude now and then.
> They were all vetted by dieticians who spoke more strictly than I but to the same effect. I excepted the bread on second thoughts because I agree the alternative seems small. It depressed me. But doubtless there are more depressing necessities before we serve the last potato with a pre-war Christmas tree ornament on top to make a Victory Dinner[76].
> I am now starting my sick leave. Such is the power of suggestion that I feel ill! I hope however that the really necessary things are done.[77] I can't get this typed so it comes unofficially—I meant to ring you up but people kept coming.
> Yours
> Emily Blair

Eileen's "sick leave" is curious, as it is not mentioned in any of the other letters by Orwell or in any other documentation for this period. However,

---

[73] Reproduced courtesy of BBC Written Archives Centre, R51/285/2.

[74] This is the abbreviation for the longer title of the department Eileen worked for: the Ministry of Agriculture and Food.

[75] Eileen's use of "at" rather than "to" is interesting, and again highlights her frustration with this particular listener's complaint.

[76] Eileen's natural optimism shines through. Immediately after a gloomy discussion of the privations of wartime, she turns this into a jolly image of a decorated potato to celebrate Victory. Given the war was to last three more years, this is very premature.

[77] This confession deserves more consideration. Eileen plays on the concept of "sick leave" and implies she is not feeling unwell by saying that it is just the name of the leave that is making her feel ill.

as Topp has suggested, this might be an "illness" that is less to do with diseases and viruses and more to do with Eileen's and Orwell's hopes of becoming parents, which might have been dashed by a miscarriage. Eileen attempts to make light of her illness, implying that she doesn't feel unwell, which would fit with Topp's hypothesis. However, hospitalisation would be required to carry out a dilation and curettage procedure that would have been the routine after-care in such cases. That would again fit with her glossing of the unpleasantness of the procedure as "the really necessary things". Holmes wrote back to Eileen on 3 September and adds weight to this hypothesis:

> I am so sorry not to have been able to see you before you went into hospital, but I didn't know until yesterday that you had gone. I am sure you will be glad to relax for a bit, and hope you will feel very much better after the first discomfort is over.

It would seem that Eileen and Holmes were sharing confidences, as well as ideas for the Kitchen Front, which shows how close a friendship had developed over their time working together.

It is not clear when Eileen returned to work, but the next letter from her on file is dated 13 November, and, although signed by someone else, it is sent from Eileen and shows that she has settled back into the routine work of the Ministry.

> Ministry of Food (official letterhead)[78]
> 13 November 1942
> Dear Miss Rowntree,
> This comment comes a bit late, but the script has been going the Ministerial rounds. You may remember that the script came at a time of crises and we got it after the broadcast. Mrs. Rowlands rang up on the Tuesday morning about it, but I wasn't available.
> You'll see the remarks in pencil. Nothing to be done! We've had no comeback as a matter of fact, and I hope you haven't.
> Yours,
> p.p. E. Blair

Another letter, the following day, is not printed on Ministry letterhead and appears to be on a scrap of paper. This perhaps reflects the problem

---

[78] Reproduced courtesy of BBC Written Archives Centre, R51/285/2.

of obtaining paper during the war, and a random piece of paper has served for this letter.

> 14 Nov 1942[79]
> Dear Mrs. Holmes,
> Thank you for Mrs. Johnson and Mrs. Hewitt. I am delighted about Mrs. Johnson—I was afraid she was too difficult geographically[80]. We should certainly like to use her, and the potato recipe she gave in her letter was very good. I should like to discuss the details of her script though—and in any case of course we shall have to find a place for her in the schedule.
> I gather you aren't a Hewitt enthusiast, but I don't know her earlier history. The recipes I think are rather good, but I've sent them up to the Kitchen for investigation.
> Yours,
> [signed Emily B]

Another scrap of paper is used for the following letter from Eileen to Holmes.

> Mrs. Holmes.[81]
> I suppose the attached letter arises out of a misunderstanding on the writer's part. Naturally we are not supplying Ambrose Heath's[82] book or any publication except our own. It does appear, however, that the Ministry of Food must have been mentioned, and in that case we should have seen the broadcast[83]. Indeed I think we ought to see any broadcast on current cookery books, don't you? Can you trace this one?
> 21.xi.42.

---

[79] Reproduced courtesy of BBC Written Archives Centre, R51/285/2.

[80] As noted earlier in the year, the Ministry and the BBC were keen to engage a wider range of voices, and contributions were welcomed from regional offices of the BBC.

[81] Reproduced courtesy of BBC Written Archives Centre, R51/285/2.

[82] As well as the Ministry's own Kitchen Front cookery book, another regular contributor, Ambrose Heath, had produced a cookery book in 1941 called *Kitchen Front Recipes and Hints: extracts from the first seven months' early morning broadcasts*. He wrote several other cookery books in the course of the war, which he published commercially rather than through the Ministry.

[83] It seems Eileen is being sent listener queries about programmes other than the Kitchen Front, and in an attempt to be helpful has asked the BBC to let the Ministry know of any other programmes that mention cookery books so that she can be prepared for such queries in the future.

[signed Emily Blair]

The on-going paper shortage appears to have led to Eileen's next letter again being typed on a scrap of paper.

Mrs. Holmes[84]
I have another script in from Mrs. Jungman [sic]. Am I right in thinking that she's definitely off the panel?[85]
Mr. Ranson was not here on Friday but I sent him a message and it was much appreciated. He will be telephoning you some time.
Bruce Blunt's[86] scripts are said to be coming in by hand this morning, but it begins to look as though you won't see them until Wednesday. We have been expecting them every hour for the last week or so. I gather, however, that he is producing all three.
Mrs. Martin's scripts will be over this afternoon or first thing tomorrow. Mrs. Hodge (the Devonshire Housewife)[87] is going to let me have her material by the end of this week. She is still a bit hesitant and wants to get a friend of hers who is a schoolmistress to help her to say things right, but I think all will be well. The script ought to be ready more than a fortnight in advance.
23.xi.42
[signed Emily B]

By early December, it seems the Ministry letterhead supply had been renewed. Eileen's letter of 8 December is typed on this.

Ministry of Food (official letterhead)[88]
8 December 1942
Dear Mrs. Holmes,

---

[84] Reproduced courtesy of BBC Written Archives Centre, R51/285/2.

[85] Holmes responded on 25 November that Mrs Jungmann "is definitely off the panel as a broadcaster", but with no extra information.

[86] Bruce Blunt was a well-known poet, journalist and wine expert. It is likely that it is in the latter guise of bon viveur that he was appearing on the Kitchen Front.

[87] Mrs Hodge, with her title of "Devonshire Housewife", would be one of the regional amateur cooks who appeared on the Kitchen Front at various times. Her lack of broadcasting experience here is being framed by Eileen as not a matter for concern, owing to Mrs Hodge's consultation with a more literary friend.

[88] Reproduced courtesy of BBC Written Archives Centre, R51/285/2.

I enclose a copy of Dorothy Taylor's[89] Yorkshire Cake script for Thursday week. I hope I understand correctly that you are now doing the typing in quintuplet[90]. This is the only really comforting news I have had since Mrs. Search[91] got 'flu.
Yours sincerely,
[signed Emily Blair]
Emily Blair
Public Relations Division

A second letter, dated 8 December, is more detailed about future broadcasting schedules.

Ministry of Food (official letterhead)[92]
8 December 1942
Dear Mrs. Holmes,
You will remember that it was decided that Mary Ferguson should do a short series on the Kitchen Front on shopping schemes etc. At the time it was vaguely taken for granted that her dates would be at the beginning of 1943. As the schedule has worked out a convenient time would be Mondays beginning Monday December 28—the date on which my schedule had a pencil "Don't Do It" suggestion. The Don't Do It series, if it occurs, can certainly do with more consideration. We postponed Mary Ferguson partly so that she should not coincide with the Bruce Blunt series, but that will have been forgotten, I should think and rather hope, by the 28th.
Mrs. Arthur Webb, whose series would start on Tuesday, December 29, is coming to see us on Thursday which ought to give us plenty of time.
If you agree with the Mary Ferguson date and if your Franco-Italian reporters are O.K., the schedule for the week beginning December 29 is tied up—like this:

---

[89] This may be Dorothy Cottingham Taylor, who was head of the Good Housekeeping Institute and then, from 1940, wrote for the upmarket magazine, *Homes and Gardens*. She gave public lectures on wartime food management.

[90] This would be quite an achievement in a manual typewriter. Normally, a maximum of three copies would be made, as the greater the number of copies, the lower the quality of the impression through the carbon paper, and thus the fifth copy would the one least legible in this case. However, with wartime staffing shortages, it seems Eileen is grateful for any help.

[91] Mrs Search was Eileen's secretary, and this is of course a tongue in cheek remark.

[92] Reproduced courtesy of BBC Written Archives Centre, R51/285/2.

Monday,	December	28—	Mary Ferguson
Tuesday	"	29—	Mrs. Arthur Webb
Wednesday	"	30—	Dr. Stephen Taylor
Thursday	"	31—	Your Idea—F.H.G.[93]
Friday	January	1—	Franco-Italian dialogue
Saturday	"	2—	A Cook from Croydon [handwritten] Mrs. Brown

The following week is almost filled automatically, with Mary Ferguson on Monday, Mrs. Buggins on Tuesday, Dr. Hill on Wednesday and Your Idea on Thursday. For Something New I have a couple of very good potato recipes from Berthe Grossbard[94] which will then have been waiting a long time. Would you feel strong enough to cope with her by then? We shall have had a long rest from the Central European[95]. And for Saturday, January 9, we more or less decided the other day on Mrs. Johnson, whose material can be through here by the end of the week.

Are there any points at issue? I am now rather hopelessly busy. Mrs Search's flu has turned into nervous disability, which I suppose may last for weeks, and my own flu has turned into a daily low fever and a nightly high one which I suppose will last as long[96]. It makes me slow and single-minded— I think very hard about how to copy the recipe for Christmas pudding[97]. So if more adult[98] thinking can be postponed I shall be rather glad.

Yours,

[signed] Emily Blair

Eileen had been off work several times, and her health was increasingly precarious. Lettice Cooper judged that "Eileen needed a good deal of care and George was incapable of giving it" (Coppard and Crick 1984, p. 165). Eileen, on the other hand, had long thought it more important

---

[93] An abbreviation for Freddy Grisewood's name.

[94] See note for letter of 20 March 1942.

[95] Cryptically, this could be Berthe or one of the many other European refugees that were engaged by the BBC at this time.

[96] Eileen makes light of her own illness, using the juxtaposition of contrasts high and low, day and night.

[97] Christmas pudding recipes are notoriously complicated, so Eileen's difficulty with this is not surprising.

[98] In likening her state of health as being less than adult, Eileen hints at weakness and befuddlement that come from having a flu infection.

that Orwell be the central focus for care, and, even as her own health deteriorated, she did not sway from that view.

The next letter, dated 10 December, returns to the use of scrap paper. It shows Eileen's careful editing of the radio scripts very clearly, and we can see how her years of editing her husband's and her brother's work have become useful.

[handwritten date] December 10[99]
Mrs. Holmes.
I enclose Freddie's[100] Monday script (shorter this time), and Mabel Constanduros for Tuesday and Ruth Drew[101] for Friday.
Mrs. Buggins[102] had just come in, and I find rather to my horror that one of her recipes is very like one of Ruth Drew's. Apple and potato. I don't however think this matters. They sound a good deal more different than they are, and Ruth Drew's has its own significance as part of a three-dish plan. I should imagine that the people who actually write down the Buggins recipes are not the same people who write down the Friday recipes either. I am rather unwilling to cut Ruth Drew's (the cut would the fourth paragraph) because it is a very good idea to prepare in one go a potato-apple puree for three quite different purposes. Unfortunately Ruth Drew had just left the office when I made this discovery so I haven't been able to break the news to her. I had wondered about the length of the script, as you will see from her letter enclosed. I see the jettisoning of the cheese parcels, if it has to be done, will necessitate a change in the first sentence of paragraph 2, but nothing fundamental. These are most excellent recipes from our point of view—we have no other speaker (except Mabel Constanduros perhaps) who has this sort of instinctive feeling for the nuances of our policy.
[signed] Emily B.
Savonius Billing. I don't know whether you've given her a title. If you want to, you may remember her own title is "Some Christmas Stuffings".

---

[99] Reproduced courtesy of BBC Written Archives Centre, R51/285/2.

[100] In this letter, the variant spelling of Freddy Grisewood's name is used. This may have been the choice of the person who typed this note rather than Eileen herself, as she always used the same spelling as Freddy himself employed.

[101] Ruth Drew was already an established broadcaster. She went on to be joint presenter of the long-running BBC Radio news show, Today, when it was first broadcast in 1959, co-presenting with Jack De Manio. She produced books on household hints during the war.

[102] This would be the script, rather than character.

The script contains three but it is longish and one of the three is not too popular anyway, so in the end she may well do two only, in which case I don't much like the some. Can you think of a good headline? I can't.

A memo in the BBC Written Archives file for the Kitchen Front at this time shows the collaboration between the BBC and the Ministry needing further clarification. Holmes writes that the speakers are now to be principally invited by the BBC rather than the Ministry, and that, at the meeting she had had with Eileen the previous day, they had agreed on this, and there was "no bad blood". However, there does seem to have been an on-going issue with Westerby, as Holmes comments that she will still be on hand to "bark at Westerby if he tries to slip up on our arrangement". How successful this was is partly revealed several months later when an exasperated Holmes writes, in a memo about inviting guests to present on the Kitchen Front, that it should be done quickly by the BBC lest the "irrepressible Westerby"[103] made a start without the BBC's approval.

Eileen was still at her desk at the end of December (probably on the 30th, given the reference to "before Christmas"), sending a letter to Holmes on another scrap of paper.

> Mrs. Holmes[104]
> I tried to turn out various corners the other day and found this script. We could not use the recipes or I think any of Mrs. Gottlieb's.
> I have also had down from the Kitchen Anne Beaton's[105] recipes. You may remember I wrote to you about her before Christmas. The recipes are good and new though made of carrots. I suppose they are Polish in inspiration as she says so, but they need not be called Polish. You were not enthusiastic so far as I remember, but I don't think we ever had any specific conversation about her. What letter do you suggest she should have now? As a matter of fact, of course, she may never be able to come to London anyway. She broadcast last time from Glasgow and probably thinks she could do so again.
> 3?.xii.42s [signed Emily Blair]

---

[103] Reproduced courtesy of BBC Written Archives Centre, R51/285/3. Memo of 10 May 1943 from Holmes to Director of Talks, BBC.

[104] Reproduced courtesy of BBC Written Archives Centre, R51/285/2.

[105] Anne Beaton published *Success Cookery* in 1951.

Orwell seems to have been impressed by Eileen's work on the Kitchen Front and, towards the end of 1942, he suggested that this be adapted for the Eastern Service broadcasts to appeal to Indian housewives, for a programme called In Your Kitchen. Venu Chitale, one of Orwell's assistants at the BBC, was very impressed by what Eileen came up with:

> Mrs Blair has a reservoir of quiet humour, and again and again some of it seems to come out in between an amused smile and a penetrating remark. (Davison vol 14, p. 250)

The In Your Kitchen programme continued until July 1943, when it was "paused" but never resumed. In retrospect, this seems understandable, as 1943 is also the year in which a famine in Bengal led to the deaths of more than three million people. To continue to broadcast a cheerful programme about food economy would have been in bad taste, to say the least. The Kitchen Front, on the other hand, continued in its six-episodes-a-week format in Britain.

At the start of the new year of 1943, little had changed in terms of the war. However, there does seem to have been a warming of the friendship between Eileen and Winifred Holmes. The first letter of 1943 that we have shows her using the salutation "Winfred" rather than "Mrs Holmes", and Holmes reciprocated (not always) by using the salutation "Emily" and signing it "Winifred".

> 18 Jan 1943[106]
> Winifred
> We had these recipes tested, and they aren't very good. And by the way, Miss Sparrow[107] heard Mrs. Johnson's broadcast and thought that pretty bad too, though comprehensible. The Sparrows are a good source of information for us because Mrs. Sparrow really <u>uses</u> the K.F. in her catering.
> What do you think? Mrs. Brigman has taken such an interest that one doesn't like to be discouraging. On the otherhand [sic], there is no point in struggling with Mrs. Johnson if, as seems likely, she hasn't got another <u>good</u> recipe. I don't imagine that anyone thought she was outstanding as a broadcaster.

[106] Reproduced courtesy of BBC Written Archive Centre, R51/285/3.

[107] Mrs Sparrow was a regular listener and referred to by Eileen as a trustworthy source of feedback.

Passed to you now.
[signed Emily]

By 1943, when Eileen and Lettice had a secretary to do their typing, they had more time to talk, and Lettice reports that they spent a great deal of time in the coffee shop at Selfridge's (Cooper 1984, p. 19). This means that, when coupled with the worsening paper shortage, we have far fewer letters on file from this time onwards. However, there are some, and it is worth looking at these as they can tell us more about the nature of the work Eileen engaged with. We can see that the telephone was used more often, and it crops up in various letters from the BBC relating to their work on the Kitchen Front, for instance when following up a telephone call from Eileen, or else when assuring the recipient that Mrs Blair will call back. There is, in fact, one telephone message, typed up, in the files:

Telephone messages. 28.5.43[108]
Mrs. Blair would like you to ring her in the afternoon.
She has found an Ernie Bunker[109], shop steward at a tanks-parts factory in Gray's Inn Road, whom she thinks would be suitable for a Kitchen Front 'Man in the Kitchen'.
She wants to discuss the next xxxxx [sic] Men in the Kitchen meeting, June 9, and who will be there—Mr. Khan and Mr. Walker?—also new arrangements for factory people. As they lose time through coming four times for audition, script talk, rehearsal and broadcast, could not the audition and script talk, at least, be combined?

This note shows Eileen to be busy developing ideas and finding new speakers. Her socialist outlook is also evident in that she has clearly expressed concern for lost earnings of factory workers who would be required to attend the BBC studios, and offers a partial solution to this. The Men in the Kitchen series was her idea, and was used as a vehicle for Freddy Grisewood to act as a roving reporter.

[108] Reproduced courtesy of BBC Written Archive Centre, R51/285/3.

[109] A later memo from Holmes to another BBC colleague gives us a bit more information about Ernie Bunker. He had been introduced to Eileen by her sister-in-law, who also worked at the same factory. Interestingly, Holmes's memo also includes reference to his voice, which she describes as that of a "husky working man", and thus would be more acceptable to female listeners who might otherwise think men helping in the kitchen was a sign of effeminacy, here referred to as "pansy".

At the same time as developing new ideas, Eileen was also continuing to liaise with the BBC about the more mundane aspects of her job, such as the regular requirement for the BBC to accommodate the needs of the Ministry, as the following letter shows.

Ministry of Food (official letterhead)[110]
5 June 1943
Dear Mr. Salmon[111],
I enclose the text of Monday's Kitchen Front closing announcement as we received it last night, with a note on the two amendments that our legal department think necessary. You will see that the first one at least is not important to the lay eye, but that there is a logical distinction.
I am so sorry to pester you about this, but I should be most grateful if you would put the alterations through.
Yours sincerely,
[signed Emily Blair]
Emily Blair
Public Relations Division

Eileen seems to have resorted to writing rather than telephoning, as the official Ministry announcement appears to have been important enough for a sense of some urgency to creep into her letter.

By July 1943, it was announced that Holmes would be replaced by Anne Harris in September. This infuriated Eileen, but Holmes responded that it might prove to be a blessing in disguise for her as she could now spend more time at home with her children. We might get some idea of the shared wit of both Holmes and Eileen in the opening sentences of this letter:

2 July 1943[112]
Dear Emily,
I am so glad you have sheathed the hatpin, because I have really enjoyed working with you and am very sorry to hear you have been hiding up all kinds of grievances. I hope you won't resign, and certainly not on my account.

---

[110] Reproduced courtesy of BBC Written Archive Centre, R51/285/3.
[111] Mr C. V. Salmon was part of the production team at the BBC.
[112] Reproduced courtesy of BBC Written Archive Centre, R51/285/3.

As with Eileen's exaggerated claims of murdering her husband in her letter to Norah shortly after her marriage, this threat of violence is taken as intended: as a strong emotion but without violent action. This episode is notable because Lettice Cooper later claimed to have used it as a scene in her 1947 novel, *Black Bethlehem*, where her lead female, Ann, organises a rebellion against the BBC. This mirrors Eileen's earlier organised rebellion when working at Gurney's after leaving Oxford.

Eileen sent another letter to Holmes, dated 3 July, typed on a scrap of paper rather than official letterhead. We get another glimpse of the precarious health Eileen suffered, and of her close friendship with Holmes that allowed her to share some details, although with her usual self-deprecating humour.

> 3/7/43[113]
> Winifred
> I came in to drop my "unfit to follow her occupation" chit and have been following my occupation since then without drawing breath[114]. Robert[115] though will follow it tomorrow and for the rest of the week.
> For Friday the 30th I'm suggesting Ragna Martin[116]—I did a note about her for Robert and there is a copy attached. I think that's the only doubtful billing.
> The Palanque[117] script is to reach both of us tomorrow. She is "petting it up" at the moment. I think there's a chance that it may be very good, but you may need some of my new strychnine[118] medicine nevertheless.
> The Grossbard[119] script for Friday the 16th is just in and will be on its rounds tomorrow.

---

[113] Reproduced courtesy of BBC Written Archive Centre, R51/285/3.

[114] Eileen's love of word play is clear once more.

[115] Robert Westerby.

[116] Ragna Martin was born in Norway but lived in England during the war, where she was employed to translate messages from Quisling, a Norwegian Nazi supporter. Her husband's family owned vineyards in Portugal, which may have been one of the topics she spoke about on the Kitchen Front.

[117] The Palanque is probably a dramatic script for use on the Kitchen Front.

[118] Strychnine is a highly toxic pesticide, and so in this context is another example of Eileen's overly dramatic sense of humour at play.

[119] Berthe Grossbard. See note of 23 March 1942.

So I think there are no very likely difficulties. Mrs. Search[120] knows where everything has got to.
I can't really take in the news about your leaving—my head is very peculiar and I am doing an odd sort of day by day thinking[121]. But I know I do think it's a) a pity and b) a good thing because you have looked too tired towards the end of every day when I've seen you since your pneumonia. I think I'm going to take two weeks, so I'll see you on Monday the 17th[122] one good thing is that I think we'll have gotin [sic] all the series we were after, except the distinguished guests one. You wanted Clark Gable[123] most—perhaps you'd like to get him and let him be the whole series, five concentrated minutes. Or what about two talks, C. G. and the Queen?
[signed Emily]

The telephone appears to have been the main means of communication from Eileen at this time. This was not always the most efficient method, as this memo from Miss Ouston hints:

18 August.[124]
Mrs Holmes
Men in the kitchen dates, etc.
I go on to Miss Harris and then to Mrs. Blair about this. The confusion seems to have been caused by Mrs. Blair asking over the telephone for various dates to be changed, to fit in with her absence on leave. The position now is:
Roy Rich[125]. Coming to M. of Food with or without Grisewood at 11.30 Thursday 19th for scripting talk. Broadcast to be on Thursday 26th, recorded or if possible live. Miss Harris' letter, to which his was a reply,

---

[120] Eileen's secretary at the Ministry.

[121] Eileen's health problems are here expressed as a form of delirium.

[122] This is probably the wrong date. If Eileen is talking about Friday 16 July, then the Monday can't be 17, nor could it be Monday 17 August.

[123] On-going correspondence between the Ministry and the BBC showed a growing list of starry celebrities that they wished to invite on the Kitchen Front. There is no evidence that any of these people actually accepted, although the process for inviting them was carefully noted in several BBC memos.

[124] Reproduced courtesy of BBC Written Archive Centre, R51/285/3.

[125] Grisewood had suggested Cadet Officer Roy Rich as a Man in the Kitchen contributor and Rich had suggested a talk about "Good and Bad Messes". This is set out in a letter from Holmes to Eileen, dated 4 August 1943. BBC Written Archive Centre, R51/285/3.

mentioned 'possibly record' and gave Sept. 2nd as broadcast date, so this needs correction. As he has a message to ring up Ex. 561, this can be explained to him from Room 201 today.
Mr. Cooling. Has agreed to change date. Going to scripting talk with Grisewood at M. of Food on Wednesday 25th August. Broadcast date September 2nd.
These arrangements have been confirmed with Mrs. Blair, by telephone.
S. Ouston.

A further telephone message gives us a glimpse of the political tightrope Eileen was walking at this time, as the issue of the talk by Roy Rich proved problematic.

To: Mrs. Holmes 20 August 1943[126]
Subject: GETTING KITCHEN FRONT SCRIPTS PASSED BY OTHER MINISTRIES
To: D. T.[127]
Mrs. Blair telephoned me yesterday afternoon to tell me that in the scripting talk for Men in the Kitchen on August 26 Roy Rich was very critical of the attitude of W.A.A.F.[128] cooks in many canteens and suggested to me that the Air Ministry might not pass the script, and that Roy Rich would say just that or nothing. Further conversation with Mr. Westerby, who had done the scripting, led to our mutual agreement that he would send me the script early today, and that after I had read it, I should have a preliminary consultation on the telephone with Flight Officer Higgins and ask her advice as to whether the Air Ministry and W.A.A.F. authorities would be likely to pass the script; after which I should either send it to her to be passed in the usual way or we should start looking out for another Man in the Kitchen to do the programme, instead.
I have not yet received the script (4.45 p.m.) and have telephoned enquiries to Mr. Westerby's office. These revealed that he has already sent the script to Flight Officer Higgins himself[129].
Handwritten response by Salmon: I saw Shelton Smith[130] this morning (21/8) and gave him the gist of your complaint which I said I endorsed.

---

[126] Reproduced courtesy of BBC Written Archive Centre, R51/285/3.

[127] D. T. would be "director of talk", Mr Salmon.

[128] Women's Auxiliary Air Force. This part of the armed services was staffed by women but was largely restricted to home service.

[129] It seems the irrepressible Westerby was at work again.

[130] W. Shelton Smith worked at the Ministry of Food as a senior civil servant.

He said he did too, and promised to raise the matter with Westerby. Under the circumstances I said we wouldn't use him.

As we can see, the telephone was the main means of communication used by Eileen from early 1943 onwards. This was undoubtedly to help save paper, as the shortage of paper was so acute at times that scraps were used rather than official letterhead. However, as we have also seen, there were occasional episodes of miscommunication. Nevertheless, Eileen was very hard at work at the Ministry, and her name appears in the circulation list of meeting minutes from the BBC all through 1943 and into October 1944. The last letter from her on file comes from February 1944 and she is writing to Miss Quigley at the BBC, enclosing a Ministry poster. The letter is handwritten rather than typed.

Ministry of Food (official letterhead)[131]
[handwritten]
17.2.44
Dear Miss Quigley,
I'm sorry the Vegetabull[132] has been so slow moving, but here he is. If you've ever seen "the Ministry's" other posters you'll understand that there is considerable competition for these.
Yours sincerely
Emily Blair.

Eileen can't resist an element of playfulness in this letter. She personifies the cartoon bull, and uses the metaphor of bovine sluggishness to excuse the tardiness of her own response to the request for a copy of the poster. Eileen also seems to be very proud of the creativity in the Ministry's posters, and her comment about "considerable competition" indicates just how in demand copies of these were.

In all of this, Eileen and Orwell were meeting new people and seeing less of one another as they both worked long hours. Orwell in particular had never really given up pursuing other women, summing this up thus:

---

[131] Reproduced courtesy of BBC Written Archive Centre, R51/285/5.

[132] The vegetabull was a poster designed by Jan Lewitt and George Him for the Ministry of Information in 1941. It shows a composite bull made up of different vegetables and was intended to encourage the use of vegetables, dried eggs and milk rather than meat during wartime shortages.

> I don't much care who sleeps with whom [...] It seems to me what matters is being faithful in an emotional and intellectual sense. (letter to Anne Popham 18 April 1945, Davison 2001i, p. 249).

Amongst these women were novelist Inez Holden, who had a relationship with Orwell lasting several months around this time. Another was writer Stevie Smith, and then there were secretaries at the BBC and, later, at the *Tribune,* where he was literary editor. In all of this, Eileen is mute, seemingly accepting the established dalliances of her husband. However, Celia Paget Goodman records one occasion on which Eileen appears to have minded. Orwell had begun an affair with a secretary at the *Tribune*, Sally McEwan, and this distressed Eileen so much that there was "a fiendish row", at the end of which she had persuaded Orwell to break it off. (Shelden 1991, p. 393).

In Eileen's case, the possible affair with Georges Kopp is the only one for which there could be said to be any evidence. Eileen continued to maintain her rejection of Kopp, who in the end married Gwen's sister, Doreen, and so stayed close to Eileen for the rest of her life. There are also rumours of Eileen having an affair with Harman Grisewood whilst working with him at the BBC, but there are no relevant letters from this time. Instead, there is an oblique reference made by Orwell in a letter from 1946:

> I was sometimes unfaithful to Eileen, and I also treated her very badly, and I think she treated me badly too at times, but it was a real marriage in the sense that we both had been through awful struggles together and she understood all about my work, etc. (Davison 2001i, p. 249)

There is a division between "affairs" and "treated badly" that implies these are not the same thing, and so it would appear from this letter that Orwell wrote after her death that he believed Eileen had not been serially unfaithful to him. However, he had seen Kopp's letters to Eileen, and thus was aware of this flirtation. There is elliptical gap in the "etc.", where his behaviour could be said to have required understanding beyond his role as a writer, and perhaps it is here that his dalliances linger. As we have seen in other chapters, Eileen was very well connected through her friendships at Oxford and beyond. Many of these friendships were with men, and her naturally vivacious character might have led others to think she was more flirtatious with these male friends that she actually intended.

In any case, Eileen and Orwell remained married and no one has recorded that there was ever any notion of divorce. In fact, 1943–44 turned out to be a year in which they collaborated on a novel once again, this time a political satire called *Animal Farm*.

Animal Farm

Anyone who knew Eileen and Orwell, or who had read *Homage to Catalonia*, would have seen the clear passion they had for socialism, whilst also distinguishing this from Stalinist communism. The underlying ideology of *Animal Farm* would, therefore, not be a surprise. However, the story of this masterpiece is more complicated than a simple anti-Stalinist argument would indicate.

By the end of 1943, a combination of ill health and stifled creativity whilst working at the BBC led to Orwell resigning. He also left the Home Guard with a medical discharge at this time. Eileen was fully supportive of him in this and, indeed had been imploring him to make time to indulge in his creative writing again. In a letter of 21 March 1945, she wrote, "I think it's essential that you should write some book again"[133] (Davison 2001, p. 99,). Orwell took on part-time work as literary editor at the *Tribune*, for which he also contributed a regular column, "As I Please", and reviewed a huge number of books. This allowed him the space to work on a short novel, which quickly became *Animal Farm*. By 9 March 1944, Orwell was able to write to his agent that the manuscript was being typed, the passive tense indicating that it was being typed by someone else, most likely Eileen.

Orwell once described the inspiration for *Animal Farm*:

> I saw a little boy [...] driving a huge cart-horse along a narrow path [...] It struck me that if only such animals became aware of their strength we should have no power over them. (Meyers 2001, p. 248)

Animal Farm is very unlike any other book that Orwell wrote. Gollancz had the rights to his next two novels, but he didn't want to publish *Animal Farm*. It was not merely a whimsical fairy tale: it was a political allegory that sought to criticise Stalin and Communism. This was a long-standing argument that we have seen can be traced back to Eileen

---

[133] See Chapter 9 for full version of this letter.

and Orwell's time in Barcelona during the Spanish Civil War. In 1944, Russia was still part of the Allied forces fighting a war against fascism, in the form of Hitler, and Gollancz was not willing to publish a novel that was essentially critical of an Ally. Orwell was prepared for this, and immediately sent a copy of the manuscript to a different publisher. However, they also rejected it, as did the next and the next, all on the grounds that Russia was an Ally. Even his friend, T. S. Eliot, as reader at Faber & Faber, rejected the novel. Orwell complained in a letter to an American friend: "I am having hell and all to find a publisher for it here though normally I have no difficulty in publishing my stuff" (Davison 2001g, p. 174). Having exhausted the list of prominent publishers, Orwell approached Fredric Warburg, although he doubted that Warburg's small publishing house would be able to muster sufficient paper to print the novel, even if they accepted it. However, Warburg did accept the manuscript for publication, and managed to find a printer who could gather enough paper to print 4,500 copies. By February 1945, Eileen and Orwell had received the proofs for checking. However, further delays, primarily with paper supply, meant that the book was not finally published until 17 August 1945. Unfortunately, Eileen died on 29 March 1945 and was thus unable to appreciate the very favourable response this book received.

But what was it that the publishers were so wary of printing? How could a book be so powerful and potentially dangerous? And what was Eileen's part in all this?

In that cold winter of 1943–44, Eileen and Orwell resorted to going to bed early and sitting up reading in the evening. As the writing of *Animal Farm* progressed, Orwell would read out extracts to Eileen, and she in turn would make enthusiastic suggestions. Lettice Cooper recalls Eileen recreating and retelling scenes from the book for the entertainment of her colleagues and friends at work. "She saw at once that it was a winner [...] And she would quote bits out of it when we were having our coffee [...] It was very exciting" (Lettice Cooper in Crick archive). Later, after reading *Animal Farm* herself, Cooper commented that she "could recognise touches of Eileen's humour in some of the episodes. Whether she had directly suggested them, or George had unconsciously assimilated some of his wife's whimsical ways of talking and viewing things [...] I have little doubt that Eileen had collaborated in the creation of *Animal Farm*" (Jackson 1960, p. 123). Tosco Fyvel also noticed how different *Animal Farm* was from anything else Orwell had produced, and he ascribed this to Eileen's influence:

> It has so often been remarked that, unlike Orwell's other works, *Animal Farm* is a tale so perfect in its light touch and restraint (almost 'unOrwellian'), [that] I think some credit is due to the conversational influence of Eileen and the light touch of her bright, humorous intelligence. (Fyvel 1982, p. 134)

We might also look at the creative use of animals in this allegory, and in particular the use of pigs to be the most devious of the ones selected for anthropomorphising. Orwell's favourite Beatrix Potter book was *The Tale of Pigling Bland*, which is in the anthropomorphising tradition of Potter's books. It's the story of a pig who outwits evil farmers to escape "over the hills and far away", rescuing his love, Pig-Wig, *en route*. The pigs, typical of Potter's animal characters, stand on their hind legs, as Aunt Pettitoes reminds them:

> Mind your Sunday clothes, and remember to blow your nose [...] beware of traps, hen roosts, bacon and eggs; and always walk upon your hind legs. (Potter 1913, pp. 17–18)

But, in this story, the pigs are the moral heroes throughout.

As we have seen, Eileen retained her university nickname "Pig" throughout her life when corresponding with her close friend, Norah Myles. Orwell noted elsewhere that pigs were "the most annoying destructive animals, and hard to keep out of everywhere because they are so strong and cunning" (Meyers 2001, p. 248). That view would make them appealing to him as lead villains. If Eileen was in agreement, and surely she must have been, then she could not have seen it as a personal insult based on her own nickname. This would give further credence to the view that she acquired this name because of her own untidy habits, and it was used ironically and without malice by her university housemates. In that way, she would have no personal investment in the sanctity of her nickname, as it was linked to another facet of pig habits: a perception of them being untidy and dirty.

Elsewhere, Eileen's understanding of psychology can be seen in the details of the characters. Boxer, in particular, seems to be a character whose death is seen from the point of view of one who had witnessed her own husband's haemorrhaging over the years. Eileen's playfulness with language, apparent in her very earliest contributions to her school magazine, can be seen in the committees Snowball forms: the Clean Tails

League for the cows and the Wild Comrades Re-Education Committee to tame the rats and rabbits both carry the sort of whimsical humour that Eileen was very fond of. Also, in the context of the wartime deployment of women to do men's jobs on the home front—and being found to be more than capable—Eileen could quite possibly have suggested changing the ending of one rule, adding, after "All animals are equal", the words "but some animals are more equal than others".

As this chapter shows, Eileen's professional role in the Ministry of Food often drew on the literary world she was also part of. The letters held in the BBC Written Archive clearly show how well-connected Eileen was. From her Oxford friends, the Grisewoods, back to her Old Girls network and Nell Heaton, Eileen was able to draw on a wide range of friends and acquaintances from her past to enhance her newer literary contacts, all in the cause of the "war effort". She was very highly regarded by those she worked with, and created her own individual identity, helped in part by her use of the name "Emily". Outside of work, she was still grieving for her brother and suffering bouts of serious ill-health, but she continued to support her husband's writing, collaborating with him on *Animal Farm*. As the year came to a close, Eileen's health was worsening. However, she and Orwell decided on a major change in their lives: to adopt a child. The next chapter explores this in more detail.

References

Benney, Mark (1966), *Almost a Gentleman*. Peter Davies, London.
Bowker, Gordon (2003), *Inside George Orwell*. Palgrave Macmillan, New York.
Cooper, Lettice (1984), "Eileen Blair", *The PEN: Broadsheet of the English Centre for International PEN*, no. 17, Spring 1984.
Coppard, Audrey, and Crick, Bernard (eds) (1984). *Orwell Remembered*. BBC, London.
Crick Archive. Birkbeck College, University of London. Extracts are used by kind permission of the executors of the late Sir Bernard Crick at Birkbeck University Archive.
Crick, Bernard (1980), *George Orwell: a life*. Little, Brown; Boston.
Davison, Peter (2001c), *The Complete Works of George Orwell. Vol 12: A patriot after all, 1940–1941*. Secker & Warburg, London.
Davison, Peter (2001e), *The Complete Works of George Orwell. Vol 14: Keeping our little corner clean, 1941–1943*. Secker & Warburg, London.
Davison, Peter (2001h), *The Complete Works of George Orwell, Vol 17: I Belong to the Left, 1945*. Secker & Warburg, London.

Davison, Peter (2001i), *The Complete Works of George Orwell. Vol 18: Smothered Under Journalism, 1946.* Secker & Warburg, London.
Davison, Peter (2010), *Orwell: A Life in Letters.* Random House, London.
Didley, Douglas (2010), *Dunkirk 1940: Operation Dynamo.* Osprey, London.
Fyvel, T. R. (1982), *George Orwell: A personal memoir.* Weidenfeld and Nicolson, London.
Jackson, Lydia (1960), "George Orwell's First Wife", *The Twentieth Century Magazine.* Vol. 168, August 1960.
Meyers, Jeffrey (2001), *Orwell: Wintry Conscience of a Generation.* W. W. Norton, New York.
Nilson, A. R. (letter dated 5 December 1983). Crick Archive.
Potter, Beatrix (1913), *The Tale of Pigling Bland.* Frederick Warne, London.
Ray, John (1996), *The Night Blitz: 1940–1941.* Cassell Military, London.
Richards, Denis (1974), *Royal Air Force 1939–1945: the Fight at Odds. Vol 1.* HMSO, London.
Shelden, Michael (1991), *Orwell: the authorized biography.* Harper Collins, New York.
Sheridan, Dorothy (ed) (1990) *Wartime Women: a Mass Observation Anthology 1937–45.* Orion Books, London.
Sitwell, William (2016), *Eggs or Anarchy? The remarkable story of the man tasked with the impossible: to feed a nation at war.* Simon & Schuster, London.
Topp Sylvia (2020), *Eileen: the making of George Orwell.* Unbound, London.
Wadhams, Stephen (ed) (1984), *Remembering Orwell.* Penguin, Harmondsworth.
Ziegler, Philip (2002), *London at War, 1939–1945.* Pimlico, London.

CHAPTER 9

Last Letters (1945)

This chapter deals with the last few months of Eileen's life. Unlike the other chapters in this collection, it includes several letters from Eileen to Orwell. It would seem the only reason they are still in existence is because he kept them following her death. However, they do offer a glimpse at the sort of letters Eileen sent to him through the years, and how they differ from the correspondence with her friends.

The year 1944 saw a change in the Second World War as the Allies started to get the upper hand across Europe. Eileen and Orwell began to make plans for a post-war future. They were both keen to move out of London as soon as they could, and Orwell had starting making enquiries for an "ideal" house for them. However, this plan was on hold until the war could be declared over and, in the meantime, Orwell had another idea: they should adopt a baby. Both he and Eileen seem to have concluded that they would never have a child of their own, and recent changes in the law relating to adoption had drawn their attention to that as a possible route.

Until 1926, adoption in the UK was generally an informal arrangement between individuals, sometimes mediated by charities or the Poor Law Guardians. However, as the century developed and the state started to take a closer interest in the personal lives of the population, there was a shift away from such informal networks, and in 1926 the Adoption of Children Act was passed for England and Wales. This Act was primarily aimed at giving more rights to the adoptive parents. Up until then, it was not uncommon to see advertisements in local newspapers putting children up for adoption in "a good home". However, there were often disagreements between the birth parents and the adoptive parents when, after the adoptive parents had spent many years and much expense in bringing up a child to the point of wage-earning years, the birth parents would re-appear and take the child back. The rights of the child were nowhere to be seen in the legislation. The Act gave the adoptive parents legal guardianship of the child and thus safeguarded their investment (although there is a distinction between legal adoption and legal guardianship). There was no requirement for the adoptive parents to be a married couple, and many single people were able to adopt (although there was a general expectation that single men would not be allowed to adopt female infants). If a married couple were the adoptive parents, then only the name of one of them would appear on the papers (Keeting 2013), and, in patriarchal society, by default this was usually the husband's.

However, the pre-1926 haphazard system of informal adoption did not disappear completely, and, even ten years after the passing of the Act, there were still advertisements appearing in local newspapers offering children up for adoption. The Adoption of Children (Regulation) Act of 1939 started the process of regulating adoption and giving local authorities much of the responsibility for adoption services. This Act also prohibited personal advertisements for adoption, which was the way that the least affluent still tended to put children up for adoption. The start of the Second World War meant that the Act wasn't put into practice until June 1943. It was also at this point that "secrecy" in adoption became enshrined in law. Up until then, the identities of both birth and adoptive families would appear in court papers (Keeting 2013). By 1943, there were so many babies being advertised for adoption (many of them by unmarried women who had been seduced by the peril and sexual liberty of war) that the more rigorous regulation of adoption needed to be hastened into practice. Gwen O'Shaughnessy had adopted a baby daughter, Mary Catherine, at this time. Her job as general practitioner had given her an insight into the increased number of unwanted pregnancies, and the case of one young woman in particular touched her and so she adopted the infant.

Orwell was very keen to have a son, but Eileen was more ambivalent about adopting a child. She had long argued that she was not sufficiently maternal, and the war had given her a career and a job she loved at the

Ministry of Food. A decision was more or less imposed on them when Gwen alerted them to a baby boy who was coming up for adoption. His mother, Nancy Robertson, had given birth when her husband had been away from home fighting for more than a year. Richard Horatio Blair was born on 14 May 1944, and Eileen collected him from the hospital and took him back to the flat in Mortimer Crescent four weeks later (Fig. 9.1).

The war appeared to be turning much more strongly in favour of the Allies at this time. On 6 June, 155,000 Allied troops had landed on the beaches of Normandy in France on what became known as D-Day. The movement of the troops continued into the summer, with the liberation of Paris on 25 August 1944. Meanwhile, just as Eileen and Orwell were discovering how to be parents to an infant, the first V-1 flying bomb attack on London took place on 16 June. This marked the start of two months of bombing of the capital, more intense than anything since the blitz. It resulted in more than 6,000 deaths as well as damage to around one million buildings. The Mortimer Crescent property was badly damaged by a V-1 bomb on 28 June, collapsing the roof and bringing down the ceilings. By some miracle, Eileen, Orwell and Richard were staying with Gwen in Greenwich that night, so were unharmed, but their belongings were either damaged or destroyed. The terror of the V-1 s, which were unpiloted and were characterised by the sound of their engines that would cut out just seconds before exploding, saw Eileen react with less insouciance: she had a baby to care for now. Lydia Jackson recalls that Eileen "seemed at the end of her tether [...] it was the first—and only—occasion in which I saw Eileen lose her poise on account of an air-raid" (Jackson 1960, p. 124). The combination of having another life to look after, along with the grinding tedium of the war years, made this near-miss resonate more than any other bombing raid for Eileen. The V-1 and then V-2 raids continued throughout 1944, expanding to targets along the East Coast of England.

Eileen and Orwell moved around, staying with Richard in various friends' flats and houses over the next few months. Eileen was still working at the Ministry of Food at this time, and so, when Orwell took Richard to his sister's flat in Bristol, Eileen must have remained in London. Eventually, they took Richard to Wallington. The cottage had been used by various friends who had been bombed out of their London homes, with Lydia in particular taking up residence from 1940. In the summer of 1944, Eileen was joined by a nurse for Richard, a woman who

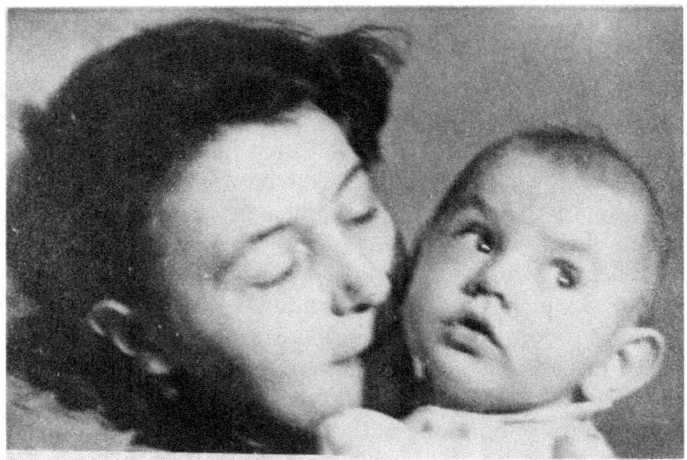

Fig. 9.1 Eileen Blair with Richard Blair (July/August 1944). UCL Orwell Archive ORWELL/T/3/B/1/14

was the nanny for Mary Catherine[1] and young Laurence O'Shaughnessy,[2] who had returned from Canada earlier in the year.

Early in August, Eileen wrote to Lydia, explaining the situation.

[*Typewritten*]
Wednesday [9? August 1944]
Ministry of Food
Portman Court
Portman Square
London WI
Dear Lydia,
I didn't know where to write to you and indeed I don't know whether this is a very good idea because one of Gwen's letters to Florrie[3] took ten days in transit.[4] However we'll hope.

---

[1] Gwen's adopted daughter, Mary Catherine, was first called Mary and later Catherine.

[2] Gwen and Eric O'Shaughnessy's son.

[3] A nanny of the children.

[4] Amongst all of the other privations of the war, the disruption to the postal service was one that rankled many people. Prior to the war, most people could expect regular deliveries

So far as I can see the cottage is going to repeat its Disney[5] act. Two babies are now supposed to be going into residence, one with a mother and father the other with a mother (fortunately the father is in Normandy or somewhere).[6] I pity them but it's satisfactory to have the space so well used. Mrs. Horton[7] has seen the space now so it's her responsibility. And about that, I thought I might come down for an hour or two while you're there and pack away some of our oddments—papers chiefly. I've arranged that the old tin trunk can stay locked but I think it would be a good idea to put it in the bottom of the larder (if it'll go) and also that the linen chest will be used for our things or yours. They're providing their own linen of course and will bring it in something in which it can be kept. I expect they will move most of the furniture about and the two passage rooms will go into use again. By the way, do you...

(There was a long interruption on the telephone and I can't at all remember what this important enquiry was.)

But I have remembered what I really wanted to write to you about. It was a confession. Lettice Cooper and her sister went down to the cottage for the week-end. Barbara the sister is in the act of recovering from a nervous breakdown and this life is not good for her. She won't go away without Lettice and Lettice couldn't free herself for the week-end, until just before it came. Then she did but of course it was too late to make any ordinary arrangements. They had a lovely time they say. Mrs. Anderson[8] swore she would clean on Tuesday and I hope she did but Lettice has a curious liking for housewifery, and doubtless did clean quite well herself; the real crisis was about the sheets as usual—they carried one but couldn't well do more than that. Anyway I hope you don't mind. It seemed a pity to have the place empty for the bank holiday and I couldn't contact you. Seeing how much they enjoyed it and how well they looked I rather hoped that all these babies wouldn't like the place after all. It would be fun to send

---

of mail twice or even three times a day, and, in a world where domestic telephones were still uncommon, the postal system was a vital means of communication.

[5] In keeping with Eileen's whimsical style, this appears to be a humorous description of the small cottage being the home of many people, as could be found in many fairy tale adaptions by Disney at this time.

[6] An example of dark humour of which Eileen was capable, but typical of the "keep smiling" propaganda that was encouraged by the government.

[7] It is not clear who this is, but it may be a villager who was helping to look after the cottage whilst Eileen and Orwell were in London.

[8] A neighbour who often helped out.

people down all the time[9] and I don't think it need have been empty for a night for the rest of the summer anyway. But of course it won't be empty! Can I come to tea? It's a bit of a job because we are going North with Gwen on the 17th [August] to help with the luggage primarily. But I could manage Saturday or Monday—or Sunday I suppose but the travelling back is so ungodly.[10] It'll have to be a compressed trip because we are also more or less in the act of moving. We have a flat in Canonbury Square—at least references are now being taken up and we shall have it unless the bombs beat us to the post which is rather likely.[11] It's a top floor flat and there have been numbers of bombs in the vicinity though the square itself has lost nothing but a window or two. I rather like it, in fact in some ways I like it very much indeed. The outlook is charming and we have a flat roof about three yards by two which seems full of possibilities. Disadvantage is that to get to it you climb an uncountable number of stone stairs—to get to the flat I mean[12]; to get to the roof you climb one of those fire-escape ladders with very small iron rungs.[13] I don't know how Richard will be managed if the bombing ever stops. I thought we might have a crane and sling and transport him the way they do elephants in the films but George thinks this unsuitable.[14]

Which day? With preference Saturday or Monday. No. Posts being as they are, I think I'll come on Saturday unless I hear to the contrary, and hope to see you. I expect I shan't get on the bus anyway[15] but I'll come some time in the afternoon and leave in the late afternoon, having put away the papers and possibly collected one or two things. When and if Richard comes I'll be wanting a few things but probably the best thing to do will be to leave them for the moment in the linen chest so that they don't get bombed before they're used. I meant to brood on this when I went over

---

[9] Eileen's irrepressible desire to be hospitable is clear here.

[10] As with the postal system, the railways were in a state of confusion and timetables were largely non-existent.

[11] Eileen's gallows humour is much in evidence here.

[12] Co-author Sylvia Topp visited this flat in 2022. The long climb up the stone staircase was certainly tiring for her, even without a heavy child to carry.

[13] This idea appeared to Topp to be a wild thought, an almost impossible task to climb those rungs.

[14] Eileen did end up carrying Richard up those difficult steps many times.

[15] Her plans would involve a walk of three or so miles back and forth from the train station to the cottage.

with Mrs. Horton but she had to get back and we only had half an hour in the cottage which didn't leave much time for brooding.[16]
See you on Saturday I hope.
With love
Eilee.[17]
[*Handwritten postscript*] (One thing I want to do with you is to check up on the things you want out of the garden. Kay wants you to have the crops of course but she'd better be forewarned so that the apple disaster[18] isn't repeated the day they arrive.)
Also I want to arrange to buy the coal and the Calor Gas.

Meanwhile, another option was becoming possible for them. Orwell had found his "ideal" home: an isolated farmhouse on the desolate isle of Jura in the Scottish Inner Hebrides. The house, Barnhill, had no telephone and mail was delivered twice a week to a neighbour's home. The nearest shop was 25 miles away, and it took two days for mail to arrive from London. Orwell regarded Barnhill as a house in a perfect state of isolation where he could write his next novel. Eileen was apparently ready to start again and proposed that they plan to spend the summer of 1945 there. But, before that, they had to negotiate the end of 1944.

The couple moved into the new flat in Canonbury Square, Islington in October. Eileen finally gave up her job at the Ministry of Food at the end of October and devoted herself to the care of Richard. She doted on the infant, and even started to deploy some of her child psychology knowledge on her observations of him. Lydia Jackson observed a sort of domestic idyl: "As we drank tea in front of the fire [...] and Richard lay on his back on the couch, cooing happily and playing with his toes, his adoptive parents looked more serene, more relaxed and happier than they had done for some time past" (Jackson 1960, p. 124). But Eileen was not well. By the winter of 1944/45, she was often finding it very difficult to carry Richard up and down the stone stairs. Gwen O'Shaughnessy and another doctor friend, George Mason, advised Eileen to have a course of injections in an attempt to increase her strength. However, this had little effect.

[16] A charming example of Eileen's typical humour based on her love of word play.

[17] Her signature is scrawled.

[18] An unexplained "disaster", which may have involved the unexpected harvesting of apples by a previous incumbent.

Early in 1945, Orwell managed to get himself a job as a war correspondent for the *Observer*, which required him to go to Europe for two months. Gwen had recently inherited a substantial property, Greystone, in Country Durham, and she persuaded Eileen to leave London and go up to Greystone, where care for Richard could be shared with the staff who were employed there to look after Mary Catherine and Laurence. Greystone was about half a mile out of the village of Carlton, Stockton-on-Tees. The village had a post office, pub, shop, and a railway station. The station offered links with the main London-Edinburgh railway line run by LNER at this time, and so was easily accessible for travellers to and from London Kings Cross. Eileen, Orwell, and Richard travelled up together around 10 February, before Orwell left for Paris on 15 February.

Eileen had been in debilitating pain for several months, with excessive vaginal bleeding that had kept her in bed for days at a time. Despite this, she was still typing manuscripts, not just from Orwell, but from other people as well, and at this time she had just completed working on Evelyn Anderson's book, *Hammer or Anvil: The Story of the German Working-Class Movement*. In other words, Eileen was never able to enjoy absolute bed rest.

As we know, Orwell had the practice of discarding all of Eileen's letters. One letter that did survive was dated by Peter Davison as written on March 21. Co-author Topp believes it was written over a month earlier, on February 14, 1945, as explained below. However, this earlier letter also survived because Orwell had already left for France, and he didn't see it until he returned from Germany, after learning that Eileen had died.

> Mary[19] calls Richard Which or Whicher or Which-Which. I suppose he'll call himself something like that too. Whicher I find rather attractive. She is better with him now and I must say I am proud to see that she is more apt to be frightened of him than he of her, sad though it is. I actually heard her say to him yesterday 'No no Whicher, no hurt Mamie'.[20] She takes things from him but she runs away from him, relying on her mobility; once he can move himself I don't believe she'll dare to—she never stays within his reach once she has the thing in her hand. She tries to gain confidence for herself by saying Baby wet all the time—generally with truth because he has now got to the stage of rejecting his pot (this is the usual preliminary

---

[19] Catherine initially went with the name Mary.
[20] Mary calls herself Mamie.

to being 'trained' and I hope we'll reach that stage soon though at present I see not the slightest indication of it[21]), but when she dirtied her pants for the second time today I heard this conversation with Nurse: 'No cross with Mamie Nurse?' 'Yes I am cross this time' 'Iodine no cross?' 'Yes, Iodine's cross too.' 'Whicher cross?' 'Whicher says he'll have to lend you some nappies.' 'No.... Baby's.' And she began to cry—so she's not sure of her superiority even in this. She isn't so superior either. This has been a bad day, but she never gets through one with dry pants poor little wretch.[22]

Dearest thank you very much for the books—Psmith in the City[23] has been making me laugh aloud. By the way, he arrived yesterday and the other three this afternoon although according to your letter you posted the three first.[24]

The oranges came too, and the fats. I think you're being too generous but as the oranges have come I'm going to eat them. Blackburn got some the other day and I gave all mine and most of Richard's to the children so they're all right for the moment. Richard has the juice of half an orange every other day and Mary has his other half and Laurence a whole one.[25]

This is being typed under difficulties as Mary is on my knee and trying to contribute.

Tomorrow I'm going to Newcastle[26], primarily to see the man in charge of Welfare Foods for the North of England. So far as I can see I can't get Richard's back orange juice as Stockton Food Office has stolen the coupons[27], but I hope to arrange that they won't bring off the same coup again. I now have some reason to think that they take orange juice out of stock on these extra coupons and sell it but of course I'm not proposing to

---

[21] Eileen is careful not to be critical of Richard.

[22] Eileen's comic description of toilet-training young children is also making fun of herself, through the childish rendition of her name as "Iodine".

[23] A comic novel by P. G. Wodehouse, to whom Orwell was introduced by his friend Malcolm Muggeridge whilst in Paris.

[24] The goods Orwell is sending seem to affirm that this letter was written weeks (rather than days) before Eileen went in for her operation on March 29. Also, Orwell would not have sent books, etc., to Eileen from France.

[25] Food rationing meant that there was a shortage of many things, such as fat/butter. Oranges would have been imported by ship, and this made them extremely hard to come by because of German blockades.

[26] Also, Eileen wouldn't be going to Newcastle for two days to run errands and get supplies just a week before her operation.

[27] Rationing for young children would include some of the precious fresh fruit that Eileen mentions here.

mention this theory to Watkins[28]. I'm also going to three food meetings and two infant welfare clinics with Nell.[29] If I stay the course. It will be very interesting and I hope profitable because I ought to lay hold of some Ostermilk[30] somewhere.

Don't bother about blankets.[31] I've bought two from Binns' in Sunderland[32]—they cost 22/- each and are more like rugs than blankets but they'll do quite well. I hope to make one into a frock for myself. They're dark grey which isn't I think the colour of choice for blankets but they'll come in useful one way or another and they're certainly cheap. I hope you have enough at home[33] and are not economising by leaving out the underblanket because without that you'll be cold if you have a dozen on top of you[34].

The playpen has come and all the children are entranced by it. Richard laughed heartily as soon as he was put in and then the others joined him

---

[28] The rationing system meant that parents could collect additional coupons for young children from special Food Offices, and it seems here that Eileen is complaining that her local food office in Stockton has not been able to supply the ones needed for Richard.

[29] Nell is likely to be Nell Heaton. Nell was a food writer and had joined the war effort in 1940 to help the Ministry of Food in its communications about food and nutrition. She probably met Eileen there, and they bonded over a shared Sunderland Church High School background. Nell appeared on Kitchen Front in 1943/44 at the time that Eileen was working on this programme, so it is likely that they had a long-standing friendship. As Eileen doesn't expand on Nell's name in her letter to Orwell, it can be assumed that she was well enough known to him for this to be clear. In fact, in her 1947 book, *The Complete Cook*, Heaton lists "Emily Blair and George Orwell" in the acknowledgements. While working at the Ministry of Food, Eileen went by the name Emily. See Chapter 8 for suggestions as to why she might have used this name. In using the pen names of both Orwell and Eileen, it seems that Heaton is focusing on their professional lives rather than their private lives.

[30] This is a fortified powdered milk, produced in the UK by Farley, formulated for infants.

[31] Orwell would not have sent blankets to Eileen from France, so the letter must have been written before he left.

[32] It is not clear why Eileen was in Sunderland. The Binns store there had been badly damaged by bombing in 1940, and there was a less disrupted Binns store in Stockton, which was closer to Greystone. It may be that Eileen was in Sunderland with Nell for one of the infant welfare or food meetings she was organising as part of a national tour.

[33] This detail seems to clarify that Orwell was still in London, getting ready to leave England and follow the British troops as they moved east through Germany.

[34] In the days before duvets, the convention would be to have a blanket between the mattress and the sheet to add extra warmth. As always, Eileen believes that Orwell needs her help looking after himself.

and there was a riot. I don't know how he'll take to it when he is left alone but I think he'll be OK. I have made him some strings of beads which he passionately loves and he will now play by himself quite happily for as long as you like. He's had more trouble with his teeth but no more are through. He might have another couple by the 21st though[35]. As for his appetite, he ate for his lunch the same food as Mary and very nearly the same quantity, but he didn't want his milk. I'd just announced that I was going to replace the midday milk by water so this came very aptly. But I've had to replace the cereal after his evening bath. I gave him Farex[36] for a couple of nights and the last two he has had MOF[37] again made much thinner. When he had just milk he was restless at night and screaming for his late feed by nine o'clock. So I'm just going to risk his getting overweight—he's still below the average for his age and length I'm sure. He's beginning to drink cows' milk instead of Ostermilk but I can't go ahead with this as fast as I might because I'm terrified that he'll turn against the Ostermilk and we'll be dependent on that when we're in London.[38] The other thing that doesn't progress well is his drinking. He's much worse at it since he had the teeth. But I think part of the trouble is that he can't manage the mug which he's supposed to use now. I'll try to buy one or two cups or mugs in Newcastle (I'm staying the night there and coming back on Friday to fit all these things in).

I've been dressed every day since you went away but I've done very little else except give Richard most of his food and have him for his social between five and six and play with Mary for half an hour or so after feeding Richard because she's so jealous of him, quite naturally. This morning

[*Handwritten*] At this point typing became impossible—I am now in the train but I got your wire last night (Wed). I hope you'll be able to do the Court[39] but of course you mustn't mess up the French trip.

Could you ring me up on Friday or Saturday evening? It's quite easy—Stillington, Co. Durham, 29. A trunk call of course—you dial TRU & ask

---

[35] Eileen would not say that Richard would have two more teeth by March 21 in a letter written on March 21.

[36] A baby food made with rice.

[37] This abbreviation would seem to stand for "Ministry of Food", and relate to a generic baby food given out at the clinics Eileen visited with Richard.

[38] Eileen is looking forward to the time when Orwell returns and the family lives together in London.

[39] Eileen hoped that Orwell would handle the adoption papers for Richard, which was scheduled for February 21, before he left for France. And he should certainly have had the time to fit this in, to save Eileen the chore. However, in the end, Eileen had to take Richard to court herself.

for the number. Then we can talk about the plans. Unless of course you're coming up this weekend which would be nice.[40] I'll be home at Greystone on Friday afternoon.
Eileen

On 21 February, since Orwell hadn't taken care of this chore, as he could easily have, Eileen took Richard to London for the finalisation of his adoption, which had to be done in court. In order to create a positive impression of efficient motherhood, Eileen had dressed as smartly as she could, and had even bought a new hat (according to Lettice Cooper in Wadhams 1984, p. 131). After the hearing, she took Richard into the Ministry of Food offices to show him off to her former colleagues. However, this all proved too much for her, and she collapsed and so was forced to spend a few more days in London than she had planned. Eileen returned to London again on 9 March for a dental appointment, but when she called in to the Canonbury Square flat, she discovered that Georges Kopp had failed to sort out the mail as promised, and some of it needed to be attended to urgently. Eileen's illness returned with a vengeance, and her friends in the Ministry were so alarmed that several of them wanted to recall Orwell from Paris. What should have been a two-day visit ended up being nearly a week.

Eileen wrote the following letter—the longest extant letter of hers—to Orwell on 21 March, 1945. It also survived because Orwell didn't get it until after Eileen had died. Aside from the gossipy content of the letter, what is also interesting to note is the length of it. In the hundreds of letters Eileen must have written to her husband over the years, the sad fact that only these few still exist is testimony to a relationship that was literary at its heart.

[Typewritten and handwritten]
Wednesday 21 March 1945
Greystone
Carlton
Dearest your letter came this morning—the one written on the 7th after you got my first one. I was rather worried because there had been an

[40] Eileen wished that Orwell would visit them before he left for France, more proof that this letter was written in February. However, he doesn't manage this visit, and there's no record of whether he did make the phone call. Tragically, by not arranging to visit Eileen before he left, Orwell didn't get to see Eileen one more time before her death.

interval of nearly a fortnight, but this one took 14 days whereas the last one came in 10 so probably that explains it. Or one may have gone astray[41].
I am typing in the garden. Isn't that wonderful? I've only got a rug for myself and typewriter and the wind keeps blowing the paper down over the machine which is not so good for the typing but very good for me. The wind is quite cold but the sun is hot. Richard is sitting up in his pram talking to a doll. He has the top half of a pram suit[42] on but he took off the rest some time ago and has nothing between himself and the sky below his nappies. I want him to get aired before the sun gets strong so that he'll brown nicely. That's my idea anyway. And he is enjoying the preliminaries anyway. I bought him a high chair—the only kind I could get. It sort of breaks in half and turns up its tail like a beetle if you want it to, and then you have a low chair attached to a little table, the whole on wheels. As a high chair it has no wheels and the usual tray effect in front of the chair. He loves it dearly and stretches out his hands to it—partly I'm afraid because what normally happens in the chair is eating. When it is being a low chair Laurence takes him for rides round the nursery and down the passage—indeed Laurence wheeled the whole contraption home from the station and I found it very useful myself on the way up as a luggage trolley. I came by night in the end so that George Kopp could see me off at King's X[43] which was very nice, but there were no porters at all at Thornaby or Stockton—and only one at Darlington but I got him. There is no real news about Richard. He is just very well. I was sorry to be away from him for a week because he always stops feeding himself when I don't act as waiter, but today he did pick up the spoon himself from the dish and put it in his mouth—upside down of course, but he was eating rather adhesive pudding so he got his food all right. I bought him a truck too for an appalling sum of money. I had to forget the price quickly but I think it's important he should have one[44].
We're no longer in the garden now. In fact Richard is in bed and has been for some time. Blackburn[45] came and told me all about his other jobs and

---

[41] This hints at the chaos in the postal system at this time.

[42] This would be a two-part knitted outfit, designed to keep a baby warm when in its pram. It seems Richard has removed the "trouser" part of the outfit.

[43] Eileen still had a soft spot for Kopp, a man who was quite visibly in love with her. Here she recounts how he escorted her to King's Cross Station, the main railway station out of London to the North of England.

[44] Eileen's concern with money is here ameliorated with her characteristic humour.

[45] The gardener at Greystone.

how Mr. Wilson fished and Sir John[46] once had to go to his office on August 12th[47] but the car went with him full of guns and sandwiches and they got to the moors by 1.30. And Blackburn's predecessor here shot himself[48]. I think perhaps the general shooting standard was rather lower than at Sir John's, because this man shot a wood pigeon and tried to pull it out of the bush into which it had fallen with his gun (this might be better expressed but you can guess it). Naturally the bush pulled the trigger and there was another shot in the other barrel and the ass was actually holding the barrel to his belly, so he might as well have been an air raid casualty. This convinced me not that Richard must never have a gun but that he must have one very young so that he couldn't forget how to handle it.

Gwen rang up Harvey Evers[49] and they want me to go in for this operation at once. This is all a bit difficult. It is going to cost a terrible lot of money. A bed in a kind of ward costs seven guineas a week and Harvey Evers's operation fee is forty guineas. In London I would have to pay about five guineas a week in a hospital but Gwen says the surgeon's fee would be higher. The absurd thing is that we are too well off for really cheap rates—you'd have to make less than £500 a year. It comes as a shock to me in a way because while you were being ill I got used to paying doctors nothing. But of course it was only because Eric[50] was making the arrangements. I suppose your bronchoscopy would have cost about forty guineas too—and I must say it would have been cheap at the price, but what worries me is that I really don't think I'm worth the money.[51] On the other hand of course this thing will take a longish time to kill me if left alone and it will be costing some money the whole time. The only thing is, I think perhaps it might be possible to sell the Harefield house if we found out how to do it. I do hope too that I can make some money when I am well—I could of course do a job but I mean really make some money

---

[46] It is not clear who these people are, although they may be wealthy neighbours, well enough known to Orwell to not need further explanation in Eileen's letter.

[47] August 12 is traditionally the date on which grouse shooting starts in the UK, referred to as "The Glorious Twelfth".

[48] Eileen's humour here links the shooting of birds for sport with the incompetence of those who pull the trigger and end up shooting themselves.

[49] The doctor in Newcastle who was going to do the operation.

[50] Eileen's brother.

[51] It's unbearably sad to realise that Eileen is worrying about the cost of a necessary operation. In a pre-NHS world (the NHS started in 1948), Eileen's concerns about the cost of basic health care would have been a very common sentiment for many people.

from home as it were.[52] Anyway I don't know what I can do except go ahead and get the thing done quickly. The idea is that I should go in next week and I gather he means to operate quickly—he thinks the indications are urgent enough to offset the disadvantages of operating on a bloodless patient; indeed he is quite clear that no treatment at all can prevent me from becoming considerably more bloodless every month. So I suppose they'll just do a blood transfusion and operate more or less at once.

While I was in London[53] I arranged to take Evelyn's manuscript[54] in to Tribune. I set off with it all right, broke the journey to go to the bank and was taken with a pain just like the one I had the day before coming North, only rather worse. I tried to have a drink in Selfridges' but couldn't and all sorts of extraordinary things then happened but after a bit I got myself into the Ministry. I simply could not do any more travelling, so Miss Sparrow[55] rang up Evelyn for me and they arranged between them about the transfer of the manuscript. People from Tribune then rang up in the most friendly way, offering to come and look after me, to bring me things and to get you home. I was horrified.[56] But yesterday I had a phase of thinking that it was really outrageous to spend all your money[57] on an operation of which I know you disapprove, so Gwen rang Tribune to know whether they had means of communicating with you quickly and could get your ruling.[58] They hadn't but suggested she should ring the Observer, which she did and talked to Ivor Brown[59]. He said you were in Cologne now he thought and that letters would reach you very slowly if at all. He suggested that they would send you a message about me by cable and wireless, like their own. Gwen says he couldn't have been nicer.

---

[52] Eileen regularly typed books in order to make more money for the couple.

[53] To handle the adoption papers.

[54] A book Eileen had worked on and then delivered to the *Tribune*, which was a well-established socialist magazine. According to Bernard Crick, Orwell had "volunteered Eileen's help... in correcting [Anderson's] English for a book" [Crick, p.446].

[55] Presumably a secretary at the Ministry of Food.

[56] Eileen was apparently so ill that her friends thought Orwell should come back from Germany to be with her. As we have seen in the past, she downplays her own illness and focuses on the response of others around her.

[57] A sad, ironic phrase when Eileen had just mentioned a manuscript she herself had typed for money. In fact, she was often doing typing jobs to increase the couple's income.

[58] At this time, it would have required a husband's authority to permit such a major operation to take place. In Eileen's case, the major surgery was a hysterectomy, and it seems Orwell wasn't in favour of this radical operation.

[59] Ivor Brown was the London drama critic of the Sunday paper, the *Observer*.

But I'm not having this done. It's quite impossible to give you the facts in this way and the whole thing is bound to sound urgent and even critical. I have arranged with Gwen however that when the thing is over she'll ask the Observer to send you a message to that effect. One very good thing is that by the time you get home I'll be convalescent, really convalescent at last and you won't have the hospital nightmare you would so much dislike. You'd more or less have to visit me and visiting someone in a ward really is a nightmare even to me with my fancy for hospitals—particularly if they're badly ill as I shall be at first of course. I only wish I could have had your approval as it were, but I think it's just hysterical[60]. Obviously I can't just go on having a tumour or rather several rapidly growing tumours. I have got an uneasy feeling that after all the job might have been more cheaply done somewhere else but if you remember Miss Kenny's[61] fee for a cautery, which is a small job, was fifteen guineas so she'd certainly charge at least fifty for this. Gwen's man might have done cheaper work for old sake's sake, but he's so very bad at the work and apparently he would have wanted me in hospital for weeks beforehand[62]—and I'm morally sure I'd be there for weeks afterwards. Harvey Evers has a very high reputation, and George Mason[63] thinks very well of him and says Eric did the same, and I am sure that he will finish me off as quickly as anyone in England[64] as well as doing the job properly—so he may well come cheaper in the end. I rather wish I'd talked it over with you before you went. I knew I had a 'growth'. But I wanted you to go away peacefully anyway, and I did not want to see Harvey Evers before the adoption was through in case it was cancer[65]. I thought it just possible that the judge might make some enquiry about our health as we're old for parenthood and anyway it would have been an uneasy sort of thing to be producing oneself as an

---

[60] Eileen is clearly showing more concern for her husband than for herself here.

[61] This may be a female surgeon whose help Eileen had previously sought. It might help us explain her prolonged absence from her Ministry job in September 1942 when she may have had a miscarriage. In the course of the subsequent D&C, any obvious anomaly in the uterus would have been discovered and this cautery might be an attempt at treating it. Follow-up appointments would have monitored this, and a year later resulted in the diagnosis of what Eileen calls "the growth".

[62] Eileen decided to rush through with this operation instead of allowing doctors in London to strengthen her ability to withstand the serious procedure.

[63] A surgeon colleague of Eric O'Shaughnessy's.

[64] An unbearably sad statement.

[65] Eileen's urgent desire to complete the adoption is painfully sad when we read that she delayed treatment for her own serious ill-health in case this jeopardised their chances.

ideal parent a fortnight after being told that one couldn't live more than six months or something[66].

You may never get this letter but of course it's urgent about the house in the country.[67] Inez [Holden] thinks we might do something together with her cottage near Andover. It's quite big (6 rooms and kitchen) but it has disadvantages. The 25/- a week rent which she considers nominal I think big considering there is no sanitation whatever and only one tap, no electricity or gas, and expensive travelling to London. She and Hugh [Slater] (incidentally they are more or less parting company at present but they might join up again I think) hire furniture for another 25/- a week which wouldn't be necessary if we were there, and it might be possible a) to get a long lease for a lower rent and b) to have modern conveniences installed. I am now so confident of being strong in a few months that I'm not actually frightened as I should have been of living a primitive life again (after all when you were ill soon after we were married I did clean out the whole of Wallington's sanitation and that was worse than emptying a bucket) but it does waste a lot of time.

So we can consider that. Then George Kopp has a clever idea. Apparently people constantly advertise in the Times wanting to exchange a house in the country for a flat in London. Most of these, probably all, would want something grander than N.1[68], but we might advertise ourselves— asking for correspondingly humble country accommodation. In the next few months people who have been living in the country for the war[69] will be wanting somewhere in London and we might do well like that. Meanwhile there is a letter from the Ardlussa[70] factor enclosing the contractor's estimate for repairing Barnhill[71]—which is £200. I found to my distress that George was not forwarding letters to you, although I gave him the address by telephone the day I got it, because he had not heard from you. I opened one from the Borough and found it was to say that the

---

[66] Again, Eileen is showing awareness of the needs of others over her own health. In this case, she was so eager for Richard's adoption to go ahead that she put off her medical appointments until the adoption had been finalised.

[67] Eileen is still thinking of finding somewhere else for them to live rather than at the cottage.

[68] This is the post code district that Eileen and Orwell had moved to. It was not the best area, but was also by no means the worst, covering both Islington and King's Cross.

[69] This provides more evidence that the war was coming to an end, and people were starting to make plans for their future.

[70] Ardlussa is a hamlet on Jura.

[71] Eileen was aware of Orwell's visit to Barnhill, and of the possibility of moving there.

electricity supply would be cut off as soon as the man could get in to do it. I paid that bill and decided I'd better look at the rest of the mail. There was nothing else quite so urgent except perhaps a letter from the BBC Schools about your two broadcasts for them. They want the scripts as soon as possible! There's also a contract. I didn't send anything on at once because I thought you might be moving and in view of Ivor Brown's news of you I'm not sending them now, but I've written to say that you are abroad but expected home next month. The broadcasts aren't till June after all. If you don't come next month I'll have to think again, but there may be a firmer address to write to. I can do nothing with this except send it to the Hotel Scribe and hope they'll forward it.[72] To get back to Barnhill. I'm going to write to the factor to say that you're away and I'm ill and will he wait till you get back. He's very apologetic about having kept us waiting and I'm sure they won't let the house to anyone else. I think this £200 can be very much reduced, but the house is quite grand—5 bedrooms, bathroom, W.C., H & C[73] and all, large sitting room, kitchen, various pantries, dairies etc. and a whole village of 'buildings'—in fact just what we want to live in twelve months of the year. But we needn't have all this papered and painted. I put my hopes on Mrs. Fletcher[74]. The only thing that bothers me is that if it's thought worth while to spend £200 on repairs the kind of rent they have in mind must be much higher than our £25-£30, let alone David's £5. Incidentally I had a letter from David [Astor][75] who just missed you in Paris.

It's odd—we have had nothing to discuss for months but the moment you leave the country there are dozens of things. But they can all be settled, or at least settled down, if you take this week's leave when you get back. I don't know about Garrigill.[76] It depends when you come. But at worst you could come here couldn't you?[77] If you were here we should stay

---

[72] Eileen is taking care of all the mail that she had expected Kopp to handle for her. The Hotel Scribe is where Orwell stayed while in Paris.

[73] The luxury of an indoor toilet (WC) and hot and cold running water (H&C) appears to greatly appeal to Eileen.

[74] Their contact on Jura.

[75] David Astor was an old Etonian friend of Orwell's, who was working as journalist for the *Observer*. It is a matter of some speculation how someone as ill as Orwell was at this time could be sent to the Continent to cover the final days of war (he was hospitalised when in Paris and again when in Germany). Some Orwell scholars believe it may have been connected with Astor's work for British Intelligence.

[76] A village in the south of England, were Orwell hoped to go fishing.

[77] Eileen apparently isn't sure whether Orwell will decide to take the time to visit her and Richard, so she is hypothesising a plan that could permit this.

mainly in my room, indeed I suppose I'll be there for some time after I get back in any case, and Richard will be available. Mary and Laurence both spend a lot of time with me now but they could be disposed of. Laurence by the way has improved out of recognition. He has three passions: farms, fairy tales, Richard. Not in that order—Richard probably comes first. So you ought to get on nicely. He has begun to invent fairy tales now, with magic cats and things in them, which is really a great advance. The pity is that the country isn't better but almost any country is good round about May and if I'm still at the picturesque stage of convalescence you could go out with Blackburn who knows every inch of the countryside or perhaps amuse yourself with Mr. Swinbank the farmer who would enjoy it I think. Or you could go over to Garrigill for a weekend's fishing on your own.

I liked hearing about Wodehouse. And I'm very glad you're going to Cologne. Perhaps you may get East of the Rhine before you come home. I have innumerable questions.

I think it's quite essential that you should write some book again.[78] As you know, I thought Tribune better than the BBC and I still do. Indeed I should think a municipal dustman's work more dignified and better for your future as a writer. But as I said before I left London, I think you ought to stop the editing soon, as soon as possible, whether or not you think it worth while to stay on the editorial board or whatever it's called. And of course you must do much less reviewing and nothing but specialised reviewing if any. From my point of view I would infinitely rather live in the country on £200 than in London on any money at all. I don't think you understand what a nightmare the London life is to me[79]. I know it is to you, but you often talk as though I liked it. I don't like even the things that you do. I can't stand having people all over the place, every meal makes me feel sick because every food has been handled by twenty dirty hands and I practically can't bear to eat anything that hasn't been boiled to clean it. I can't breathe the air[80], I can't think any more clearly that [stet] one would expect to in the moment of being smothered, everything that bores me happens all the time in London and the things that

---

[78] In the spirit of post-war planning that was already creeping into people's conversations, Eileen is insistent that Orwell write another book rather than continue reviewing books by others.

[79] This is the first time we see Eileen complaining about living in London. It may be that she felt she needed to make a stronger case for moving to the country.

[80] London had notoriously poor air quality, owing to the huge number of houses and office buildings that were heated by coal.

interest me most don't happen at all and I can't read poetry[81]. I never could. When I lived in London before I was married I used to go away certainly once a month with a suitcase full of poetry and that consoled me until the next time—or I used to go up to Oxford and read in the Bodleian and take a punt up the Cher[82] if it was summer or walk in Port Meadow or to Godstow if it was winter. But all these years I have felt as though I were in a mild kind of concentration camp. The place has its points of course and I could enjoy it for a week. I like going to theatres for instance. But the fact of living in London destroys any pleasure I might have in its amenities and in fact as you know I never go to a theatre. As for eating in restaurants, it's the most barbarous habit and only tolerable very occasionally when one drinks enough to enjoy barbarity. And I can't drink enough beer.[83] (George Mason took me out to dinner the night after I got to London and gave me to drink just what I would have drunk in peacetime—four glasses of sherry, half a bottle of claret and some brandy[84]—and it did cheer me up I admit.) I like the Canonbury flat but I am suicidal every time I walk as far as the bread shop, and it would be very bad for Richard once he is mobile. Indeed if the worst comes to the worst I think he'd better go to Wallington for the summer, but it would be better to find somewhere with more space because you and Richard would be too much for the cottage very soon and I don't know where his sister[85] could go. And I think the cottage makes you ill—it's the damp and the smoke I think.

While this has been in progress I have read several stories to Laurence, dealt with Richard who woke up (he has just stopped his 10 o'clock feed), dealt with Mary who always cries in the evening, had my supper and listened to Mrs. Blackburn's distresses about Raymond[86] who has just got a motor bike. That's why it's so long. And partly why it's so involved. But I should like to see you stop living a literary life and start writing again and it would be much better for Richard too, so you need have no conflicts

---

[81] Eileen's love of poetry was life-long, and, as we have seen, she carried poetry books with her everywhere she went.

[82] This is a common abbreviation for the River Cherwll.

[83] Orwell only drank beer, and perhaps Eileen believed she shouldn't drink the kind of liquor she preferred when she was with him.

[84] Eileen apparently had quite a capacity for alcohol.

[85] Eileen would not have been able to get pregnant after the operation, so she must be suggesting that they adopt a daughter.

[86] The Blackburns' son.

about it.[87] Richard sends you this message. He has no conflicts. If he gets a black eye he cries while it hurts but with the tears wet on his cheeks he laughs heartily at a new blue cat who says miaow to him and embraces it with loving words. Faced with any new situation he is sure that it will be an exciting and desirable situation for him, and he knows so well that everyone in the world is his good friend that even if someone hurts him he understands that it was by accident and loses none of his confidence. He will fight for his rights (he actually drove Mary off the blue cat today, brandishing a stick at her and shouting) but without malice. Whether he can keep his certainties over the difficult second year[88] I don't know of course but he's much more likely to if he has the country and you have the kind of life that satisfies you—and me. I think Richard really has a natural tendency to be sort of satisfied, balanced in fact. He demands but he demands something specific, he knows what he wants and if he gets it or some reasonable substitute he is satisfied; he isn't just demanding like Mary[89]. I'm not protecting him. That is, he takes the troubles I think proper to his age. He gets no sympathy when his face is washed and very little when he topples over and knocks his head and I expect him to take in good part the slight sort of bumps he gets when the children play with him. But he can be tough only if he knows that it's all right really.

Now I'm going to bed. Before you get this you'll probably have the message about this operation[90] and you may well be in England again if you keep what Ivor Brown calls on the move. What a waste that would be.

All my love, and Richard's.
E.

In response to this, Mary Catherine and Richard were kind enough to send us their reactions to the above letter. Richard's response, as shown below, relays his understanding as given to him by relatives in later life. He told us that he knew this letter well. "In fact", he wrote, "I have it open in front of me with a view to reading it again. I'm not sure that Eileen's attitude to Catherine and myself was quite as "black and white". After all she had three children to look after, with the help of Joyce Pritchard.... My mother was bound to be more attuned to me as we had been bonding

---

[87] Eileen again stresses her belief that Orwell should write a new book, even suggesting that Richard agrees with her.

[88] Eileen is here anticipating the stereotype of the "terrible twos".

[89] Poor Catherine is often compared negatively to Richard by Eileen.

[90] This is unfortunately prophetic.

for the best part of nine and a half months, in spite of her reservations at the beginning of the adoption. Children at that age can be so different from each other, yet later get on so well. Laurence sadly had a bit of a break down when he was at Trinity College Dublin, but Catherine and I have always been the best of friends, as we are with Quentin and Mary. We saw each other during the fifties at Cranglegate in Swaffham and always played well together. I think that by and large my mother got on well with Catherine, after all she was sitting on my mother's knee, whilst she was typing. Yes, Catherine and I had different temperaments at the young age, but I'm pleased to say that has all come good over the years. However everybody has different ways of interpreting the same thing, but my feeling, for what it's worth, was young and old got on well enough, bearing in mind that my mother was ill and probably found child rearing and caring damn hard work".

Mary Catherine, being slightly older than Richard, has first-hand memories of this period of their lives, although she also has relied heavily on recollections by family and friends.

She told us that she had "gleaned more about Eileen from this letter than from all the talk about her from the family. I knew she was always worried about money but not to the extent she verbalizes in this letter. Here is a woman who grew up in middle class England, went to good schools, supported herself until she was nearly 30 and managed quite well as far as we know, then she marries and becomes obsessed about money. I don't follow the reasoning. I know they were short but surely they had friends and family who could have helped them out. Almost the whole letter is about cost. Do you think her character changed after she married Eric? She seemed to completely give herself over to his needs.

"As I have said before I don't know why Mummy recommended she go up to Newcastle to have her operation unless Eileen was so stressed about the money situation that she, Gwen, gave in and let her go. Eileen was obviously much sicker than anyone knew."

"As the letter says Dr Evers was highly recommended by George Mason and apparently Eric as well. I met George Mason and his wife when I was 17ish. Mummy took me up to see them in Northumberland where they had a beautiful home. Very cheery man who, unfortunately, had a son my age with a sports car which rather took my attention away from his father. If you google George Alexander Mason, Newcastle, England you will see he worked with Eric at the college of surgeons. I didn't know he was a thoracic surgeon. I thought he was OBG."

"Eileen was obviously, by this time, in love with Richard and naturally she thought him the best of the bunch, what mother wouldn't. He was a very lovable child. Easy to get along with, wasn't a "fusser" and fit right in anywhere and everywhere he went. Eileen was right, he was always a good child. As far as my memory goes Rick and I have always been friends."

"I, on the other hand, was not so pliant. I wasn't adopted until I was 6 months old (Mummy couldn't make up her mind) and I think wrenching a child away from her mother at that age probably had an adverse effect. Everything I have read about myself at that age states 'she was crying'. I wonder why Eileen was left to look after all those children when she was so sick."

"I was interested to read that Laurence was a helpful child and that he was into fairy tales! That was not the Laurence I knew growing up. He didn't want a sister and made that abundantly clear. It wasn't until I was well into my teens that we became friends."

"What a shame all these people died before we could ask them the questions that pop into our heads now."

We would actually take the view that Eileen and Orwell were not so keen to be seen relying on family and friends for money, as they both seem to be very independent (the self-sufficiency they worked hard to maintain at the cottage, for example). However, they did have that very big safety net to call on if they needed it, as they often did. As for being treated in Newcastle, that would be easier to reach from Greystone than London, and it was where they were living in relative safety with the children, so that could be a contributing factor in all of this. The focus on money in the letters could perhaps be seen in light of there being so few letters remaining, so it might give an unbalanced view if we say that Eileen became obsessed with money on the basis of these letters. As we have seen, her other letters to friends do not seem to show anything like this obsession.

Eileen was now planning to get her "illness" sorted out so she could devote her energies to looking after Richard and Orwell. On Gwen's recommendation, she contacted the surgeon Harvey Evers, who was well-respected in Newcastle and had been acquainted with Eric O'Shaughnessy. He had a private nursing home, Fernwood House, in Jesmond, Newcastle. Eileen knew how seriously ill she was but hid it from just about everyone. She needed a hysterectomy, a major operation even now. Perhaps only Lettice and Gwen knew of the seriousness of her condition, and certainly her letters to Orwell downplay the danger. Eileen needed her husband's permission to undergo the operation, part of the latent patriarchal structure of health care that continued well after the NHS was established three years later. She telegraphed him to request this, again playing down the seriousness of her illness. However, Orwell was very ill himself at this time, but he eventually responded to give his consent when he was in hospital in Cologne following another of his haemorrhages.

Eileen wrote the following letter to Lettice Cooper on 23 March. Lettice was one of the people from the Ministry that Eileen kept in touch with, and her letter here indicates a friendship with shared gossipy news that was mutual.

[Typed and handwritten]
23 March 1945 or thereabouts
Greystone
Carlton
Dear Lettice,
I'm sorry about the paper and the typewriter but Mary got at both. You practically can't buy paper here[91] so I can't waste that and although I could do something about the machine I am bored with it after about twenty minutes spent in collecting the ribbon and more or less replacing it. A typewriter ribbon is the longest thing in the world. It will go round every chair leg in a good sized house. So I've just discovered.
Richard was delighted with his coat and it will see him through the summer. He was just getting very short of jackets because he is so large. Mary's castoffs will hardly go on, knitted things anyway. He took over her nightgowns the day after she inherited some pyjamas of Laurence's and even those aren't at all too big. He's still backward but has great charm which will be a lot more useful to him than talent. And he is not so stupid as Mogador[92] because he found out about pulling trucks by their strings before he was ten months old and is now investigating the principles of using one object to drag nearer or to pick up another. He's a hard worker. I really would have written sooner but I came up to London about a fortnight ago to see my dentist so I thought I'd ring you up. Then I got ill and rang no one up and finished with all kinds of dramas at the

---

[91] The paper the letter was typed on was very crumpled, and it seems Mary was responsible for that. However, Eileen points to the national paper shortage, which explains her use of what would otherwise be unsuitable paper.

[92] Davison suggested that this could be a reference to Eileen's blue cat named Moggie.

Ministry[93]. On the way up I went to see a Newcastle surgeon because as Richard's adoption was through I thought I might now deal with the grwoth (no one could object to a grwoth)[94] I knew I had. He found it or rather them without any difficulty and I'm going into his nursing home next week for the removal. I think the question about the hysterectomy is answered because there is hardly any chance that the tumours can come out without more or less everything else removable. So that on the whole is a very good thing. It was worth coming to the north country because there is to be none of the fattening up in hospital before the operation that I was to have in London.[95] London surgeons love preparing their patients as an insurance against unknown consequences. I think they're all terrified of their knives really—probably they have a subconscious hope that the patient will die before getting as far as the theatre and then they can't possibly be blamed[96]. In London they said I couldn't have any kind of operation without a preparatory month of blood transfusions etc.; here I'm going in next Wednesday to be done on Thursday. Apart from its other advantages this will save money, a lot of money. And that's as well. By the way, if you could write a letter that would be nice. Theoretically I don't want any visitors, particularly as I can't get a private room; in practice I'll probably be furious that no one comes and no one can because such friends as I have in Newcastle will be away for the school holidays.[97] So if you have time write a letter to Fernwood House, Clayton Road, Newcastle. It's a mercy George is away—in Cologne at the moment.

George visiting the sick is a sight infinitely sadder than any disease-ridden wretch in the world.

[Handwritten]

I hate to think that you are no longer at the Ministry & that this will be the last extract from Miss Tomkins' conversation[98]. I clearly remember the sweetly pretty painting of snowdrops.

Tell me whether the flat materialises. It sounds perfect. Incidentally if you want somewhere to work or to live for that matter, use our flat which

---

[93] Eileen is repeating information she has already told Orwell in a previous letter.

[94] This is Eileen's typing mistake, which she teases about after making it.

[95] Of course, Eileen should have chosen to be "fattened up" before the operation, since if she had she might have survived.

[96] A perverse use of Eileen's knowledge of psychology, but perhaps also an attempt to downplay the possible dangers of her operation.

[97] Lettice didn't get this letter until after Eileen had died. She said later that, if she had received it earlier, she would have gone to Newcastle to be with Eileen.

[98] Eileen is presumably referring to something Lettice had written to her.

is rotting in solitude. Doreen Kopp[99], who lives at 14A Cannonbury[100] Square, has the key. Ours is 27B Cannonbury Square. And her telephone number is CAN 4901. She has a son, very large, with the hair and hands of a talented musician. I expected to be jealous but find that I didn't prefer him to Richard, preferable though he is.[101] To return to the flat, Doreen can tell you whatever you don't know about its amenities, which don't include sheets. The last lot have disappeared since I came North. But you could have a peat fire which is a nice thing.

Raymond Blackburn is going to Stockton & he must carry this in his hand. It has taken about a week to write...[102] But all this time we have been thanking you for Richard's present, he & I.

Lots of love
Emily[103]

Eileen wrote a letter to Orwell dated 25 March. It shows that she is concerned about her forthcoming operation, but eager to share the minutiae of their son's life. Eileen maintains her humorous approach to life, together with a keen eye for whimsical detail.

25 March 1945
Greystone
Carlton
Dearest

I'm trying to get forward with my correspondence because I go into the nursing home on Wednesday (this is Sunday) & of course I shan't be ready. It's impossible to write or do anything else while the children are up. I finish reading to Laurence about a quarter to eight (tonight it was five to eight), we have supper at 8 or 8.15, the 9 o'clock news now must be listened to & lasts till at least 9.30 (the war reports the last two nights have been brilliant)[104] & then it's time to fill hotwater bottles etc. because we come to bed early. So I write in bed & don't type. Incidentally I did while explaining the poaching laws as I understand them to Laurence make

---

[99] Wife of Georges Kopp.

[100] Eileen has misspelled Canonbury Square.

[101] A sweet version of Eileen's whimsical humour.

[102] Nothing is omitted; the elliptical dots are in the original letter.

[103] The name Eileen was called by at the Ministry of Food, which Eileen continued to use in correspondence with the friends she made there.

[104] Davison suggests that Eileen might be referring to Operation Plunder, an offensive across the Rhine, which began on March 23.

my will—in handwriting because handwritten wills are nearly always valid. It is signed & witnessed. Nothing is less likely than that it will be used but I mention it because I have done an odd thing. I haven't left anything to Richard. You are the sole legatee if you survive me (your inheritance would be the Harefield house which ought to be worth a few hundreds, that insurance policy, & furniture). If you don't, the estate would be larger[105] & I have left it to Gwen absolutely with a note that I hope she will use it for Richard's benefit but without any legal obligation. The note is to convince Richard that I was not disinheriting him.

But I've done it that way because I don't know how to devise the money to Richard himself. For one thing, there has been no communication from the Registrar General[106] so I suppose Richard's name is still Robertson. For another thing he must have trustees & I don't know who you want & they'd have to be asked. For another, if he is to inherit in childhood it's important that his trustees should be able to use his money during his minority so that he may have as good an education as possible[107]. We must get all this straightened out properly when you come home but I thought I must cover the possibility that you might be killed within the next few days & I might die on the table on Thursday. If you're killed after I die that'll be just too bad but still my little testament will indicate what I wanted done. Gwen's results in child-rearing have not been encouraging so far but after the war she will have a proper house in the country containing both the children & herself, she loves Richard & Laurie adores him. And all the retainers love him dearly. I'm sure he would be happier in that household than with Marjorie though I think Marjorie would take him on. Avril I think & hope would not take him on anyway. That I couldn't bear.[108] Norah[109] & Quartus would have him & bring him up beautifully but you've never seen either of them. Quartus is in India & I can't arrange it. So in all the circumstances I thought you would agree that this would be the best emergency measure.

---

[105] This implies that Orwell has some money saved, even though he always acts as if he is in need.

[106] Despite the adoption being finalised, it seems there is still a backlog in the paperwork and Richard's birth surname is still officially the one he has.

[107] Eileen's insistence on education being so important as to be singled out above other considerations is interesting, and shows how much she must have valued her own education.

[108] After Orwell died, Richard did live very happily with Avril.

[109] Norah was Eileen's classmate at Oxford, and they wrote many letters back and forth through the following years. Six of them were recently discovered.

RICHARD HAS SIX TEETH.¹¹⁰ Also he got hold of the playpen rail when I was putting him in & stood hanging on to it without other support. But he doesn't really know at all how to pull himself up so don't expect too much. Yesterday Nurse & I took all three to the doctor for whooping cough injections. He lives about 2½-3 miles away, partly across fields. We got lost & had to cross ploughland. The pram wouldn't perambulate¹¹¹ & neither would Mary. She sat in a furrow & bellowed until carried. Laurence cried to be carried too...¹¹² Laurence however didn't cry when the needle went in but Mary did and made an enormous pool on the surgery floor. Richard was done last. He played with a matchbox on my knee, looked at the doctor in some surprise when his arm was gripped & then turned to me in astonishment as though to say "Why is this apparently nice man sticking needles into me? Can it be right?" On being told it was he looked up at the doctor again rather gravely—& then smiled. He didn't make a sound & he was perfectly good all day too, though his arm is sort of bruised. The other two unfortunately remembered that they'd been injected & screamed in agony if either arm was touched. It was a happy day.

But Richard did a terrible thing.¹¹³ He will not use his pot¹¹⁴, nearly always goes into a tantrum when put on it & if he does sit on it does nothing more. The tooth upset his inside a bit too. After lunch I sent the other two to bed & left Richard in his playpen while I helped wash up. Then there were cries of agony. He had done what Mary calls tick-tocks¹¹⁵ for the third time, got his hands in it & put his hands in his mouth. I tried to wash his mouth out, hoping he'd be sick. But no. He seemed to swallow most of the water I poured in, so it was worse than useless. In the end I scoured his mouth with cotton wool, gave him some boiled water & hoped for the best. And he is very well. Poor little boy. And I was sorry for myself too. I was sick. Blackburn however says a lot of children do this every day.¹¹⁶

---

¹¹⁰ Eileen's huge pride in her son's achievement is evident through the use of block capitals here.

¹¹¹ Eileen's love of word play is evident even when recounting a particularly trying story.

¹¹² Nothing has been left out.

¹¹³ The first criticism of Richard.

¹¹⁴ This seems to refer to his early toilet training.

¹¹⁵ Here, Eileen is using Mary's childish euphemism for defaecation.

¹¹⁶ Nothing has been left out here. The elliptical lines are in the original letter.

I haven't had a copy of Windmill[117] & I haven't had a proof. Surely you said they were sending a proof. And I failed to get the Observer[118] one week which must have been the relevant one. I've also failed to get today's but shall get it I hope.

Your letter with the Animal Farm document came yesterday & I've sent the enclosure on to Moore[119]. He will be pleased. This is much the quickest exchange we've had.

I suppose I'd better go to sleep. By the way the six teeth are 3 top & 3 bottom which gives rather an odd appearance, but I hope the fourth top one will be through soon.

All my love & Richard's
E.

Eileen wrote one final letter to Orwell, while sitting on her hospital bed as she waited for the anaesthetic to take effect for her operation. This letter is a mixture of Eileen's habitual attempts to make light of a situation, even when it was very serious and potentially dangerous, and also a touching realisation that this might actually be her last letter.

[handwritten] 29 March 1945
Fernwood House
Clayton Road
Newcastle-on-Tyne
Dearest

I'm just going to have the operation, already enema'd, injected (with morphia in the right arm which is a nuisance[120]), cleaned & packed up like a precious image in cotton wool & bandages. When its[121] over I'll add a note to this & it can get off quickly. Judging by my fellow patients it will be a short note. They've all had their operations. Annoying—I shall never have a chance to feel superior[122].

I haven't seen Harvey Evers since arrival & apparently Gwen didn't communicate with him & no one knows what operation I am having! They

---

[117] The journal in which "In Defence of P. G. Wodehouse" was to appear.

[118] This seems to refer a specific report, possibly written by Orwell himself, which appeared in the *Observer* newspaper, but in an edition that Eileen had missed buying.

[119] Orwell's agent.

[120] Eileen is right-handed and the injection has reduced her ability to write.

[121] As Eileen wrote the word, omitting the apostrophe.

[122] Even in her anxiety about her operation, she is able to resort to gallows humour.

don't believe that Harvey Evers really left it to me to decide—he always "does what he thinks best"![123] He will of course. But I must say I feel irritated though I am being a model patient. They think I'm wonderful, so placid & happy they say. As indeed I am once I can hand myself over to someone else to deal with.

This is a nice room—ground floor so one can see the garden. Not much in it except daffodils & I think arabis but a nice little lawn. My bed isn't next the window but it faces the right way. I also see the fire & the clock.

The letter ends here. No note was added. Eileen suffered a heart attack and died under the anaesthetic. She was 39. Orwell was in Germany when he received the news that Eileen had died; he got to Greystone on Saturday, 31 March[124]. Eileen was buried in St Andrew's and Jesmond Cemetery, Newcastle upon Tyne. The grave is number 145 in Section B. Co-author Topp found Eileen's overrun and untended grave with great difficulty, in 2011, when she began research for her biography of Eileen. Since then, the gravesite has been cleaned up and is now well taken care of by Orwell Society member, Brian Thompson.

In this letter, Eileen mentions that she has not seen Harvey Evers. This is puzzling, as a surgeon would usually see his patient and check on her before surgery. In Eileen's case, she was expecting to receive a blood transfusion, knowing that she was anaemic (with frequent mention of being "bloodless" in her letters), and believing that this transfusion would be a substitute for the "fattening up" that would have been expensively carried out in a London clinic. No blood transfusion nor last-minute check of the conscious patient was made by Harvey Evers. Eileen suffered a fatal heart attack when on the operating table. The coroner's report shows that the medical team tried for 40 minutes to resuscitate Eileen, but to no avail. Eileen Maud O'Shaughnessy Blair died on 29 March 1945.

Orwell received the telegram informing him of her death whilst still in hospital in Cologne. He managed to muster the strength and contacts to get on a military plane and fly back to England. Eileen's funeral took

---

[123] It is certainly upsetting to know that she didn't even see Evers before going in for the operation.

[124] Eileen's death is recorded in *The Chronicles*, her school magazine, as being "in April". It may be that Nell is responsible for sending in this information, and the actual date of Eileen's death—at the very end of March—has been confused by the postal disruption that everyone had become used to in the course of the war.

place on 3 April, and Orwell's novel *Nineteen Eighty-four* starts: "It was a bright cold day in April", perhaps in homage to her. We have her letters to Orwell for this period because, in the chaos of the wartime postal service, they reached him after her death. We know, therefore, that he treasured them and her memory embedded in them, as he didn't throw any of them away, which he must have done with countless other letters they had exchanged. The couple had been in frequent correspondence with one another over the previous nine years of marriage, but this most unsentimental of couples kept none of these letters, apart from the last few that Orwell received after Eileen's sudden death.

Orwell travelled to Paris the day after the funeral, burying himself in his work as a way to cope with his grief. His final novel, which he had been working on for many years with Eileen's help, was published in June 1949. Aside from various areas of the novel which are clearly related to Eileen—such as the descriptions of the Ministry of Information and of the secret bedroom where Winston and Julia make love, which is a recreation of the bedroom in the Wallington cottage—there are other links. The novel begins in early April, immediately following the day of Eileen's funeral. The last letter Eileen wrote ends with the word "clock", and this mundane feature makes its way into the devastating first sentence of the novel. Also, the title of the novel itself may be the strongest link with Eileen. Originally, Orwell had called the book *The Last Man in Europe*, but his American publishers didn't like this title and asked him to reconsider it. He replaced it with the title *Nineteen Eighty-four*. No explanation was ever given by Orwell, and for many years people assumed he had simply transposed the numbers of the year in which he finished the manuscript, 1948. But the title of a novel is never so randomly and carelessly contrived. A stronger theory could be that Orwell was honouring Eileen, in that her poem of that title had been published in her school magazine just before they met, and the poem itself has elements of the dystopian world that Orwell was building in the novel. Dorien Lynskey (2019) shows that the original manuscript contains Orwell's own amendments to the title, where he first uses 1980, then 1982, before settling on 1984. Lynskey and others argue that this is proof that he was not influenced by Eileen's poem, but we would suggest that it is the reverse: he settled on a date dredged up from his memory, a date that relates to his recently deceased wife. If this is indeed the inspiration behind the title, then this masterpiece of English literature is a fitting tribute to one of the most remarkable women to have existed in the shadows of literary greatness in the twentieth century.

References

Jackson, Lydia (1960) 'George Orwell's First Wife', *The Twentieth Century Magazine*. Vol 168, August 1960.

Keeting, Jenny (2013) *History of Adoption and Fostering in the United Kingdom*. Oxford Bibliographies https://doi.org/10.1093/OBO/9780199791231-0083. Accessed 17 August 2024.

Lynskey, Dorian (2019) *The Ministry of Truth: the biography of Orwell's Nineteen Eighty-Four*. Doubleday, London.

Wadhams, Stephen (ed) (1984) *Remembering Orwell*. Penguin, Harmondsworth.

Bibliography

Ackroyd, Peter (1984) *T.S. Eliot: a life*. Penguin, London.
Bell, Rudolph and Virginia Yans (2008) (eds) *Women on their Own: interdisciplinary perspectives on being single*. New Brunswick, Rutgers University Press.
Benney, Mark (1966), *Almost a Gentleman*. Peter Davies, London.
Bowker, Gordon (2003) *Inside George Orwell*. Palgrave Macmillan, New York.
Boyd, Brian (2016) *Vladimir Nabokov: the American Years*. Princeton University Press, Princeton.
Brittain, Vera (1997, first published 1933) *Testament of Youth: an autobiographical study of the years 1900–1925*. Virago, London.
Charlton, John and Murphy, Mike (1997) *The Health of Adult Britain 1841–1994. Vol 2, Infection in England and Wales 1838–1993*. Chapter 13. Office for National Statistics, London.
Civilservantorg.uk Women in the Civil Service: a history. https://www.civilservant.org.uk/women-history.html [Accessed 27 July 2022]
Cooper, Audrey and Bernard Crick (eds) (1984) *Orwell Remembered*. BBC Books, London.
Cooper, Lettice (1984), "Eileen Blair", *The PEN: Broadsheet of the English Centre for International PEN*, no. 17, Spring 1984.
Coppard, Audrey, and Crick, Bernard (eds) (1984). *Orwell Remembered*. BBC, London.
Crick, Bernard (1980), *George Orwell: a life*. Little, Brown; Boston.
Davison, Peter (2001c), *The Complete Works of George Orwell. Vol 12: A patriot after all, 1940–1941*. Secker & Warburg, London.

Davison, Peter (2001e), *The Complete Works of George Orwell. Vol 14: Keeping our little corner clean, 1941–1943.* Secker & Warburg, London.
Davison, Peter (2001h), *The Complete Works of George Orwell, Vol 17: I Belong to the Left, 1945.* Secker & Warburg, London.
Davison, Peter (2001i), *The Complete Works of George Orwell. Vol 18: Smothered Under Journalism, 1946.* Secker & Warburg, London.
Davison, Peter (ed) (2000) *The Complete Works of George Orwell. Vol 11.* Secker & Warburg, London.
Davison, Peter (ed) (2011) *George Orwell: a life in letters.* Harvill Secker, London.
Davison, Peter (ed). (2000) *The Complete Works of George Orwell.* Secker & Warburg, London. *Volume 10: A kind of compulsion,* 1903–1936.
Davison, Peter (ed). (2006) *The Lost Orwell.* Timewell Press, London.
Didley, Douglas (2010) *Dunkirk 1940: Operation Dynamo.* Osprey, London.
Diggins, John P. (1975) *Up from Communism: Conservative odysseys in American intellectual history.* Columbia University Press: New York.
Essex, Rosamund (1977) *Woman in a Man's World.* London, Sheldon Press.
Fussell, Paul (1975) *The Great War and Modern Memory.* Oxford University Press: Oxford
Fyvel, Tosco. (1982) *George Orwell: A personal memoir.* Weidenfeld and Nicholson, London.
Gelb, Norman (1990). *Dunkirk: the incredible escape.* Michael Joseph, London.
Gramsci, Antonio (1971) *Selections form the Prison Notebooks,* trans Quentin Hoare and Geoffrey Nowell Smith. Lawrence & Wishart, London.
Holden, Katherine (2007) *The Shadow of Marriage: singleness in England 1914–60.* Manchester, Manchester University Press.
Israel, Betsy (2002). *Bachelor Girl: the secret history of single women in the twentieth century.* New York, William Morrow.
Jackson, Lydia (1960), "George Orwell's First Wife", *The Twentieth Century Magazine.* Vol. 168, August 1960.
Jackson, Lydia (writing as Elisaveta Fen) (1976) *A Russian's England.* Paul Gordon Books, Warwick.
Jackson, Lydia (writing as Elisaveta Fen) 'George Orwell's First Wife' in *The Twentieth Century Magazine* vol 168. August 1960.
Kaufman, Andrew (2021) *The Gambler Wife: A True Story of Love, Risk, and the Woman Who Saved Dostoyevsky.* Riverhead Books, New York.
Keeting, Jenny (2013) *History of Adoption and Fostering in the United Kingdom.* Oxford Bibliographies https://doi.org/10.1093/OBO/9780199791231-0083. Accessed 17 August 2024.
Lynskey, Doreen (2019) *The Ministry of Truth: the biography of Orwell's Nineteen Eighty-Four.* Doubleday, London.

McNab, Richard (2013) *Retreat from Riviere: The Dunkirk Diary of Major George McNab*. Digital Print Media.
Meyers, Jeffrey (2001) *Orwell: A Wintry Conscience of a Generation*. W.W. Norton, New York.
Orr, Charles A (1984) *Homage to Orwell—as I knew him in Catalonia*. Unpublished pamphlet.
Orwell, George (1936) *Keep the Aspidistra Flying*. Victor Gollancz, London.
Orwell, George (1952) *Homage to Catalonia*. Harcourt Brace, New York.
Payne, Stanley G. (2011) *The Franco Republic (1936–1975)*. University of Wisconsin Press: Madison.
Popoff, Alexandra (2010). Sophia Tolstoy: a biography. Free Press, New York.
Potter, Beatrix (1913), *The Tale of Pigling Bland*. Frederick Warne, London.
Ray, John (1996), *The Night Blitz: 1940–1941*. Cassell Military, London.
Rees, Richard (1962) *George Orwell: Fugitive from the Camp of Victory*. Southern Illinois University Press, Carbondale.
Richards, Denis (1974), *Royal Air Force 1939–1945: the Fight at Odds. Vol 1*. HMSO, London.
Sayers, Audrey B. (1984) *Sunderland Church High School for Girls: a centenary history*. Privately printed.
Sayers, Dorothy L. (1988, first published 1935) *Gaudy Night*. Hodder and Stoughton, London.
Shelden, Michael (1991) *Orwell: The Authorized Biography*. Harper Collins, New York.
Sheridan, Dorothy (ed) (1990) *Wartime Women: a Mass Observation Anthology 1937–45*. Orion Books, London.
Sitwell, William (2016), *Eggs or Anarchy? The remarkable story of the man tasked with the impossible: to feed a nation at war*. Simon & Schuster, London.
Smith, Angela (2013) *Discourses Surrounding British Widows of the First World War*. London, Bloomsbury.
Stansky, Peter and William Abrahams (1979) *Orwell: The Transformation*. Constable, London.
Struther, Jan (1939, 2001) *Mrs Miniver*. Virago, London.
Todman, Daniel (2016) *Britain's War: Into Battle, 1937–1941*. Oxford University Press, Oxford.
Topp, Sylvia. (2020). *Eileen: the making of George Orwell*. Unbound, London.
Vicinus, Martha. (1985) *Independent Women: work and community for single women 1850–1920*. London, Virago.
Wadhams, Stephen (ed) (1984) *Remembering Orwell*. Penguin, Ontario.
Whyte, Bert and Hannant, Larry (2011) *Champagne and Meatballs: Adventures of a Canadian Communist*. Athabasca University Press, Edmonton.
Wildemeersch, Marc. (2013) *George Orwell's Commander in Spain: the enigma of Georges Kopp*. Thames River Press, London.

Ziegler, Philip (2002) *London at War, 1939–1945*. Pimlico, London.

Primary sources

Crick Archive. Birkbeck College, University of London. Extracts are used by kind permission of the executors of the late Sir Bernard Crick at Birkbeck University Archive.

Nilson, A. R. (letter dated 5 December 1983). Crick Archive.

Obermeyer, Rosalind. Letter of 12 November 1974. Crick Archive.

St Hugh's Archive. Collection of submissions for Penny Griffin (ed) *St Hugh's: One Hundred Years of Women's Education in Oxford*, Palgrave Macmillan, 1986. Reproduced here by kind permission of the Principal and Fellows of St Hugh's College, Oxford.

The Chronicle (School magazine for Sunderland Church High School) (November 1917, November 1918, June 1922, November 1923, June 1924, November 1924, November 1927, June 1934) Additional primary sources from Sunderland Church High School's archive held at Sunderland Antiquarian Society are reproduced with the consent of that organisation.

INDEX

A
Adie, Kate, 16
Adoption. *See* Blair, Richard
Adoption law. *See* Blair, Richard
Anderson, Eveyln, 212
Anti-fascism, 2, 87, 123, 125, 137, 167
Anti fascists, 7
Aunt Nellie, 52, 67, 87
Avery, Desmond, 156

B
Barnhill, 211, 221
BBC
  Blunt, Bruce, 186, 187
  Mrs Buggins radio show, 158, 159, 162, 164, 170, 188, 189
BBC India Service, 156, 191
BBC policy(ies)
  accent/accents, 164, 170, 171
Bengal famine, 191
Benney, Mark, 156
Berthe Grossbard, 160
Binns store, 214

Blair, Avril, 60, 122, 157, 231
Blair, Eileen. *See* St Hugh's College
  accent, 16
  affair, 47. *See also* Grisewood, Harman; Kopp, Georges
  appearance, 4, 46, 74, 169
  Bussey, Edna, 41, 42
  communist spy, 81, 95
  degree, 38
  editing work, 17, 20, 23, 25, 29, 42, 44, 53–55, 57, 58, 61, 101, 157, 189, 223
  employment, 3, 39–41, 44, 47, 54, 66, 67, 74, 102, 142, 147, 152, 171, 194
  euphemisms, 97
  evacuation, 68
  Fernwood House Nursing Home, 227, 229, 233
  funeral, 234, 235
  governess, 11
  grief, 146, 148, 156
  health, 5, 7, 22, 38, 52, 79, 83, 86, 90, 102, 104, 107, 108, 112,

113, 116, 120, 121, 126, 127, 130–133, 136, 140, 141, 147–149, 151, 152, 156, 166, 169, 182–184, 188, 189, 194, 195, 199, 202, 216, 218–221, 227, 228
homes, 143, 148, 151, 152, 155, 211, 230
honeymoon, 53
Jura, 2, 211, 222
living accommodation, 5, 39–41, 61, 63, 66, 94, 96, 151, 152, 155, 169, 207, 212, 214, 216–218, 227, 228, 230, 231, 234
living accommodation plans, 110, 115, 116, 136
marriage, 1, 2, 4, 6, 7, 18, 19, 30, 31, 39, 47, 51–58, 60, 88, 96, 102, 104, 114, 141, 194, 198, 235
menstruation, 149
money concerns, 61, 93, 108, 109, 111, 142, 151, 169, 181, 219
music, 12, 16, 55, 71
nickname, 201
pacifism, 96
pen name origins, 158
pet dog Marx, 93, 99, 102, 119, 124, 126, 133, 135, 140
poetry, 35, 44, 45, 92, 224
politics, 25, 29, 43, 47, 51, 57, 60, 71, 90
School magazine *The Chronicles*, 234
Shelley's pub, 164
shorthand, 40, 42, 66, 110, 111, 142
smoking, 57, 77, 107, 145, 169
social class, 12, 27, 52, 129, 226
South Shields, 4, 5, 11, 12, 36, 53, 67

St Hugh's College, 28, 29, 34, 38, 40, 100
surname, 5
The Stores, Wallington, 6, 7, 30, 52–54, 57, 60, 61, 63, 66, 78, 83, 92–94, 96, 104, 108, 109, 112, 114–116, 118, 119, 123, 131, 136–138, 140–143, 146, 147, 169, 207, 221, 224, 235
Tioli, Georgio, 95
Westerby, Robert, 157, 162, 167, 169, 171, 178, 179, 190, 194, 196, 197
Westgate House, 4
whimsical style, 7, 26, 199, 200, 202, 209, 230
Windermere, 116, 117
Blair, Marjorie, 119, 123, 124, 135, 149, 231
Blair, Richard, 207, 210–215, 221, 222, 225, 232, 233
adoption, 207, 216, 226, 229, 231
Blitz, 150, 155, 156, 207
Bowker, Gordon, 146, 157, 202
Branthwaite, Jock, 95
Bristol, 69, 93, 119, 126, 133, 135, 140, 147, 150, 152, 207
Brockway, Archibold Fenner. *See* Spanish Civil War
Brown, Ivor, 219, 222, 225

C

Cadbury, Dame Elizabeth, 41
Canada, 148, 151, 208
evacuation, 148, 151, 208
Casablanca, 119, 120, 122
Casalis, Jeanne de, 168
Censorship, 142, 156
Chamberlain, Neville, 123, 125, 128, 142, 144
Cheltenham Ladies' College, 13
Churchill, Winston, 144–146

Cologne, 219, 223, 228, 229, 234
Common, Jack, 60, 103, 104, 116–119, 126, 127, 130, 136, 137, 140
Common, Mary, 129
Communist press, 92, 110
Communist spy, 95
Cooper, Lettice, 55, 65, 143, 158, 167, 188, 192, 194, 200, 201, 209, 216, 228
Coppard, Audrey and Crick, Bernard, 188, 202
Cottman, Stafford, 91–93
Courtneidge, Cicely, 167
Crick archive, 158, 200
Crook, David. *See* Communist spy
Czechoslovakia, 123, 139

D
Dakin, Henry, 169
Davison, Peter, 8, 51, 52, 60, 61, 78, 96, 97, 99, 101, 115, 117, 134, 135, 138, 140, 145, 146, 148, 156, 191, 198–202, 212, 228, 230
Dostoevskata, Anna, 3
Dunkirk, 144, 145, 202. *See also* O'Shaughnessy, Eric
Operation Dynamo, 144, 145, 202

E
editor, 7, 17
Egypt, 150, 153
Eliot, TS, 3, 156, 200

F
Fascism. *See* Anti-fascism
Fierz, Mabel, 54, 66, 157
Franco, General, 60, 67, 68, 71–73, 87, 128, 187, 188

Funder, Anna, 5, 6
Fussell, Paul, 71
Fyvel, Tosco, 137, 138, 146, 153, 200, 201

G
Gellhorn, Martha, 73
Gollancz, Victor, 48, 61, 62, 64, 82, 83, 93, 110, 140, 199, 200
Gorer, Geoffrey, 54, 66, 127, 128
Greystones
 Blackburn, 213, 217, 218, 223, 224, 230, 232
Grisewood, Freddy, 157, 162, 188, 189, 192
Grisewood, Harman, 157, 198, 202
Grossbard, Berthe, 160, 188, 194

H
Harrods Department Store, 171, 173
Harvey Evers, 218, 220, 227, 233, 234
Heaton, Nell, 166, 170–172, 202, 214
Hemingway, Ernest, 73
Hitler, Adolph, 44, 68, 123, 147, 156, 200
Holden, Inez, 12, 27, 198, 221
Homage to Catalonia, 91, 93, 95, 102, 109–111, 119, 199

I
Independent Labour Party, 39, 43, 60, 74, 75, 81, 84, 88, 167

J
Jackson, Lydia, 38–40, 46, 50, 51, 54, 68, 113, 137, 138, 140, 145,

148, 156, 200, 202, 207, 211, 235
Jacob, Naomi, 167

K
Keep the Aspidistra Flying, 50, 51, 56, 58, 67
King-Farlow, Denys, 111, 114, 116
Koestler, Arthur, 72
Kopp, Doreen, 198, 230, 235
Kopp, Georges, 75, 76, 78, 79, 84, 88–91, 93, 94, 97, 98, 133, 137, 141, 146, 147, 150, 198, 216, 217, 221, 222, 230
imprisonment, 94, 97, 98, 125, 133

L
Langdon-Davies, John, 97
Lewis, C.S., 35

M
MacDonald, Ramsay, 39
Mannin, Ethel, 167, 174
Masefield, John, 92
McNair, John, 60, 66–68, 74, 77, 79–81, 91, 94, 95
Morocco, 72, 115, 116, 119, 120, 122–124, 128, 133, 134, 138, 139, 141
Mussolini, Benito, 68
Myers, L.M., 141, 142
Myles, Nora, 1, 34, 36, 38, 49, 56, 57, 67, 96, 99, 101, 102, 119, 132, 135, 136, 148–151, 194, 201, 231

N
Nabokov, Vera, 3

Newcastle, 5, 12, 67, 213, 215, 218, 226, 227, 229, 233, 234
Nineteen Eight-Four, 235
Lynskey, Doreen, 2, 235

O
Obermeyer, Rosalind, 46, 49, 50, 67
Orr, Lois, 74, 81, 87
Orwell, George
affairs, 198, 121, 134. *See also* Jackson, Lydia; Salkeld, Brenda
bronchiectasis, 110, 114, 115
chickens, 52, 116, 118, 123, 129
Eric Blair, 1, 5, 49, 50, 66, 89, 158, 226
family at Southwold, 55, 57, 59, 66, 98, 119, 140
goats, 52, 54, 60, 93, 116, 117, 121, 123, 127–129, 131, 135
haemorrhages, 102, 103, 108, 201
history of enslavement, 59
Home Guard, 143, 147, 152, 199
hospital visits, 8, 16, 75, 79, 80, 88, 90, 102, 103, 108, 109, 111, 136, 140, 146, 151, 173, 184, 207, 218, 220, 228, 229, 234
illness, 107, 110, 114, 133
Sanatorium Maurin, 88
The Observer, 80, 110, 113, 219, 220, 233
The Tribune, 198, 199, 219, 223
tuberculosis, 107, 108, 115
O'Shaughnessy, Catherine, 206, 227
O'Shaughnessy, Eileen. *See* Blair, Eileen
O'Shaughnessy, Elsie. *See* Blair, Eileen
O'Shaughnessy, Eric
Greenwich house, 5, 42, 46, 51, 58, 64, 66, 67, 86, 103, 137, 139–141, 143, 151, 152, 207

Royal Army Medical Corps, 126, 142
O'Shaughnessy, Gwen, 5, 42, 77, 79, 87, 133, 137, 142, 148, 151, 198, 206–208, 210–212, 218–220, 226, 227, 231, 233

P
Pickles, Wilfred, 164
Potter, Beatrix, 201
The Tale of Pigling Brand, 201
Power, Esther, 34, 35, 38

R
Rees, Richard, 49, 56, 66, 67, 91, 157

S
Salkeld, Brenda, 141, 146
Sayers, Dorothy L., 33, 34, 47, 48
Second World War
  Normandy Landings, 207, 209
Shelden, Michael, 54, 134, 147, 198
Smith, Angela, 27, 55, 68
Spanish Civil War
  arrests, 90, 91
  Huesca Front, 76, 83
  International Brigade, 74, 85, 87
  Madrid, 60, 72, 73, 81, 85
  POUM, 74, 80, 85, 87, 90, 91, 97
  Siétamo, 62
Stalin, Josef, 72, 81, 199
St Hugh's College, ix, 29, 34
Stockton, 212–214, 217, 230
Stopes, Marie
  Married Love, 48
Struther, Jan
  Mrs Miniver, 139
Sunderland Church High School, 4, 11, 12, 14, 16–18, 25, 27, 29, 30, 38, 39, 42, 46, 171, 214

Ironside, Ethel, 13, 14, 16–18, 20–23, 26–29, 39, 41, 171
Old Girls' Guild, 16, 17, 28, 30
Sayers, Audrey, 13, 14, 17
Symes, Norah. *See* Myles, Norah

T
The Road to Wigan Pier, 7, 53, 58, 60, 61, 64, 66, 68, 74, 82, 83, 101
Thompson, Brian, 234
Tioli, Georgio. *See* Blair, Eileen
Tolkien, J.R.R., 35, 38
Tolstaya, Sofia, 3
Topp, Sylvia, 1, 3, 34, 36, 40, 50, 56, 61, 114, 116, 137, 145, 156–158, 164, 169, 184, 202, 210, 212, 234

V
Vera, Brittain, 33

W
Wadhams, Stephen, 54, 55, 69, 156, 201, 216, 235
Wartime London
  air raids, 123, 148, 152, 156, 218
  Bombed out, 147, 207, 210
Wartime rationing, 8, 142, 157, 159, 161, 165, 168, 169, 213, 214
  cheese, 130, 157, 166, 168, 179–181, 189
  Lord Woolton, 157
  milk, 197, 214, 215
  nutritional values, 165, 166, 171, 214
  Vegetabull poster, 197
Wartime refugees, 160
Wodehouse, P.G., 213, 223, 233
Wordsworth, William, 3, 92

GPSR Compliance

The European Union's (EU) General Product Safety Regulation (GPSR) is a set of rules that requires consumer products to be safe and our obligations to ensure this.

If you have any concerns about our products, you can contact us on

ProductSafety@springernature.com

In case Publisher is established outside the EU, the EU authorized representative is:

Springer Nature Customer Service Center GmbH
Europaplatz 3
69115 Heidelberg, Germany

www.ingramcontent.com/pod-product-compliance
Lightning Source LLC
LaVergne TN
LVHW012037070526
838202LV00056B/5522